Anderson, Charles Roberts, 1902–
The magic circle of Walden [by] Charles R. Anderson. [1st ed.] New York, Holt, Rinehart and Winston [1968]

x, 306 p. 22 cm.

Bibliographical references included in "Notes" (p. 281–298)

1. Thoreau, Henry David, 1817–1862. Walden. I. Title.
II. Walden.
818.31 T48wza 818'.3'08 68-10098

Library of Congress [5]

oks by Charles R. Anderson include: / *Melville in the South Seas* / *The Centennial Edition Sidney Lanier* / *Emily Dickinson's Poetry: Stairway of Surprise* / *The Magic Circle of lden*

The Magic Circle of Walden

HOLT,
RINEHART
AND WINSTON

New York   Chicago
San Francisco

CHARLES R. ANDERSON

The Magic Circle

of Walden

In his own magic circle wanders
The wonderful man, and draws us
With him to wander, and take part in it.

—GOETHE, *Torquato Tasso*

 Published simultaneously in Canada by Holt, Rinehart and Winston of Canada, Limited.
Library of Congress Catalog Card Number: 68-10098

First Edition

Designer: Ernst Reichl
8657009
Printed in the United States of America

To Mary Pringle Anderson

Preface

Since Thoreau wrote *Walden* as a deliberately radical book, perhaps the way to read it should be equally radical. This is an attempt to read it *as if* it were a poem. While my critical study was in progress several articles have appeared showing that a similar approach has occurred to others, and these have proved encouraging. But no one has attempted a strictly literary interpretation of *Walden* as a unified whole, and no one has carried out such a study full scale. My book attempts both, and goes one step further. Taking *Walden* to be not only Thoreau's masterpiece but the central focus of his life and works, I have combed the twenty volumes of his collected *Writings* for everything relevant and have brought all this to bear on a close reading of his one great book. Also, since Thoreau was one of the most erudite of nineteenth-century American authors, his wide reading has been used to gloss the text, whenever pertinent. Finally, in the last decade a number of basic factual studies of Thoreau have been published, and these have solved many problems for the literary critic. I have tried to read everything that has been written on Thoreau and to use whatever was suitable for my purposes. My indebtedness to all my predecessors is hereby gratefully acknowledged. I would also like to thank several friends and colleagues for a critical reading of the manuscript of this book, in whole or in part: Stanley Burnshaw, Walter Harding, John Magnus, J. Hillis Miller, Georges Poulet, and Earl R. Wasserman.

The text used for quotation and citation is that of the "Walden Edition" of *The Writings of Henry David Thoreau* (Boston: Houghton Mifflin and Co., 1906), 20 volumes. Since most of my references are to these writings, it seemed pointless to send the reader to notes at the back of the book just to be given volume and page. Instead, they are placed in parentheses immediately following the quotation or citation. References to *Walden* are by page numbers only (*e.g.*, 137); to the other formal writings by volume and page (*e.g.*, III, 422); to the *Journal* by initial, volume, and page (*e.g.*, J, II, 151–152). (The *Journal* comprises Volumes VII to XX of the *Writings*, but is renumbered separately I to XIV; the latter numbering is used here.)

References to all other writings may be found in the end notes.

—C.R.A.

Contents

The Magic Circle of Walden

Walden: Table of Contents

Thoreau and "I"

The trouble with Henry Thoreau, said urbane Dr. Holmes, was that he insisted on "nibbling his asparagus at the wrong end." The fault went far deeper, according to Professor Lowell of Harvard, who in referring to the famous experiment at Walden Pond accused him of irresponsible posturing as a savage and childishly rejecting the benefits of civilization. This misunderstanding by contemporaries was kept alive by R. L. Stevenson, that romantic lover of life, who called Thoreau a prig for his otherworldliness and a skulker for renouncing his obligations to humanity. Even his best friend, Emerson, misconstrued his lack of ambition and lamented, in an often reprinted essay, that he refused to use "his rare powers of action" for the good of society. In fact the reputation of this author, and his one great book, has had a curious history. During his lifetime and for many years after, Thoreau had little recognition, being usually dismissed as an eccentric or a minor disciple of transcendentalism. In our century he has gradually come into fame until today he is widely acclaimed as a major author, largely on the strength of *Walden*, yet it has never been shown satisfactorily just how this is a masterpiece of literature.

Neither of the main lines of interpretation used so far—treating it as nature essays or as social criticism—has succeeded in discovering its meaning as a work of art. To claim that the chief purpose of Thoreau's flight from civilization was to make a scientific study of the natural world, as some have done, is to diminish his stature. In comparison with the great forerunners of modern biological science, such as Darwin and Linnaeus, he fades into insignificance. If he is merely counted as one of the vast army of observers and cataloguers, he is consigned to limbo. Even when placed, more properly, with that remarkable group of amateur naturalists who flourished in the nineteenth century, he can only be reckoned a less systematic Audubon or a less dedicated Burroughs. Though a unique anthology of vignettes of the natural world can be culled from *Walden*, and there are many such collections, they leave the central vision untouched.

The second approach, more congenial in recent decades, assumes that Thoreau retreated to the woods merely to find a vantage point for his criticism of civilization. The long introductory chapter on "Economy" may so mislead the unwary. And throughout the rest of the book the most memorable passages, for non-literary readers, may well be his thrusts at capitalism and the American worship of material progress. But in comparison with the revolutionary critics of his own century—economic and political theorists like Marx, Mill, and Auguste Comte—his criticisms seem fragmentary and ineffectual. True, he lifted his voice against the complacency of the times, seeing more clearly than most the drift toward collectivism in modern society. Taken all together his protests make a brave credo for the despairing individualist in any age, but they do not add up to a program for society. Finally, both these lines of interest begin to suffer somewhat as the twentieth-century world view defines itself more clearly. The trend toward a collective social order, today an accomplished fact, reduces Thoreau's one-man strike to a rhetorical gesture. The radical shift of science in recent years from descriptive to theoretical research makes his nature commentary seem quaint and outmoded.

On the other hand both lines of interpretation do apply in varying degrees to Thoreau's life, and even to a few of his shorter works. His reaction to certain aspects of contemporary civilization, for example, was so violent that it led him into dramatic actions on two notable occasions. In mid-career, by way of protest against the Mexican War and the extension of slavery, he refused to pay his taxes and thus forced the Concord jailer to lock him up—for one night in the summer of 1846. (Actually, he had refused to pay his taxes once before, in 1844, but had not been jailed for it.) There is an apocryphal story that Emerson visited him in jail and asked, "Why are you here?" only to get for a reply, "Why are you not here?"—a tale that is true in spirit if not in fact. The episode itself formed the basis of his essay on "Civil Disobedience," which was published in 1849 and has been astonishingly influential ever since. It has served in this century as a model for Gandhi's campaign of passive resistance in India and as a handbook for the anti-Nazi underground in Occupied Europe. Near the end of his life Thoreau again defied society by being almost the first to come out in defense of the anarchist raid on Harper's Ferry, outdoing the most fanatical Abolitionists in his "Plea for Captain John Brown," delivered as a speech in 1859 and published the next year. He could indeed on occasion give himself passionately to questions of the day.

As for science, though he shied away from commitment to research, he did furnish specimens of plants and animals to the Harvard professors, and at least once he wrote an article that is wholly scientific, "The Succession of Forest Trees," praised today as an original contribution to ecology. Further, the penchant for observing and cataloguing the phenomena of nature grew on him until it became almost obsessive in his later years. But his overall attitude is made clear by the *Journal* entry at the time he refused to fill in the questionnaire sent him by the Association for the Advancement of Science. It is impossible, he wrote, to define his specialty for people who do not believe in "a science which deals with the higher law." (J, V, 4)* Natural history, like social criticism, was only a subordinate part of the man and his writings.

Another way of reading *Walden*—usually combined with one of the above—is to treat it as literal autobiography. Though the outward form suggests such a possibility, this approach does not lead to what sensitive readers feel is original and timeless in the book. There was a real person named Henry David Thoreau, to be sure, who was born and died in Concord, Massachusetts (1817–1862), who lived alone in the woods for two years at

* The method of reference to Thoreau's *Writings* and *Journal* is explained on p. vii, above.

Walden Pond (1845–1847), and wrote an account of his experiences there which he later published (1854). But the flesh and blood man and the actual place are of interest to students of literature only as points from which to measure the author's imaginative projection—his mythical world of *Walden* and the fictive "I" who serves as both the narrator and the subject of that book. In the pages that follow it is important to keep these distinctions clear. As an aid to readers of this study the actual person and place will be presented first, in a brief sketch.

Since Thoreau's life was simple and uneventful, the biographical facts can be set down compactly. Few major writers have centered themselves on such a small plot of earth. Thoreau left Concord only on rare occasions, such as his years at Harvard, his lecture trips to neighboring towns, and a few more extended excursions—to Cape Cod, to the Maine woods, to Canada. He was not a traveler but a rooted villager, first and last. His college career, though undistinguished, brought him two gifts: discovery of the world of books and friendship with Emerson. He read avidly in literature, both classical and English; then in philosophy and religion, oriental as well as Western; finally in a variety of genres including natural history, world travel, and Indian lore. He became one of the most widely read Americans of his time, erudite in a limited sense. One piece of his college reading proved seminal, Emerson's *Nature,* so that he was prepared for the full impact of the "American Scholar Address," the challenge flung down to his graduating class in 1837. These and other basic Emersonian ideas certainly played a large part in orienting the young Thoreau.

Friendship between the two ripened to the point that the potential disciple went to live as a member of Emerson's household from 1841 to 1843, and for another year in 1847. Through this connection he came to know Bronson Alcott, Margaret Fuller, William Ellery Channing, and other members of the Transcendental Club, as well as literary figures tangential to the "fellowship," like Hawthorne and Horace Greeley. Thoreau was associated in varying degrees with several projects sponsored by this group, such as Brook Farm and *The Dial.* He took an active part in the magazine helping Emerson edit it and contributing a number of his own poems and essays to it. These relations provided his first incentive to authorship and his first outlet as a creative writer. But he was a detached friend and participant at best, and he was never a disciple in any true sense. It is when Thoreau moved farthest away from Emerson that he is most interesting. He alone tried to practice in his life what with the transcendentalists was largely a theoretical faith. And his uniqueness as a writer lies in what distinguishes him from them—replacing their tendency to abstract thinking and moralizing with the concreteness of poetry and the exuberance of wit. His essay praising Carlyle, written during the Walden residence, was a sort of disguised preface to his own emergent style (worthy of comparison with Melville's famous essay on Hawthorne's *Mosses*). Though Carlyle was not a poet, according to this full-scale analysis of his works he was a vigorous humorist. Thoreau intended to make up the former lack and to emulate the one great talent, as a way of transforming his Concord heritage. "Transcendental philosophy needs the leaven of humor to render it light and digestible," he concluded; it is the "indispensable pledge of sanity." (IV, 333–334)

Finding a vocation was a real problem for many of the transcendentalists, particularly acute for Thoreau. After graduating from Harvard he ran a private school in Concord with his brother for several years (1838–1841). Then, after serving as Emerson's handy man, he tried tutoring on Staten Island for a few months. From time to time he engaged in his father's business of manufacturing pencils. When at one point he succeeded in making one better than any then in use, so the story goes, his friends congratulated him on opening his way to a fortune. But his reply, that he would never make another pencil, shocked them. "I would not do again what I have done once," he said disconcertingly. He was misunderstood by family and fellow townsmen because his goal was simply one that could not be fitted into any normal trade or profession. He was a dedicated poet. But authorship of any sort was a precarious way to make a living at that period, and since Thoreau's writing was especially limited in its audience, he could not make a self-supporting business of it. His famous experiment-in-living, the residence at Walden Pond in 1845–1847, was partly for the purpose of solving this problem. He wanted to see if he could support himself in a minimum way with light manual labor so as to free most of his time for writing. When he left the pond he had completed the manuscript of his first book, *A Week on the Concord and Merrimack Rivers*, and an early draft of what was to become *Walden.*

For the rest of his life Thoreau continued in this vocationless vocation, making a bare living by doing such odd jobs as ditching and surveying. This was his solution of how, in a materialistic world, he could devote himself to non-paying authorship and still have time for the endless walks that furnished the staple of his meditations and writings. He never made a living by his pen, though his works fill twenty volumes. His first book was a spectacular failure. Published (or more accurately, printed) at his own expense in 1849, the *Week* sold only 219 copies in all out of an edition of 1,000. When in 1853 the unsold ones were returned to him, Thoreau took them up to his attic room and noted in his *Journal:* "I have now a library of nearly nine hundred volumes, over seven hundred of which I wrote myself." (J, V, 459) One may admire his laconic wit and his indifference to success, but the consequences to his career as an author were serious. The publication of *Walden* was postponed for several years. When it finally appeared in 1854, under the imprint of a well-known Boston publisher, though it received a number of good reviews, five years were required to dispose of an edition of two thousand copies.

These two books, together with some poems and a good many essays (most of which were published posthumously), make up the body of Thoreau's formal works, only five volumes in all. The great bulk of his writings consists of his *Journal*, not published until nearly half a century after his death. This was not written for the public but for his own use. It was not a diary but an artist's workbook, serving several purposes: to record his observations and thoughts, to experiment with literary "miniatures," to provide a storehouse of material on which he could draw for essays and books. Because of this last use, especially for *Walden* and *A Week,* the surviving journal text for the first ten or twelve years is greatly reduced from the much longer original. Also, the later volumes are somewhat clogged with tedious lists of flowers and birds observed during his nature rambles. But in spite of these limitations, the *Journal,* covering the whole of his mature life from 1837 to 1862, makes fascinating reading. One could even argue that his greatest achievement as a writer is this remarkable record of a remarkable man's view of the world. With the publication of these fourteen volumes in 1906, Thoreau at last came into his own as a major author.

During his lifetime he was considered an eccentric by most of the townspeople—a caustic wit, a "come-outer" who frequently took a stance on public issues that startled his neighbors, a man whose whole mature life was marked by whimsical gestures and unconventional acts. Even in Concord, which had more than its share of eccentrics, he stood out as a queer New England "character." But his keen common sense and extraordinary talents soon won admiration from those who had thought him only an oddity. His knowledge of nature was so precise, he boasted, that if he were to wake up from a trance in Beck Stow's swamp he could tell by the plants what time of year it was within two days. His feats of manual dexterity, his skill at weighing and gauging by eye, his uncanny knack with things—all these talents made him a legend even during his lifetime. With such wide-ranging faculties and original opinions on all subjects, great things came to be expected of him, but none of his contemporaries caught the quality of his greatness. One reason for this misunderstanding is that he was hard to get close to. His plain manners and blunt speech had a chilling effect on conversation. His ingrained habit of negations and renunciations made him difficult in social situations: he never went to church, never voted, ate no meat, drank no wine, used no tobacco. Though he wrote much on the ideal of friendship, one of his close friends said: "I love Henry, but I do not like him"; another remarked: "As for taking Thoreau's arm, I should as soon take the arm of an elm tree."

Thoreau never married, and there is only tenuous evidence

that he was ever in love. When he was twenty-two he is said to have had a short-lived romance with Ellen Sewall, a girl of seventeen. He is even believed by some to have proposed to her in a letter, though nothing came of it. The whole affair seems to have been more literary than real, to judge from the vague record that has come down. (None of their correspondence has survived, and she is not mentioned by Thoreau in his *Journal* or elsewhere.) At any rate the experience, if actual, stands alone in his life.

By the age of thirty he was a confirmed bachelor. His stand on the matter is underscored in his response to a reverse proposal made to him in 1847, shortly after he left Walden. As the climax of a "tragic correspondence," so he reported to Emerson, a Miss Sophia Ford asked him to marry her. "I sent back as distinct a *no* as I have learned to pronounce after considerable practice," Thoreau declared. Since she was an unbalanced spinster, seventeen years his senior, this seems reasonable enough. What is striking about the episode is his appended comment: "I really had anticipated no such foe as this in my career." The meaning is clear. There was no place for love and marriage in the way of life he had chosen. The women he felt drawn to (in addition to his sisters and his mother) were usually a generation older than he, such as Emerson's wife, Lydian, and his sister-in-law, Mrs. Lucy Brown. It may sound ridiculous to call Thoreau a bachelor of nature, as many have done, but there is an entry in his *Journal* for 1856 that supports the epithet in a most astonishing way: "I love and could embrace the shrub oak with its scanty garment of leaves. . . . I felt a positive yearning toward one bush this afternoon. There was a match found for me at last. I fell in love with a shrub oak." (J, IX, 146) This is a curious New England version of the myth of Apollo pursuing the chaste Daphne only to find her transformed into a laurel tree to escape his ravishing embrace. The myth is here inverted.

As Thoreau's way of life diverged from that of his fellows, he gradually withdrew to a small circle of family, young people interested in nature, and close friends—most of whom were outside Concord's well-known literary group. Except for his years at the pond, at Emerson's, and at Harvard, he always lived at home. Though he was more and more alone, in his attic study and in his solitary walks, he never became a recluse. But when, at the age of twenty-eight, he took up residence at Walden Pond it seemed to his worldly townsmen sheer perversity that he should give up the advantages of civilization for a hermit's cabin and support himself by raising beans. Yet the visitors came, not only friends but the curious and the scornful. What they saw was commonplace enough: a rude but well-built one-room hut, situated on a wooded hillside, overlooking one of those pleasant ponds that abound in New England; their host the same prickly character they had known all their lives, his behavior simple, his dress as plain as his house was bare of furniture. There was nothing remote or romantic about it. After all, this was not a frontier outpost on the edge of the western wilderness. It was within an easy half-hour's walk of Concord—a trip Thoreau himself made several times a week—and it was surrounded in all directions by other centers of a civilization that went back two centuries. Other settings as beautiful as this could be found in the neighborhood, and it would be hard to imagine a less picturesque hermit.

In the winter of 1847, for the benefit of villagers who did not come out to see for themselves but were still incredulous or bewildered, Thoreau delivered several lectures at the Concord Lyceum on his life at the pond, the first one being entitled "A History of Myself." The substance of these lectures was later incorporated in "Economy," the first chapter of his book. It was this practical side of the experiment that interested his fellow townsmen, and even after the book was published, they seem to have paid little attention to the other aspects of it. Few of Thoreau's contemporaries understood the man or the significance of his quest—Channing, Alcott, maybe Emerson?—and most readers of *Walden* during the century following 1854 have been content with the literal narrative. If this were its chief value, then a comparison of his actual life from July 4, 1845, to September 6, 1847, with the account of it in his book would be interesting indeed.

In the first place, however, the full story of Thoreau's residence at Walden Pond is hard to come by. The *Journal*, by his own admission, is not autobiography, and only fragments of it have survived for this period. The *Correspondence* adds next to nothing, and supplementary records are scarce. Even the industry of his most recent biographer could discover only twenty pages of "facts" for these years. More than half of these are simply transcribed from *Walden* (and the *Journal*), so that they are of no help in solving the problem of the book's autobiographical content. The few pages of objective facts, from sources outside Thoreau's literary texts, are mostly concerned with surface matters: groups who came out for picnics, children to whom he showed wildflowers and woodland creatures, the commercial side of the episode about ice-cutting on the pond, and so on. The chief effect of this prosaic picture is to diminish one's sense of the solitude and wild beauty of Walden, but also to increase the reader's admiration for the magical "world" Thoreau created in his book. In the second place, even if the whole story of his outward life during these years could be known, it would probably be just as dull as the few facts listed above, and the hero of a new American myth would be reduced to a plain but quirky man who lived a simple "Life in the Woods"—the subtitle Thoreau dropped after the first edition of *Walden*. Finally, it makes no difference that a few of the events in the book can be proved to have occurred in real life, because in each instance the actuality has been thoroughly transformed by the writer's art.

All these matters surveyed here in brief must be dealt with by Thoreau's biographers, of course—his obsession with botanizing, his violent protests against society, the extreme oddity of his personality, his relations with Concord and the transcendentalists. The literary student of *Walden* may also make use of them for the light they throw on this extraordinary book, since it includes in one way or another all these facets of the author. But overemphasis on them has tended to make previous critics read it as a document to prove or disprove a thesis, instead of treating it as a created work of art. If it is a masterpiece of literature it must be something quite different from amateur natural history, dated social criticism, or the autobiography of a transcendental crank. Before the mythical world of *Walden* can be distinguished from the literal setting of pond and woods and township, we must learn to separate the actual Henry Thoreau, citizen of Concord, from the fictive character who is both the persona and the voice that speaks to us in the book.

I
The Web

Walden is a unique book. There is nothing quite like it in literature. Though it made its way slowly at first, after publication in 1854, by the turn of our century it had found a small but ardent audience. This has been steadily increasing and will probably continue to do so in the future because, once "discovered," it has proved to be a book with unusual drawing power. It may never be widely popular, but it attracts devotees of many kinds in addition to those with a zeal for literature. Reading it is always an unforgettable experience, and what is chiefly remembered is its uniqueness.

Readers of the general sort, as well as more specialized students and critics, have difficulty in deciding exactly what type of book it is. One reason is that Thoreau's masterpiece does not fit easily into any standard literary genre—novel, drama, poem, or lesser categories like autobiography and informal essay. This has been both a curse and a boon. For many years the problem of identification kept *Walden* hovering outside the great house of world literature, a sort of country cousin. Now, at last admitted, there is still some apprehension about where it fits in. But, as ample compensation for this lack of definition, every reader faces a fresh challenge: to define the quality of its greatness without benefit of a label. As a result *Walden* will undoubtedly remain a controversial book, constantly subjected to reinterpretation—a fate Thoreau would have welcomed.

It has already been approached from a variety of angles, with a resulting enrichment of its meaning. But each of them has tended to be partial, that is, incomplete, for the very reason that it reflects the specific slant of the critic instead of taking the book on its own terms. Those who read it as social criticism find the last half largely irrelevant. Those who assume it to be a book about nature find little in the first half to hold their interest. If one takes it as autobiography, he is constantly losing track of the story line. If it was the program for a new and better economy of living, why did Thoreau give up his experiment after two years and return to civilization?

The one point common to all these divergent approaches has been their concern with style, an agreement that the distinction of *Walden* may lie more in its manner than its matter. But this concern has not usually been pursued beyond a general eulogy. Perhaps it is through language that all the seemingly disparate subjects of this book are integrated into wholeness. Commenting in "Higher Laws" on the limited success of literal fishermen at Walden Pond who are content with a mere string of fish, Thoreau says they have not yet found "the hook of hooks with which to angle for the pond itself." (236) Would style be the hook of hooks, or rather the net with which to catch the whole book? Why not try an entirely new approach and read *Walden* as a poem—the transformation of a vision into words, designed so as to contain and reveal it?

That Thoreau thought of himself primarily as a poet is clear from many comments in his *Journal*. One of his first entries, just four days after he began keeping it in 1837, strikes this key-note:

> In his own magic circle wanders
> The wonderful man, and draws us
> With him to wander, and take part in it. . . .

These are Goethe's lines in praise of Tasso as the representative poet. Copied down in the *Journal* that was to become the record of Thoreau's quest for truth and for a way of life, they stand as the dedication of his career and a prophetic description of his one great book. If communication can be achieved without losing integrity, Goethe seemed to promise, the problem of the self and society, the poet and his audience, can be resolved. The artist's magic circle is both the inviolable privacy of his creative life and the enchanted world he creates in his art.

Walden was to be such a "world," foreign to normal eyes

until the reader is drawn into its circle by the poet's magic language to wander with him and take part in his wonderful experience. Thoreau did care deeply about reaching an audience, despite his protests to the contrary and his strict refusal to compromise with the public. His mode of communication was decided on early, as recorded in the quotation from Goethe's definition of the poet. Fifteen years later in this same *Journal*, just a month after he had taken up again the manuscript of *Walden* and was driving it through to completion, he expressed concern that his writing was becoming too factual and commonplace. Then he concluded, rounding out the quotation from Goethe: "I see that if my facts were . . . transmuted more into the substance of the human mind,—I should need but one book of poetry to contain them all."

The years in between, 1837–1852, comprise the main period of Thoreau's creative life. And of all his writings his "one book of poetry" can only be *Walden* (1854). He composed a good deal of verse, mostly in the early years, but no one, the author included, would offer this as his claim to distinction. The only other book published during his lifetime, *A Week on the Concord and Merrimack Rivers* (1849), is generally considered a trial run. During his last decade, a period of diminished creativity, his sole productions were those miscellaneous essays later to be collected and issued as *Cape Cod*, *The Maine Woods*, and other posthumous volumes, distinguished only in flashes. Thoreau's present high literary reputation, if it is to be sustained, must be pinned on a single book—plus the extraordinary *Journal*.

Yet the question as to whether *Walden* is a created work of art—the central one if he is to be ranked with authors like Melville and Dickinson—has with few exceptions been approached gingerly, then quickly dropped. It has style, all agree, then they rest content with quoting a few aphorisms and an occasional sentence that gleams like an Emersonian nugget. And it does have a kind of structure, some have claimed less confidently: the chapters swing loosely around the cycle of the seasons—surely not a very original or impressive unifying device. Or, as others have pointed out, the sequence of essays may seem casual but it is knit together by transitional sentences and paragraphs—that is to say, the Harvard freshman has passed his rhetoric and composition course. After such perfunctory gestures in the direction of literature, the whole question has usually been left hanging in the air while admirers of *Walden* turn to other matters which they consider more important. It was the prime American protest against materialism; it has been the bible of poor scholars and a handbook for prophets of freedom; it furnishes a calendar of the rural year for nature lovers. This is all well and good, but how does it bring the author into the circle of literary immortals any more than do Caesar's *Commentaries* or Lincoln's *Gettysburg Address?*

To call *Walden* a poem is not to say that its best passages should be extracted and rearranged as free verse, or to suggest the flowery vagueness associated with the hybrid term "prose-poem." What is needed is not a vocabulary for praising Thoreau's style but a technique for reading his masterpiece. To discover a way into the heart of *Walden* one should begin by trying for a new definition that will justify the analogy with poetry. What fittest name can be found for a book which is this, that, or the other thing, yet none of them exactly? It can be likened to a work of fiction, since it is an imaginative projection of setting, characters, and "action," although from known bases in fact. But how does this make it a poem when most fiction is prose, in essence as well as in form? The great majority of novels, such as *Vanity Fair* and *The Deerslayer*, are simply straightforward narratives whose meanings are made manifest in the resolution of their plots, though as created works of art even these rise above the prosaic level of exposition. But there are some fictions of a very different sort, much closer to the mode of poetry, like *The Scarlet Letter*. Hawthorne's meanings are revealed by indirection and irony, by dramatic scenes and ambiguous symbols. Melville, after adapting all these techniques to his own purposes, adds yet another dimension. Starting from personal experiences, he transforms them into mythical quests (in lieu of conventional plots)—simply in *Typee*, more complexly in *Moby-Dick*. Finally, the autobiographical story can find expression in outright poetry, like the blank verse of Wordsworth's *Prelude*, when inward exploration instead of outward narrative is the author's real subject.

These analogues, drawn from the writings of Thoreau's contemporaries, suggest ways in which his masterpiece also can be thought of as poetry rather than prose, if one does not insist on the mechanical distinction of verse as opposed to paragraph form. *Walden* employs all the above techniques and more besides. To read it as a poem is to assume that its meaning resides not in its logic but in its language, its structure of images, its symbolism—and is inseparable from them. Exploring it in these terms, one finds that the social satire and the naturalist's observations are literary counters, just as "autobiography" is the author's effective mask. In this way the reader can avoid being taken in by the pretended subjects (like the argument against railroads) and so discover the true poetic subjects (like the meaning of solitude). The book has long been recognized as both a negative and an affirmative one, but the definition of these two aspects and the emphasis accorded them depend on the approach. Its dual purpose has generally been taken to be merely the rejection of an economy of abundance in favor of a simple natural life. Viewed instead as a poem, *Walden* reveals itself as an experience recreated in words for the purpose of routing the World altogether and discovering the Self. Its real theme is the search for perfection, for a life of holiness, though it is certainly not rendered in Christian terms. Thoreau's own words state the paradox. In a letter of December 1852, at the very period when major revisions were transforming *Walden* from a factual to a symbolic book, he said: "My writing at present is profane, yet in a good sense, and, as it were, sacredly, I may say; for, finding the air of the temple too close, I sat outside."

Two modes of language, wit and metaphor, serve Thoreau as the negative and positive means of his quest. These set up the direction of the book and open out its multiple contrasts. Not only are society and solitude juxtaposed but the civilized and the primitive, complexity and simplicity; also matter and spirit, animal faculties and the higher laws, earth and heaven, nature and God. Man cannot achieve his high aims by rejecting the one and leaping into the other, but must work his way up from the sty of materialism to the perfection he seeks. His weapons for cutting through the jungle of the world include the whole arsenal of wit: puns, understatement, extravagance, irony, verbal surprise, parody, satire, and paradox. The goals themselves and the journey toward them are rendered in an intricate series of image-clusters: animal, leaf, food and shelter, the imagery of time, the quest or journey, the cocoon, the circle, and so on.

The overall structure of *Walden* may be likened to that of both a circle and a web. The spider's web is too geometric, but it will serve as a useful analogy to begin with. Walden Pond lies at the center as a symbol of the purity and harmony yearned for by man, though unattainable. Radial lines of wit run out from this, cutting across the attractions of the purely pragmatic or sensual life. And these radials are looped with circle after concentric circle of aspiration toward the ideal life of heaven—which is also mirrored in the central pond. But Thoreau was too much a poet to be content with a mechanical design. These figures—the spider's web and the formal Euclidian circle—are suggestive merely. Like the orientals he sought an asymmetrical pattern that would satisfy the esthetic sense of form and still remain true to the nature of experience, art without the appearance of artifice.

The circle in *Walden* is less the obvious cycle of the seasons than a number of subtly suggested circular figures, overlapping as well as concentric. (This design is treated fully in a later chapter.) The web is but another name for the intricate lines of relationship that shape the total structure. But all are so woven together that the whole vibrates when any part is touched, and the ultimate motion is toward circumference. Few works of the creative imagination are more successfully unified. Few have their meaning more embedded in a complex pattern of words. *Walden* is a poem, though rendered in the guise of prose.

The interweaving of wit and metaphor in Thoreau's introductory chapters, "Economy" and "Where I Lived," is the subject of the ensuing pages.

Wit

No book aimed at heaven ever took its start more humbly from the earth than this one. It begins with a seemingly prosaic essay on the basic necessities for maintaining physical life. Instead of considering this irrelevant, Thoreau knows it is the only way to jolt his contemporaries out of the conviction that the affairs of this world leave no time for the other. Without establishing the contrary he cannot possibly expect a hearing for his own story, whether his audience consists of men who lead lives of economic desperation or lives of complacent prosperity in the best of all possible worlds. (The early 1850's was the period of greatest prosperity in America prior to the Civil War.) So his first gambit is to slay the dragon Materialism. After feinting a head-on encounter, his actual mode of assault is a series of skirmishes to prove that the monster of mid-century is a chimera, a product of the sociological imagination, and so to rout it with laughter.

The opening gun in his battle of wit is fired in the very title of his long introductory chapter, "Economy." Readers a century ago knew what to expect, or thought they did. Either the latest defense of the capitalistic system, according to such a book as John Stuart Mill's compendious *Political Economy;* or the newest revolt against it, advocating a communal sharing of profits, for the alert few who had read Karl Marx's *Manifesto*. Both were published in 1848. Both were rationalistic schemes based on faith in materialism as the only way to achieve the greatest happiness of the greatest number, opposed as their solutions were. But Thoreau's "Economy" takes Communists as well as Utilitarians by surprise, attacking where they think themselves least vulnerable. He undermines their assumption that abundance for all is the only goal and substitutes his own program for reducing the necessaries of life to a minimum. He replaces their panaceas for the common man with a Spartan discipline for the uncommon man. His is no treatise on how to acquire possessions but a sprightly fable on how to do without them. Since the age had been filled with solemn discussions of the economic problems facing an overpopulated world, what Carlyle called the "dismal science," Thoreau also pretends to adopt the logical form of an expository essay with beginning, middle, and end. But this is merely an outward show of "argument."

Feeling the need to condition his audience before unleashing his novel attack, he allows himself a few preliminary pages of wit to accomplish this. In a first brief paragraph setting forth the purpose of his book, to recount his experience in living apart from the world, he employs a deliberate confounding of scale. Here is no long self-exile in the desert to commune with God, like that of Elijah, nor even a modern Crusoe retiring to an exotic island half a world away in the South Seas. Instead, like a straightfaced Yankee, he tells how he walked a mile and a half out of his native village, squatted in a friend's woods, and lived there alone for two years. Having returned home satisfied with his experiment, he concludes abruptly: "At present I am a sojourner in civilized life again." Such is the laconic summary of the central drama in his life, the autobiographical core of his masterpiece.

Next, in explaining why he obtrudes his private affairs on the public, he indulges in his first pun, a learned one. It is in answer to persistent inquiries by the villagers as to his mode of life, he says, "which some would call impertinent." (3) By bringing into play the Latin root of this adjective, he complicates its meaning: to be impertinent is to be rude only because it is not pertinent, that is, not relevant. But the desire of normal men to understand abnormal behavior seems to him "very natural and pertinent." This leads to his ironic understatement in apologizing for the autobiographical cast of what is to follow: "In most books, the *I*, or first person, is omitted; in this it will be retained; that, in respect to egotism, is the main difference." Such is his justification for the most self-obsessed book in the history of American literature. But the third paragraph extends this "I" to global dimensions by the language of surprise: "I have travelled a good deal in Concord." (4) And his fellow townsmen become universal men by shock metaphors, compared in their unending labors to the Greek Hercules and in their penitential lives to Brahmans. By the end of page two the reader has been launched from the simple to the complex, from local and particular to archetypal experience.

The rest of the introductory pages of "Economy" crackle with word play, aphorisms, and satirical anecdotes—the weapons of his negative mode of attack. Things are encumbrances; wage-earners are worse off than southern Negroes because self-enslaved: "The better part of the man is soon plowed into the soil for compost." (6) Since the old are no good as mentors, each man must start from scratch: "One generation abandons the enterprises of another like stranded vessels." (12) And occasionally his affirmative goal shines through in a witty image: "As if you could kill time without injuring eternity." (8) At the end of nine or ten pages the reader is presumably convinced that he has not been on the road to the good life, in any sense, and has been joked out of his resignation to his present desperate status as something inescapable. He is now ready for a serious discussion of economy. Instead, the author first gives him a low-comedy pun. One advantage of his withdrawal from the civilized way of life, he says, has been to learn what are the "grossest groceries." (13)

With such a starter, only the dullest reader would expect a treatise on the dismal science when Thoreau at last gets down to business with the basic necessaries of life: "Food, Shelter, Clothing, and Fuel." These are quickly reduced to two, since food is only internal fuel and shelter an extension of clothing; then to one, since the purpose of all is to retain vital heat, that is, life. Yet these are the necessaries men devote their whole lives to acquiring in order that they may begin to "live." The magnitude of the problem is deflated by two kinds of wit: comic exaggeration of the folly of abundance, ironic reduction of man's actual needs to a minimum. The latter is used for the more basic matters of food and shelter, the former for the lesser items of fuel and clothing.

A few striking examples will indicate the manner of his argument. "The luxuriously rich are not simply kept comfortably warm, but unnaturally hot," he says; "they are cooked, of course, *à la mode*." (15) The costly new-fangled furnace for central heating, here alluded to, would naturally be a subject for travesty by the man whose advice to anyone shivering from cold was to take a brisk walk. Again, the old adage that clothes make the man offered an easy target for caricature: "Dress a scarecrow in your last shift, you standing shiftless by, who would not soonest salute the scarecrow?" (24) The pun on "shiftless" is obvious, but the more subtle one in the previous sally should not be missed either; "cooked" originally meant simply baked at a high temperature (as in terra cotta), then was later applied to the preparation of food (à la mode). The surface reader of *Walden* will miss much of the humor of its word play.

Even when Thoreau begins his discussion with apparent seriousness he invariably ends with a fillip. For example, after equating "animal life" with "animal heat," by showing scientifically that both are maintained by a kind of slow internal combustion, he concludes: "disease and death take place when this is too rapid; or [when] for want of fuel, or from some defect in the draught, the fire goes out." (14) Again, in the midst of six pages of satire on clothes as false symbols of status, ransacking history and ethnology for outrageous examples, he interrupts himself with what pretends to be a sensible solution, but is swiftly turned into a paradox: "It is desirable that a man be clad so simply that he can lay his hands on himself in the dark." (26–27)

Shelter is a more serious problem. But the idea that it is just a roomier kind of overcoat gave him a chance to ring a new change on the fig-leaf origin of clothing in relation to the primal "tree house," both of which man found ready-made in Eden: "Adam and Eve, according to the fable, wore the bower before other clothes." (30) Next, alluding to the New Testament, he indulges in a mild bit of blasphemy. "I think that I speak within bounds when I say that, though the birds of the air have their nests, and the foxes their holes, and the savages their wigwams," he begins; then, as a substitute for the promised subversion of "the Son of Man hath not where to lay his head," he concludes with housing statistics of a sort familiar today: "in modern civilized society not more than one half the families own a shelter." (33)

Next, on the assumption that he has been too extravagant in building himself a whole cabin, one room ten by fifteen feet, he invents a classic example of *reductio ad absurdum*: "I used to see a large box by the railroad, six feet long by three wide, in which the laborers locked up their tools at night; and it suggested to me that every man who was hard pushed [for a house] might get such a one for a dollar." This is Thoreau's solution for the staggering problem of housing mankind. Of course, it is just a ruse for playing off one extreme against another. In acquiring a dwelling one must exercise a little Yankee shrewdness, he says, "lest after all he find himself in a workhouse, a labyrinth without a clue, a museum, an almshouse, a prison, or a splendid mausoleum instead." Then after an amusing elaboration of the tool-box shelter, which he decides not to buy, he brings himself up with a halt: "I am far from jesting. Economy is a subject which admits of being treated with levity, but it cannot so be disposed of." (31–32) This likewise is a dodge. What follows merely substitutes for the raillery applied to lighter matters, such as fuel and clothing, a devastating satire on men as housebuilders, with a running comparison of wigwam and mansion. Here he calls on the whole range of modes from parody to invective, then concludes on a more serious note. Primitive man, as a tent-dweller, had the advantage of being a "sojourner in nature," he says: "We . . . have settled down on earth and forgotten heaven." (41) Wit blends into metaphor as his theme shifts from negative to positive.

Food, on the other hand, is rarely subjected to Thoreau's artillery, whether light or heavy, perhaps because he thought of it as the one indispensable necessity, many animals maintaining life by this alone. And if food is the basic tie of man to his mortal life, it has also been made paradoxically a symbol of his hope for immortality. The normal use of food in *Walden* is for images that approach the sacramental, the finest example being subtly compounded with wit. As he sits down to his elemental meal during house building, he pushes his economy to the last detail and with unanswerable consistency. "I usually carried my dinner of bread and butter," he says, "and read the newspaper in which it was wrapped, at noon, sitting amid the green pine boughs which I had cut off, and to my bread was imparted some of their fragrance, for my hands were covered with a thick coat of pitch." (46–47) With water from the pond, which he drank almost ritualistically, this would suggest a kind of outdoor Eucharist, but he contents himself here with a suggestion of incense from nature's resin.

An advocate of vegetarianism, though not a fanatic on the subject, he rebukes the meat-eaters with a parable:

> One farmer says to me, "You cannot live on vegetable food solely, for it furnishes nothing to make bones with"; and so he religiously devotes a part of his day to supplying his system with the raw material of bones; walking all the while he talks behind his oxen, which, with vegetable-made bones, jerk him and his lumbering plow along in spite of every obstacle. (10)

But Thoreau goes a long step beyond vegetarianism. After reducing his regular diet by wit to the barest minimum, he answers unbelievers by declaring: "I can live on board nails. If they cannot understand that, they cannot understand much that I have to say." (72) Readers expecting a plausible essay on food economy will be certain to call this exaggerated. He meets the objection by saying that he is only afraid he "cannot exaggerate enough," that being the very style he is aiming at. "I fear chiefly lest my expression may not be *extra-vagant* enough, may not wander far enough beyond the narrow limits of my daily experience, so as to be adequate to the truth of which I have been convinced." (357) This truth is the central quest of *Walden*, the vision of which forced him into the license of poetry in order to be able to express it. To clarify, he divides the word into its two Latin components: *Extra vagance!* "Going beyond" is one of the chief stylistic devices of both the wit and the poet. And for expressing his aspiration to live in the spirit alone, "board nails" is an appropriately extravagant term for total fasting.

The long discussion of basic economies, which forms the ostensible core of his introductory chapter, is broken right in the middle by what any economist would brand as a digression—a shower of images for his own "enterprises" after the minimum necessities have been obtained. This deliberate breaking of the rational order is proof enough that his "argument" is really an anti-structure, and it points up the essentially negative purpose of the whole chapter on "Economy." There is an alternative to materialism, he says. Instead of becoming a slave to the acquisition of superfluities, it is time for man "to adventure on life now, his vacation from humbler toil having commenced." (17) At this first sounding of the affirmative note he shifts from wit to metaphor as his principal mode, though the dozen rockets that are shot off in rapid succession are an ingenious fusion of the two. All are images of the poet's vocation, in contrast to the normal trades and professions: "self-appointed inspector of snow storms," "surveyor of forest paths," "reporter to a journal of no very wide circulation" (his own *Journal*, circulated only to intimates, eventually filled fourteen volumes), and so on. (19–20)

The cluster of images begins with a cryptic symbol of what he is still in quest of: "a hound, a bay horse, and a turtle-dove," (18) which has baffled critics so far in spite of numerous attempts to explicate it. (Thoreau's own commentary, in a letter, scarcely clarifies it.) He ends with an extended conceit for authorship, as a commerce with the "Celestial Empire," (22–23) developing his analogy from the contemporary China trade by an elaborate system of word play that leads from earth to heaven. This is the organizing pun of the whole chapter, suggesting the need of a spiritual economy. The passage comes to focus in a statement that flatly denies he was making an economic experiment in the normal sense of that term: "My purpose in going to Walden Pond was not to live cheaply nor to live dearly there, but to transact some private business with the fewest obstacles." (21)

This private business, as planned in advance, was to write his first book, *A Week on the Concord and Merrimack Rivers*. Then, as he wandered in that magic circle, came the impulse to create another book, his masterpiece, which would record the actual experience of living the poet's life. The practical lesson he wanted to learn from economy was how to be a non-selling author and survive. This central "enterprise" is rendered in *Walden* by the fable of an Indian basketweaver who came to town to sell his creations and was dismayed to find that he would have to create a market for them also, or else make something that white men already wanted to buy. Thoreau, remembering the failure of *A Week,* learns from the Indian's experience by extending the metaphor to his own productions:

I too had woven a kind of basket of a delicate texture, but I had not made it worth any one's while to buy them. Yet not the less, in my case, did I think it worth my while to weave them, and instead of studying how to make it worth men's while to buy my baskets, I studied rather how to avoid the necessity of selling them. (21)

The spiritual lesson to be learned from his residence at the pond was even more important: how "to entertain the true problems of life," (13) that is, how to seek perfection. Since his previous enterprises can be described only in metaphors, this is ample evidence that his present enterprise, the Walden experiment, is symbolic also.

With these images of the quest in mind, one returns from Thoreau's strategic digression to follow through to the end his diverting escapes from the trap of materialism. By this time the reader has been properly educated, both affirmatively and negatively, to understand the author's answers to those queries by Concord villagers concerning his mode of life with which the book began. On page forty-five Thoreau takes up again where he left off at the end of the first paragraph. "Near the end of March, 1845," his story continues with the air of straightforward autobiography, "I borrowed an axe and went down to the woods by Walden Pond." (45) His concern once more is with the basic economies, now concentrated on food and shelter as he himself sought to provide them, a shift from generalized discussion to concrete narrative. His method is still that of wit, but the best of it now takes the novel form of statistics on the expense of his house and what he ate. With a bookkeeper's flourish he lists everything that went into the cost of his house down to the least item (a penny for chalk) and to the last half-cent, coming up with \$28.12½ for the grand total. (53–54) His next house will surpass the mansions of Concord in "grandeur and luxury," he boasts —as soon as he learns how to build it for the price of the present one.

The account of expenses for food is similarly detailed. After itemizing everything he spent during a period of eight months, he confesses unblushingly, "Yes, I did eat $8.74, all told," but adds that his readers' guilty deeds would look no better in print. (66) It is probably not a coincidence that this figure tallies with the one claimed as a possible food budget by the leader of a gastronomic reform group in New England during the 1830's and 1840's. There is every reason to believe that his book, *The Young Housekeeper* (Boston, 1838), would have come under Thoreau's eye. The author was a cousin of Bronson Alcott's, and in addition to advocating simple food, natural preparation, and abstinence from meat for moral and psychological reasons, he buttressed his program with economic arguments. The vegetable and cereal diet he outlined as ample to sustain one person added up to twenty-five cents a week—less than one-fifth the usual cost, and exactly equivalent to the *Walden* total of $8.74 for eight months.

Similarly, Thoreau himself gives some comparative figures for contemporary housing that dramatize his $28.12½. The rent of a dormitory room at Harvard came to a little more than that sum, $30, for just one year; an average house in Concord cost $800, about thirty times what he paid for his own. (55, 34) Even if his figures for expenses were multiplied by ten, to arrive at some sort of modern currency equivalent, they would still be ludicrously low, as any economist today would testify—about $10 a month for food and less than $300 for a house. But such literal analyses are beside the point. The relation of Thoreau's statistics in *Walden* to the actual expenses of his experiment would be irrelevant even if they could be checked. (The *Journal* for this period was largely stripped for use in the book, and so contains no data of this sort.) They are part of his wit. Spread out in his book, like pages from a ledger, they are a shriveling satire on economic man's biggest bugbear, the high cost of living.

After this, abandoning the materialist's method of reckoning altogether, Thoreau pushes his economy to its ultimate definition: "The cost of a thing is the amount of what I will call life which is required to be exchanged for it, immediately or in the long run." (34) This is the basis of his most significant conclusion, in the final casting up of accounts to arrive at a time budget also: "I found that, by working about six weeks in a year, I could meet all the expenses of living." (76) (Two pages later he reduces the work period to "thirty or forty days.") The great merit of this is that it leaves the other forty-six weeks "free and clear." And the great advantage of these figures is that they reverse the average man's vacation and work periods. On the next page this is turned into a memorable parody of Adam's curse: "It is not necessary that a man should earn his living by the sweat of his brow, unless he sweats easier than I do."

With so much leisure and with the perspective offered by his "primitive and frontier life, though in the midst of an outward civilization," it was inevitable that he should crow over his escape from some of the absurdities that he had left behind. He satirizes the railroad, telegraph, and other recent inventions as "improved means to an unimproved end." He indulges in a tirade against philanthropists and reformers of all kinds, including utopian experiments in communal living, such as nearby Brook Farm. These attacks grew naturally enough out of his answers to quips by his townsmen: Didn't he miss the advantages of civilization? Didn't he admit that his solitary way of life was selfish? And so on. If Walden really digresses from its theme anywhere it is in passages like these. But they do not prove that its purpose was social criticism, a subject tangential to the book's chief aim. Thoreau makes himself very clear on this point. "I desire to speak," he says in disavowing the reformer's role, "as one not interested in the success or failure of the present economical and social arrangements." (62) Nor is he writing even a handbook for the individualist: "I would not have any one adopt *my* mode of living on any account . . . I would have each one be very careful to find out and pursue *his own* way." (78, 79) As for his new-found independence at Walden, it enables him to follow the "bent" of his own genius, "which is a very crooked one."

Much more pertinent to Thoreau's way is his running commentary on furniture, though it begins in the lightest vein of banter. "I would rather sit on a pumpkin and have it all to myself than be crowded on a velvet cushion," he said earlier; his later revision of this epigram merely substitutes the wit of understatement: "None is so poor that he need sit on a pumpkin. That is shiftlessness." (41, 72) But the accompanying inventory of his own possessions would make an Irishman's shack seem over-furnished. When a friend offered him a door mat he declined it, "preferring to wipe my feet on the sod before my door." Similarly he dispensed with curtains, having "no gazers to shut out but the sun and moon." (74) All of this leads to an aphorism that furnishes a key to the first third of *Walden*: "A man is rich in proportion to the number of things which he can afford to let alone." (91)

The opposite—an accumulation of superfluities—is exemplified in his amusing anecdote describing the auction of a local deacon's effects, "for his life had not been ineffectual." All the furnishings and the trumpery of two generations, including a dried tapeworm preserved in a bottle, were put up for sale instead of being subjected to the "purifying destruction" of fire. The neighbors eagerly bought everything and took it home to their garrets, where it would lie until their estates were settled. "When a man dies he kicks the dust," is Thoreau's dry comment. (75) But none of this is mere nonsense for its own sake. It all prepares the way for a conclusion pertinent to his central thesis, illustrated with a ritual practised by the Mucclasse Indians. Once a year all their old possessions were gathered in a common heap and consumed with fire, he records. This was followed by three days of fasting, then three days of feasting, as they prepared themselves for a new life. Of this purification by fire Thoreau declares: "I have scarcely heard of a truer sacrament, that is, as the dictionary defines it, 'outward and visible sign of an inward and spiritual grace.' " (76)

Metaphor

"Economy" is a witty fable on how to get rid of the material world, enriched with a few metaphorical hints of the quest that lies beyond. It is strung on a slender chronicle of his life at Walden Pond, which makes the second chapter by its very title, "Where I Lived, and What I Lived For," seem to promise only a repetition of the first. But, in addition to its intrinsic merit, this section forms an indispensable transition from the negative approach of the introduction to the positive theme of the body of his book, and a subtle shift from wit to metaphor as the dominant style. It opens with his finest display of the former skill in a classic skit on how not to buy a farm. Over the years Thoreau had been developing in his *Journal* an elaborate conceit about the ownership of property, poetic "ownership" as opposed to legal. In an entry for 25 May 1851 one may find the germ of the well-known *Walden* anecdote. During a walk he stopped to admire the view across a valley to far away hills. "I wonder that houses are not oftener located mainly that they may command particular rare prospects," he commented: "A vista where you have the near green horizon contrasted with the distant blue one, terrestrial with celestial earth." (J, II, 215–216) Then, comparing the art of nature with the art of man (as described in various books on landscape gardening he had read), he added:

> The farmer would never suspect what it was you were buying, and such sites would be the cheapest of any . . . . a noble inheritance for your children. The true sites for human dwellings are unimproved. They command no price in the market. . . . An unchangeable kind of wealth, a *real* estate. (J, II, 215–216)

The turn of wit in this final phrase provided the clue for development in the *Walden* anecdote. There the whole passage is an intricate web of puns and word play, so tightly woven the reader must be on his toes to catch them. They subvert all the terminology of property ownership, *survey*, *deed*, *price*, and so on:

> At a certain season of our life we are accustomed to consider every spot as the possible site of a house. I have thus surveyed the country on every side within a dozen miles of where I live. In

imagination I have bought all the farms in succession, for all were to be bought, and I knew their price. I walked over each farmer's premises, tasted his wild apples, discoursed on husbandry with him, took his farm at his price, at any price, mortgaging it to him in my mind; even put a higher price on it,—took everything but a deed of it,—took his word for his deed, for I dearly love to talk,—cultivated it, and him too to some extent, I trust. (90)

Such is the ingenuity of his satire on the real-estate business as to leave not only agents but all buyers and sellers of property feeling a little foolish. In this way Thoreau "owned" the Hollowell place during the term of his refusal—"the refusal was all I wanted." Before the farmer made out a deed his wife changed her mind, and he offered ten dollars to be released from his contract. This leads Thoreau to indulge in some paradoxical expense accounting:

Now, to speak the truth, I had but ten cents in the world, and it surpassed my arithmetic to tell, if I was that man who had ten cents, or who had a farm, or ten dollars, or all together. However, I let him keep the ten dollars and the farm too, for I had carried it far enough; or rather, to be generous, I sold him the farm for just what I gave for it. . . . I found thus that I had been a rich man without any damage to my poverty. (91)

After the fun is over he winds up with a shining double metaphor. Ever since deciding not to buy he has annually carried off its best crop, the landscape, without need of even a wheelbarrow. Better still, the whole farm is finally put into a poem, "the most admirable kind of invisible fence," he says, leaving the owner toiling as a serf on the land Thoreau has bought with his imagination. (92)

"The present was my next experiment of this kind," he continues, in reference to his squatting on Emerson's acres and putting together his own cabin out of a dismantled railroad shanty. (93) That is, the first was an experiment in how to own a farm without buying it, the second how to build a house not so much to live in as to grow out of. So he returns yet once again to his central autobiographical experience; but most myths come to us in several versions, as in the four Gospels. At each retelling of his own story he drops back into a simple relaxed style, as if allowing the reader to catch his breath after the elaborate displays of wit and the complexity of occasional metaphorical passages. But this third style also plays a positive role in his overall language pattern. An unadorned factual narrative is ideal to begin with when one wants to put the reader in a mood for accepting the fabulous, and it has been the traditional mode for writers of scriptures and recorders of miracles. The previous versions of his Walden story have been exactly that, apparently straightforward accounts of how he built his shelter and supplied himself with food, but with a few threads woven in that give it the strange air of a "natural" rather than a man-made house. He dug his cellar where a woodchuck formerly had its burrow, he left the bark on three sides of the studs and rafters, thus keeping them as much like trees as possible, and so on. (46, 49)

These prepare the way for stronger suggestions of the miraculous, which appear in the third and last retelling. Since he did not plaster until autumn, the walls of rough weather-stained boards were left all summer with wide chinks in them, so that "I did not need to go outdoors to take the air." (95) Then, after alluding to a passage in the Hindu scriptures praising the life of nature, he adds: "I found myself suddenly neighbor to the birds; not by having imprisoned one, but having caged myself near them." (95) The sequence reaches a climax when his own dwelling, with its "clean and airy look, especially in the morning," brings back a vision: "To my imagination it retained throughout the day more or less of this auroral character, reminding me of a certain house on a mountain which I had visited a year before. This was an airy and unplastered cabin, fit to entertain a travelling god, and where a goddess might trail her garments." (94)

The memory was of a trip to the Catskill Mountains in the summer of 1844; but it was not recorded in the *Journal*, interestingly enough, until the day after he took up residence at the pond in 1845. "*July 5. Saturday*. Walden. Yesterday I came here to live," he wrote: "My house makes me think of some mountain houses I have seen." Then he described the cabin of the miller of Kaaterskill Falls, a fascinating model for the more famous cabin of the hermit of Walden:

The house seemed high-placed, airy, and perfumed, fit to entertain a travelling god. It was so high, indeed, that all the music, the broken strains, the waifs and accompaniments of tunes, that swept over the ridge of the Caatskills, passed through its aisles. Could not man be man in such an abode? And would he ever find out this groveling life? It was the very light and atmosphere in which the works of Grecian art were composed, and in which they rest. They have appropriated to themselves a loftier hall than mortals ever occupy, at least on a level with the mountain-brows of the world. There was wanting a little of the glare of the lower vales, and in its place a pure twilight as became the precincts of heaven. (J, I, 361–362)

It is hard to say which of two facts is more interesting: that it took Walden cabin as a catalyst to precipitate the mountain cabin into Thoreau's recorded memory or that the *Journal* draft was so magically transformed when it was incorporated in the book. The *Walden* version concludes:

The winds which passed over my dwelling were such as sweep over the ridges of mountains, bearing the broken strains, or celestial parts only, of terrestrial music. The morning wind forever blows, the poem of creation is uninterrupted; but few are the ears that hear it. Olympus is but the outside of the earth everywhere. (94)

In such a dwelling anything could happen. Similar hints and gleams recur throughout the book, keeping the reader in a state of expectant wonder as he shares the narrator's anticipation of "the Visitor who never comes." (298) So he is ready to accept the advent of Thoreau's gods on their own terms when they finally do arrive, deep in the chapter on "Solitude."

Chapter 2 furnishes the transition to this spiritual life, the quest for which gradually comes to dominate the book. It does so in the first half by reversing the author's previous techniques.

Instead of defending the economy of his own way of life by wit, he uses metaphor, allusion, and fable to glorify it. The factual promise of his title, "Where I Lived and What I Lived For," is part of the game by which the literal setting is subtly transmuted into the imaginary "world" of *Walden.* First the house is fit for a traveling god. Then the pond serves "to float the earth"; and its water, "full of light and reflections, becomes a lower heaven." (96) Glancing up to the galaxy, he can say that where he lives is as far off as "some remote and more celestial corner" of the system: "Both place and time were changed, and I dwelt nearer to those parts of the universe and to those eras in history which had most attracted me." (97) Best of all, the ecstasy of his life makes each morning an invitation to renewal. A sincere worshiper of Aurora, he rises early and bathes in the pond as "a religious exercise." (98) All poets make their music like Memnon at sunrise, he says: "That man who does not believe that each day contains an earlier, more sacred, and auroral hour than he has yet profaned, has despaired of life, and is pursuing a descending and darkening way." (99) Millions wake up every day to physical labor, but only one in a hundred millions "to a poetic or divine life." (100) The Walden experience, for Thoreau, is the dawn of a new life.

In a similar way the second half of this chapter prepares for his quest by using a poetic mode to define the good life that lies beyond the basic economies. Instead of occasional denials of this and that as his purpose in withdrawing from the world, he now attempts to portray it affirmatively by multiple hints and suggestions. These radiate from a key paragraph, buried in the center of the chapter, that will repay close reading. It is a series of metaphors framed by wit:

> I went to the woods because I wished to live deliberately, to front only the essential facts of life, and see if I could not learn what it had to teach, and not, when I came to die, discover that I had not lived. I did not wish to live what was not life, living is so dear; nor did I wish to practice resignation, unless it was quite necessary. I wanted to live deep and suck out all the marrow of

life, to live so sturdily and Spartan-like as to put to rout all that was not life, to cut a broad swath and shave close, to drive life into a corner, and reduce it to its lowest terms, and, if it proved to be mean, why then to get the whole and genuine meanness of it, and publish its meanness to the world; or if it were sublime, to know it by experience, and be able to give a true account of it in my next excursion. For most men, it appears to me, are in a strange uncertainty about it, whether it is of the devil or of God, and have *somewhat hastily* concluded that it is the chief end of man here to "glorify God and enjoy him forever." (100–101)

The elaborate play on live and die comes to focus in the learned pun, "I wished to live deliberately"—not only unhurriedly but with deliberation. "Deliberately" is his first polysyllable, followed by a marked pause. This is skillful rhetoric, compelling the reader to speak the word slowly in order to take in its full weight (*de* + *librare* = to weigh). As one critic has summed up the sound effects of this passage: "The measured pace seems in exact correspondence with his carefully measured thoughts, and serves, as effective rhythm always does, to direct the fullest attention to the most important words." The only way to experience life to the full is by meditating on its true values.

At the end of the paragraph, referring to the other meaning of "deliberately," Thoreau says most men have missed the way because they have "*somewhat hastily* concluded" (the italics are his) that it is the chief purpose of man here to "glorify God and enjoy him forever." This seems on the surface to advocate glorifying man, a subversion of the Shorter Catechism. But a closer look shows his purpose to be a reinterpretation of doctrine rather than blasphemy. In the first version of *Walden* this paragraph ended by saying that it is a mistake "to glorify God and Him only." This merely implies that the transcendental chief-end-of-man—to worship the indwelling god—should be grafted on the Christian. But in the finished book he added a clarifying passage at the end of his first chapter: "Our hymn-books resound with a melodious cursing of God and enduring Him forever. . . . There is nowhere recorded a simple and irrepressible satisfaction with the gift of life, any memorable praise of God." (87) After such preparation there was no further need in his second chapter to specify the error men fall into about the purpose of life when they jump to conclusions hastily instead of arriving at them by living deliberately. The only true way to glorify God is to enjoy the gift of life.

In between lie the images that suggest how one can "live deep" enough to experience this joy, and if they seem stern they are lifted up by the hope that life may be "sublime." They are drawn from some of the chief clusters of imagery used throughout the book: food, the military life, farming, hunting, mathematics. The verbs of action are his chief source of power. Sucking marrow is a primitive act, compatible with the life of a soldier. The range of Thoreau's desire to live fully is widened by the image of harvesting and intensified by the image of closing in on his quarry. This paragraph also provides the substance of the rest of the chapter. There the same images reappear, turned into word play, and the framing wit is expanded into metaphors. Even the phrasing is echoed, but with this novel transposing of styles.

Two examples will illustrate Thoreau's ingenuity. Advocating a "more than Spartan simplicity," he introduces a rapid fire of puns with the epigram: "Keep you accounts on your thumbnail." (102, 101) Such is the lively rebirth of his statistical figure for reducing life "to its lowest terms." Again, the witty initial sentence, "I wished to live deliberately," is developed into a series of metaphors. "Let us spend one day as deliberately as Nature," he begins, and then elaborates a dozen images of haste and distraction to be avoided, of peace and reality to be sought. (108–109) "Simplicity, simplicity, simplicity!" he urges. A late *Journal* entry defines the term: "By simplicity, commonly called poverty, my life is concentrated and so becomes organized, or a κόσμος, which before was inorganic and lumpish." (J, IX, 246) To return to the focal paragraph, the sternness of its regimen is mitigated by the phrase with which it ends, "my next excursion," suggesting the relaxed pleasure of his life at Walden.

The purpose of Thoreau's experiment is clearer now in one

sense: to withdraw from the life of civilization so that he can merge with the life of nature, to leave the artificial for the real. But this was a means rather than an end. The true quest is still withheld, only hinted at in two metaphors that bring Chapter 2 to a conclusion. "Time is but the stream I go a-fishing in," he says: "I see the sandy bottom and detect how shallow it is. Its thin current slides away, but eternity remains." (109) How to cast his line for that is the theme explored in the rest of the book. For the moment he pulls himself back to earth, where he knows he must make his start, but not by working with his hands any more than is necessary. His second metaphor forms the immediate link to the chapters that follow: "My instinct tells me that my head is an organ for burrowing, . . . and with it I would mine and burrow my way through these hills. I think that the richest vein is somewhere hereabouts." (109) The way must be through nature, though the goal is heaven. *Walden* is not the diary of a day laborer who supported himself on six weeks' work and spent the other forty-six loafing on the grass. It is a manual of stern discipline, the record of a search for the buried life of the soul.

The stage has at last been set for the revolutionary alternative Thoreau has to offer as a program for living, once the problems of economy have been met: "to adventure on life now." (17) The two opening chapters, taking up nearly a third of the book, might seem unduly long for a mere introduction. But he knew there was no other way to break down the resistance of readers, then as now, to any celebration of the life of the spirit. Though challenging in their own right as a sort of modern *De Contemptu Mundi,* these attacks on worldliness are actually just a prelude to the main theme contained in the body of the book, his transcendent experience at Walden Pond. The surface disparity between the two parts has led anthologists to print "Economy" and "Where I Lived" as separable essays, but this amputation is fatal because their real goal is not social criticism. The shift from counter theme to dominant theme called for a shift in technique so radical as to threaten the unity of the whole, seemingly. The pretended expository style, so well suited as a mode of argument for proving that materialism is an encumbrance to the spirit, would not serve at all as the vehicle for a quest that could be suggested only by indirection. For the body of the book he substitutes the mode of poetry, though masked as autobiography. At the very beginning of *Walden* he had said: "I should not talk so much about myself if there were anybody else whom I knew as well. Unfortunately, I am confined to this theme by the narrowness of my experience." All he required of any writer was "a simple and sincere account of his own life." (4) Having delivered himself of this chesty dictum, he proceeds to ignore it. What he gives instead is the merest thread of an autobiographical story on which to hang his images.

But the shift in styles is more a gradual movement from one to the other than a sudden break. Several times in the introductory chapters he drops into the autobiographical vein when giving a preview of the quest to come. Occasionally, in the later chapters he returns to exposition when there is some fragment of the material world remaining to be disposed of. And both styles—expository and narrative—are really only anti-structures, as has been shown. The true stylistic mode of *Walden* is the interplay of wit and metaphor, used respectively for his negative and affirmative purposes. The fusion of the two into an intricate counterpoint is made easy by their close kinship. Many metaphors are witty and much wit tends to be metaphorical, in both the derived meaning of that term and its seventeenth-century meaning (Wit as the power of joining thought and expression with an aptness calculated to delight by its novelty). So the shift from one to the other is largely a matter of emphasis, the elaborate display of pun, irony, and satire giving way as imagery and symbolism come to dominate. The pivotal chapter, "Where I Lived, and What I Lived For," blending all these modes, forms a smooth transition between the introduction and the body of the book. With his economic needs now reduced to a minimum, he can begin to "entertain the true problems of life with freedom and a prospect of success." (13)

Patterns

What really happened at Walden Pond from 1845 to 1847 will never be known. Readers of the book are excluded from the author's outward life and given instead an inward journey or exploration. This is lightly framed in a pseudo-narrative that is made to serve his real purpose by invoking the over-image of life as a pilgrimage. It begins with Chapter 3, "Reading," and continues through Chapter 17, "Spring"—leaving the "Conclusion" as a kind of epilogue in which he allows himself to savor the fruits of his experiment. These fifteen chapters are arranged in a seemingly casual sequence in order to suggest the leisurely unfolding of experience during a year spent in the woods—the transcendental ideal of organic form. But the chronicle aspect, as indeed the whole mode of autobiography, is more a device for maneuvering than a strict form. The author himself confesses that he reduced the two years and more of his actual residence to one, "for convenience." (93–94) It can also be shown from the *Journal* that he expanded it to more than fifteen years by levying on experiences ranging from 1837 to 1854. The choice of a single year was part of the artist's search for a form he could use at least as a point of departure and return. The full unfolding of Thoreau's new structure, sprung from the circular calendar, can only come much later with an examination of the elaborate image clusters that make up the book's true form. But first there are some simpler techniques for dealing with time.

The annual cycle is an important part of the total design of Walden, but it is no mere mechanical formula of seasonal progression. True, the first ten chapters of the body of the book deal in general with summer activities, and the last five spin through the other three seasons. But just as the titles of some of the latter contain the word "Winter" or "Spring" (Chapters 14–17), the titles of some of the former, such as "Higher Laws" (Chapter 11), suggest excursions out of this time scheme and out of time itself into the Eternal Now. Besides, there are intricate interweavings of the seasons in all of the chapters. For example, Chapter 3, "Reading," is ostensibly set in summer. But Thoreau begins by leaping out of the seasonal boundary: "I kept Homer's Iliad on my table through the summer, though I looked at his page only now and then. . . . Yet I sustained myself by the prospect of such reading in future" (111)—that is, when winter would drive him indoors.

It soon becomes apparent that he is concerned with something more complex than a chronological narrative. Books, he says, are for our "*morning* hours"; they are more salutary than "the spring to our lives." (111, 119–120) The next chapter begins with a literal seasonal reference in the past tense: "I did not read books the first summer; I hoed beans." (123) Then shifting quickly to the present—"I sit at my window this summer *afternoon* . . ." (127)—it moves into his real subject: the "Sounds" (Chapter 4) that come to him from the natural world. This is followed by "Solitude" (Chapter 5), which reaches its climax of spiritual communion in "the long winter *evenings*" (152); then by its sequel "Visitors" (Chapter 6), which ranges over the whole period of his residence. All this before his actual summer activity in "The Bean-Field" (Chapter 7) brings him back to the calendar year. Clearly, spring, summer, and winter, as well as morning, afternoon, and evening are the terms of an inner timetable rather than an outer one. Similarly, in the last half of the book, where Thoreau's handling of time becomes ever more complex and significant, leading at last to his circular images for renewal and rebirth. (See pp. 228–257, below.)

Beneath such natural orderings of his story—the annual cycle and the autobiographical chronicle—there are two structures of much greater subtlety and significance. The one nearer the surface is a set of patterns in the chapter groupings, beginning with the dualities that plagued all transcendentalists in their search for unity. Thoreau had never forgotten the Phi Beta Kappa address at Harvard in 1837 when Emerson laid down his novel curriculum for the American Scholar. After challenging the young graduates to shake off their bondage to Europe, he announced his radical program for the true scholar's education: He is nourished and formed by nature, and though influenced by his cultural heritage as embodied in books, he should turn to them only when the original source of inspiration flags, and even then not as their slave. The one student who fully responded to Emerson's passion to "set the hearts of youth on flame" was Thoreau. He had read the master's famous little booklet entitled *Nature* the year before and understood that his call for a return to nature really meant a return through Nature to Spirit.

Ten to fifteen years later, when he was putting this theory of education to the test of actual experience in the residence at Walden Pond and the book that embodied it, he opened his own transcendental "essay" by coming to grips with the same twofold curriculum. But he reversed the emphasis and the order of treatment. Emerson, after a brief rhapsody on Nature as spiritual teacher, had placed his chief emphasis on the proper and improper use of books, as appropriate to an academic audience. But Thoreau, with his apprenticeship to institutional learning well in the past, first disposes of "Reading" as the lesser source of truth, to be consulted only in the scholar's idle times, then turns his present attention to the Book of Nature that speaks to him in the language of "Sounds" (Chapters 3 and 4). This leads directly into another pair of opposites, "Solitude" and "Visitors" (Chapters 5 and 6).

In spite of their search for unity, or more properly because of it, transcendentalists constantly found themselves confronted with a succession of dualities. This particular one had long been a concern of Emerson's poetry and prose though the volume using it as a title, *Society and Solitude*, came late in his career. Thoreau patterned "Solitude" and "Visitors" on such a duality. The next two chapters (7 and 8) are concrete illustrations of these concepts: the record of his solitary labors in "The Bean-Field" and a typical sally into "The Village" to report on the communal life of his neighbors. The two preceding chapters are part of this same dualism: "Reading," in books which are the records of civilization; "Sounds," which are best heard in his woodland retreat.

In this way the first six chapters of *Walden* (after the long introductory sections) are woven into a design of contrasting threads of society and solitude but with the latter dominant, for the society portrayed is largely make-believe or comic. The world of others as found in books consists of those companions from the past that can best be known in the solitude of one's study. The chief visitors to his woods are witty figments of his imagination or figures out of legend and fable, hence not representatives of actual society. On his trips to Concord the villagers are turned into caricatures lining the main street down which he runs the gauntlet to escape the clutches of merchants and bankers and then bolts into the woods, only to lose himself on the way back to his cabin. Scarcely a likelihood for such an experienced woodsman, this is instead a dramatic device constructed solely for the purpose of supporting his conclusion. "Not till we are lost," he says in parody of New Testament doctrine, "not till we have lost the world, do we begin to find ourselves." (190) All these paths, including those that pretend to be directed toward society, lead to the world of the Self.

Thoreau's goal was solitude, with an exclusiveness that dismayed and all but alienated Emerson. It is one of their main lines of divergence. For example, there was actually a threefold program laid down in his famous address to the American Scholar: he is fashioned by nature; he is indebted to the culture of the past only as its master; and finally he expresses himself in action in order to influence society. But this last point finds no echo in *Walden*. Thoreau turned a deaf ear to Emerson's closing exhortation: "Action is with the scholar subordinate, but it is essential. Without it he is not yet man." Rejecting the popular notion that the scholar should be a recluse, Emerson had declared: "I run eagerly into this resounding tumult. I grasp the hands of those next me, and take my place in the ring to suffer and to work." It is absurd, of course, to picture the sage of Concord literally in this role. The very extravagance of his language came from the pressure of his need to find a vocation for himself, now that he had stepped down from the pulpit. Though he remained a man of the study, he gradually found a way to express his thought in action by becoming the mover of other men through his lectures and essays.

The real point is that Emerson felt it to be of the first importance for the scholar to have a relation with society and to influence it. There is some irony in his envy of Thoreau who, in spite of being self-engrossed, was so useful to the community as surveyor and pencil-maker (in contrast with his own ineptness); and in his troubled admiration over an occasional bold public action by such a confirmed recluse (as in Thoreau's going to jail to protest unjust taxes). The heroic role Emerson had in mind was something quite different. His disappointment, revealing his fundamental misunderstanding of Thoreau, is clearly voiced in the funeral address over the man who had refused to become his disciple: "I so much regret the loss of his rare powers of action, that I cannot help counting it a fault in him that he had no ambition. Wanting this, instead of engineering for all America, he was the captain of a huckleberry-party."

Thoreau's purpose, at least in *Walden*, was inaction rather than action—to "spend one day as deliberately as Nature." For him, the activity of men in nearby Concord was only a subject for satire. His own work in "The Bean-Field" (Chapter 7) is anything but a eulogy of the farmer, whose labors are ridiculed throughout the book as much as those of the mechanic or business-man. Instead, the key passages in this chapter deal with his joy in walking the rows barefooted, "dabbling like a plastic artist in the dewy and crumbling sand" (173); turning up Indian relics, "an instant and immeasurable crop" (175), with his hoe; or leaning on it while listening to the sounds of nature and those from the town, the latter being diminished by distance to "popguns." (176) Though his labor had the practical end of earning a living, he reduced it to a minimum. And he is emphatic about its not being his vocation. Another summer, he vows, he will not devote so much industry to beans and corn, but will plant "such seeds, if the seed is not lost, as sincerity, truth, simplicity, faith, innocence, and the like." (181) The bean field was not his arena any more than the village was.

Perhaps as near as the scholar of *Walden* comes to expressing himself in action is in "Reading" and the related area of writing, which constituted the "private business" he had come to the woods to transact. But these were subordinate to his main purpose and so may account for this chapter's being the least satisfactory of all in terms of integration with the major theme of quest. Besides, unless books are written for some recognizable social aim, they do not measure up to Emerson's final requirement for the American Scholar. However much these chapters may owe to his writings for their pattern of polarities, they are not truly Emersonian, nor is the book as a whole. It is transcendental, but only in a special sense, as symbolized in the central chapter on the magic circle of "The Ponds." Thoreau's purpose was to express himself not in action but in words—in the poem that he wrote to himself and for himself, to illuminate the quest of a life lived deliberately in accordance with nature and the spirit.

The first half of *Walden* comes to an end with his visit to and return from the village (Chapter 8). This journey, repeated "every day or two," he says, is a kind of continuous re-enactment of his original withdrawal from the world. And just as he lost his way in the woods during this ritual flight from society, so on his return to Walden Pond he found his "Way," symbolically. It is at one and the same time the goal of his quest and the path to that goal. The stance he takes there is the epitome of inaction, meditating in his boat as it drifts in the middle of the pond, occasionally engaging in that solitary and most passive of actions as a fisherman, and a transcendental one at that, as will be seen. This is what makes "The Ponds" (Chapter 9) so important to the meaning of the whole book. Yet the focus on it is not logical but symbolic. As one goes back over the preceding chapters he is surprised to recall how casually and infrequently the pond has been mentioned until now, and it is not treated in detail again until the very end of the book. It is as if Thoreau has chosen to unveil it once at the center, then draw the curtain until he is reborn with it at spring thawing. But there is no extravagance of ritual or language attending this revelation. As he approaches it, the elaborate display of wit and metaphor subsides into simple description of its purity and serenity. At this point so successfully has the world been lost and his goal found that his former modes of rejection and seeking can be dispensed with. Walden Pond is its own sufficient symbol.

In like manner, the second half of *Walden* can be shown to follow transcendental patterns. It begins with a group of chapters that form a triad centered on "Higher Laws" (Chapter 11), Thoreau's impossibly lofty aspiration for becoming divine. Those who insist on treating him as a social critic or a nature essayist have simply skipped this chapter, yet it is as integral to the book as any other. In fact, it is the exact complement to the long introductory chapter on the lower laws of economic man and fulfills its meaning by being the polar opposite. Taken together the two chapters illustrate the "two laws discrete" defined by Emerson: "Law for man and law for thing." In *Walden*, Thoreau deals with them in reverse order. "Economy" attacks the luxury of a materialistic society as a way of life enslaved by things; "Higher Laws" espouses the ascetic life as man's highest aspiration. The latter (like the former) is deliberately extravagant, not to be taken literally as the program he set himself to live by, but it must be taken seriously if the reader is to grasp the true meaning of the Walden experiment. The "Higher Laws" are those principles one should follow in order to achieve perfection, and for a saint they might be feasible. For the author of *Walden* they point to a goal which, though impossible of achievement, is something more than a simple return to nature. They define his "Way" as a stern and Spartan discipline for approaching as near as possible to his ideal self.

Preceding this is "Baker Farm" (Chapter 10), named for a place where Thoreau once thought of living before he went to Walden. Now, John Field's way of life there is pictured as a travesty in miniature of "Where I Lived, and What I Lived For." This bog-trotter has sunk as near as man can to the level of non-being. If Thoreau's satire of the very rich was devastating in the introduction, his satire of the very poor in this chapter is equally so. Both are caught in the same trap of a false economy. For the seeker of perfection, civilization seems to by-pass the true problems of life. He can never find the proper path of his development by starting from it—whether as one of the complacent rich, the enslaved poor, or those in between who lead lives of quiet desperation. Instead of trying to reform civilized society, he must go back to nature and work his way up from there toward the life of the spirit. But there is a linking sentence in "Higher Laws" that warns the reader not to think that Thoreau is substituting the code of naturalism for that of humanism: "We are conscious of an animal in us, which awakens in proportion as our higher nature slumbers." (242) So, by the time he arrives at the last of the triad, "Brute Neighbors" (Chapter 12), the reader knows he is not going to be advised to "turn and live with the animals" even in Whitman's sense. Instead, he is given a modern bestiary, but with the notations more precisely scientific than in the medieval ones and with the meanings arrived at by wit and metaphor rather than moral allegory. It is a celebration of the virtues of sheer being in the animal world.

In these three chapters, starting from bases on earth, Thoreau has triangulated toward the divine. Taken in sequence with "The Ponds" they also faintly continue the alternating pattern from solitude to society, back and forth again, though his brief visit to the shanty Irishman and his preferred companionship with his brute neighbors mark the last fading out of the social world he has renounced. The summer chapters of *Walden* have now come to an end, and with the arrival of cold weather solitude dominates the rest of the book. It does so thematically as well as literally, solitude being the inescapable condition of a life lived in the woods during the restrictive months of fall and winter. Though the last five chapters seem to follow the seasonal cycle more closely than the first ten, they also break out of the calendar quite as often, to open up new meanings. For Thoreau's is not a mere hibernation, like nature's, waiting for resurgent spring. These are the months of his greatest travail, husbanding his energies less to keep the spark of physical life glowing at his hearthside than to kindle his spirit for the new life that will be born when the old one dies. The direction of his journey is out of time into a renewal of that immortality whose intimations he had strained to hear in his lost youth.

The Weaver

Thoreau makes use of one more unifying device in the "character" of the narrator and the "voice" in which he speaks to us, for it is he who weaves the "plot" of *Walden*. A recent critic has identified him as a modern variant of the *eiron* of traditional comedy, who confronts and outwits the *alazons* of this world. Joseph Moldenhauer's idea is so ingenious and so pertinent to an understanding of the book that it deserves elaboration here. But first a full description of the types, as defined by Northrop Frye. *Alazon* is the Greek word meaning impostor, one who pretends to be something more than he is. Sometimes actual hypocrisy makes him so, but usually it is lack of self-knowledge; hence the term includes the stupid conformist, the stolid citizen, the killjoy, and the churl. The *eiron*, on the other hand, is the man who deprecates himself, irony being a technique of appearing to be less than one is. But he is really sophisticated and immensely clever, the predestined artist, just as the *alazon* is his predestined victim. In Elizabethan plays he was the trickster (derived from the "vice" of medieval moralities), often setting actions in motion from pure love of mischief. But he goes through a great deal of disguising and many metamorphoses. He is even combined with the hero, according to Frye, "whenever the latter is a cheeky, improvident young man who hatches his own schemes." Puck and Ariel are the highest examples of the type, both spiritual beings. *Alazon* and *eiron* exist in their purest form in the standard comic skit where the former complacently soliloquizes while the latter makes sarcastic asides to the audience, confident of its sympathy. Much of this is surprisingly applicable to the narrator of *Walden* and the antagonists he does battle with.

Thoreau was well acquainted with classical and renaissance drama and certainly knew these comic types from reading Aristophanes, Terence, and Shakespeare. In creating his own, he did not need to copy or invent, for he could draw from life at least as a starting point. He clearly thought many of his fellow townsmen to be *alazons* of one sort or another, and he modeled his *eiron*-narrator on himself, though so heightened as to constitute an original fictive character. The popular notion of Thoreau's being solemn as a crow, and as ungainly, needs drastic revising. He was aware of the figure he cut in the world and made comic capital out of it. The *Journal* offers many amusing examples. Once, his anecdote takes on the full flavor of comedy:

> Trying the other day to imitate the honking of geese, I found myself flapping my sides with my elbows, as with wings, and uttering something like the syllables *mow-ack* with a nasal twang and twist in my head; and I produced their note so perfectly in the opinion of the hearers that I thought I might possibly draw a flock down. (J, VII, 258)

Again, he has left a bizarre glimpse of himself as a lecturer, "grasping at, or even standing and reclining upon, the serene and everlasting truths." On such occasions "I have seen my auditors," he says, "compassionately or timidly watching my motions as if they were the antics of a rope-dancer or mountebank pretending to walk on air." (J, IX, 237–238) There can be no doubt that some of this was conscious histrionic posing. He was even striking an attitude when he chose July 4th, "Independence Day," to leave Concord and take up residence at Walden, his special kind of firecracker calculated to startle the villagers. (94) An early *Journal* entry makes an explicit justification for his posturings:

> By spells seriousness will be forced to cut capers, and drink a deep and refreshing draught of silliness; to turn this sedate day of Lucifer's and Apollo's, into an all fools' day for Harlequin and Cornwallis . . . Like overtasked schoolboys, all my members and nerves and sinews petition Thought for a recess, and my very thigh-bones itch to slip away from under me, and run and join the mêlée. I exult in stark inanity, leering on nature and the soul. We think the gods reveal themselves only to sedate and musing gentlemen. But not so; the buffoon in the midst of his antics catches unob-

served glimpses, which he treasures for the lonely hour. When I have been playing tomfool, I have been driven to exchange the old for a more liberal and catholic philosophy. (J, I, 175–176)

Contemporaries have left many testimonials to such a Puckish figure. Once when visiting friends in New Bedford, Thoreau was asked to sing. At first he demurred—"Oh, I fear, if I do, I shall take the roof of the house off!"—but, urged again, he delivered his favorite "Tom Bowline" with such spirit that the Quaker father of the family retired from the room. Again, at his own home in Concord on a day too stormy for his usual walk, he suddenly appeared in the parlor and amazed the company by breaking into a solo dance, "spinning airily around, displaying most remarkable litheness and agility and . . . finally [springing] over the center-table, alighting like a feather on the other side—then, not in the least out of breath [continuing] his waltz until his enthusiasm abated." It was probably feats like this that made Alcott call Thoreau the "ruddiest and nimblest genius that has trodden our woods." Perhaps the most charming vignette that has survived from Concord during the fabulous forties is the one sketched by the wife of Nathaniel Hawthorne, clearly designed to glorify her husband but incidentally setting Thoreau apart from his sedate literary friends most engagingly:

One afternoon, Mr. Emerson and Mr. Thoreau went with him down the river. Henry Thoreau is an experienced skater, and was figuring dithyrambic dances and Bacchic leaps on the ice—very remarkable, but very ugly, methought. Next him followed Mr. Hawthorne who, wrapped in his cloak, moved like a self-impelled Greek statue, stately and grave. Mr. Emerson closed the line, evidently too weary to hold himself erect, pitching headforemost, half lying on the air.

The *eiron* figure of Thoreau as a man has now been sufficiently established by reference to his *Journal* and by the evidence of friends. It remains only to point out how the author as a personality in life is transformed into the leading "character" in his book. He appears in the *eiron* role on the first page and continuously thereafter through the first half of *Walden*, less so in the second half. But to make sure that no one missed the pose, Thoreau scooped a choice sentence from his second chapter and used it on the title page as an epigraph: "I do not propose to write an ode to dejection, but to brag as lustily as chanticleer in the morning, standing on his roost, if only to wake my neighbors up." (94) This swaggering is countered by disarming self-deprecation at the end of the first chapter: "I never knew, and never shall know, a worse man than myself." (86) But one of the most attractive aspects of the *eiron* is his shape-shifting skill, most remarkably illustrated in the series of metaphors for the narrator's previous "enterprises," mentioned before, that form a brilliant digression early in "Economy."

In a country of self-made men, like America, where great emphasis is put on one's occupation, it is particularly effective satire for the vocationless Thoreau to take on this Protean guise, slipping into and out of fanciful versions of all the trades and professions. In addition to those enterprises already cited in other connections, two of the dozen paragraphs may be quoted here as samples of how he answered the question, What do you do?

> So many autumn, ay, and winter days, spent outside the town, trying to hear what was in the wind, to hear and carry it express! I well nigh sunk all my capital in it, and lost my own breath into the bargain, running in the face of it . . . . At other times watching from the observatory of some cliff or tree, to telegraph any new arrival; or waiting at evening on the hill-tops for the sky to fall, that I might catch something. (19)

Then in addition to being reporter to a journal "of no very wide circulation," weaver of non-selling baskets, trader with the Celestial Empire:

> I have looked after the wild stock of the town, which give a faithful herdsman a good deal of trouble by leaping fences; and . . . I have watered the red huckleberry, the sand cherry and the nettle-tree, the red pine and the black ash, the white grape and the yellow violet, which might have withered else in dry seasons. (20)

This same nimble and slippery fellow reappears throughout the book—evading visitors to his woodland retreat (143–144), running down hill "with the rainbow over my shoulder" to go fishing at Fair Haven (230), rushing past the crowd to a fire at Breed's hut, "I among the foremost, for I had leaped the brook." (286)

Similarly the *alazon* appears in many forms. He may be only the generalized laboring man, timorous or time-serving, so often the butt of ridicule in "Economy":

> It is very evident what mean and sneaking lives many of you live, . . . always on the limits, trying to get into business and trying to get out of debt; . . . seeking to curry favor, to get custom, by how many modes; lying, flattering, voting, contracting yourselves into a nutshell of civility, or dilating into an atmosphere of thin and vaporous generosity, that you may persuade your neighbor to let you make his shoes, or his hat, or his coat, or his carriage, or import his groceries for him. (7)

Professional reformers were more formidable antagonists, a special breed of the nineteenth century, and Thoreau devotes many pages to attacking them—all by raillery and caricature:

> As for Doing-good, that is one of the professions which are full. Moreover, I have tried it fairly, and, strange as it may seem, am satisfied that it does not agree with my constitution. . . . If anything ail a man, so that he does not perform his functions, if he have a pain in his bowels even,—for that is the seat of sympathy,—he forthwith sets about reforming,—the world. . . . And straightway his drastic philanthropy seeks out the Esquimau and the Patagonian, and embraces the populous Indian and Chinese villages; and thus, by a few years of philanthropic activity, the powers in the meanwhile using him for their own ends, no doubt, he cures himself of his dyspepsia. (81, 85–86)

Sometimes the *alazon* is only a nuisance, like the busybodies who paid visits to Walden cabin out of sheer curiosity and deserved only mild castigation: "uneasy housekeepers, who pried into my cupboard and bed when I was out,—how came Mrs. —— to know that my sheets were not as clean as hers?" (169) It is for the mercenary and grasping that he saves his invective:

> *Flint's Pond!* Such is the poverty of our nomenclature. What right had the unclean and stupid farmer, whose farm abutted on this sky water, whose shores he has ruthlessly laid bare, to give his name to it? Some skin-flint, who loved better the reflecting surface of a dollar, or a bright cent, in which he could see his own brazen face; who regarded even the wild ducks which settled in it as trespassers; his fingers grown into crooked and horny talons from the long habit of grasping harpy-like. . . . I respect not his labors, his farm where everything has its price, who would carry the landscape, who would carry his God, to market, if he could get anything for him. (217–218)

It is the actual contests between *eiron* and *alazon*, of course, that provide the action in traditional comedy. In *Walden* they are usually presented in the indirect way shown above, since its mode is narrative, or poetic, rather than dramatic. But occasionally the encounter approaches a little nearer to the latter. The *Journal* itself is full of sparring with imaginary enemies. For example: "Men even think me odd and perverse because I do not prefer their society to this nymph or wood-god rather." (J, IX, 215–216) Sometimes Thoreau addresses them directly, as if present: "You think that I am impoverishing myself by withdrawing from men," and so on. (J, IX, 246) Many of the "antagonists" in *Walden* are such straw men, caught by the heel or forelock and dragged into the narrative purely for the purpose of being knocked down. But the memorable ones are sufficiently developed to pass for real "characters" and the confrontations with them have enough "action" to become miniature comic skits. Such are the scenes with the Canadian woodchopper, a natural man whom the narrator tries in vain to interest in ideas, and the meeting with the impoverished John Field, to whom he tries to give a lesson in economics—both to be treated fully in later chapters.

Two similar anecdotes will serve to illustrate the *alazon* here. The first is a simple bout with a mindless conformist, whom he mystifies with double talk:

> When I ask for a garment of a particular form, my tailoress tells me gravely, "They do not make them so now," not emphasizing

the "They" at all, as if she quoted an authority as impersonal as the Fates, and I find it difficult to get made what I want, simply because she cannot believe that I mean what I say, that I am so rash. When I hear this oracular sentence, I am for a moment absorbed in thought, emphasizing to myself each word separately that I may come at the meaning of it, that I may find out by what degree of consanguinity *They* are related to *me*, and what authority they may have in an affair that affects me so nearly; and, finally, I am inclined to answer her with equal mystery, and without any more emphasis of the "they,"—"It is true, they did not make them so recently, but they do now." (27)

The second one turns from clothes to shelter, another necessity of life. To simplify the building of his own cabin he bought for $4.25 the tumbled-down shanty of James Collins, a railroad worker, in order to dismantle it and make use of its materials:

I took down this dwelling the same morning, drawing the nails, and removed it to the pond-side by small cartloads, spreading the boards on the grass there to bleach and warp back again in the sun. . . . I was informed treacherously by a young Patrick that neighbor Seeley, an Irishman, in the intervals of the carting, transferred the still tolerable, straight, and drivable nails, staples, and spikes to his pocket, and then stood when I came back to pass the time of day, and look freshly up, unconcerned, with spring thoughts, at the devastation; there being a dearth of work, as he said. He was there to represent spectatordom, and help make this seemingly insignificant event one with the removal of the gods of Troy. (48–49)

The *alazon* here is merely a rascal, but since the *eiron* himself is a clever fellow too (though never dishonest) the rascality is winked at in the name of a larger fellowship.

Thoreau was fully aware of the role he was playing in life, as has been shown, and he confesses once outright in *Walden* to the same histrionic role there. "I had this advantage, at least, in my mode of life, over those who were obliged to look abroad for amusement, to society and the theatre, that my life itself was become my amusement and never ceased to be novel," he remarks in a casual aside: "It was a drama of many scenes and without an end." (125) Even so, the traditional comedy structured by contests between *eiron* and *alazon* is not a model for *Walden,* only an instructive analogue. Since the argument for this influence has been put most convincingly by Professor Moldenhauer, he should be heard fully at this point. The narrator of *Walden* is the *eiron,* the witty and virtuous character whose actions are directed ultimately toward the establishment of an ideal order; the *alazons* are the hecklers and impostors, those who stand in the way of this fulfillment.

In Chapter 1, "Economy" (according to this critic), Thoreau assumes a hostile audience, creates stylized individual figures who complain and try to block the action, and then "destroys" them with every kind of wit. The "plot" of *Walden* is similar to that of traditional comedy, as defined by Professor Frye. The action is a rising movement from a world ruled by conventions and the arbitrary laws of the elders to a world made free by youth, the awakened man of Thoreau's "Conclusion." The narrating "I" performs this ascent, prefiguring the spiritual transformation of the audience also. The pattern of development is a comic one, Moldenhauer sums up, contrasting two worlds: the private paradise of the narrator and the social wasteland of the audience he has left behind, inhabited respectively by happy youth and misanthropic old age. And Thoreau's rhetoric is a direct result of this debate—the dramatic status of the speaker with respect to his hostile fictive audience.

The narrator changes shapes many times. He is by turns "a severe moralist, a genial companion, a bemused 'hermit,' and a whimsical trickster," as this critic aptly puts it, at times treating the Walden experiment itself as a sly joke on solid citizens. Similarly, Thoreau uses many voices—persuasive, mocking, scolding, ecstatic. But his really distinctive voice speaks to us in paradoxes. Emerson objected to this quality in Thoreau's style. Once, in accepting an essay of his for publication in the *Dial* (1843), Emerson wrote to say that he had made numerous omissions in order to remove this "*mannerism.*" In the privacy of his *Journals* he was more outspokenly critical:

Henry Thoreau sends me a paper with the old fault of unlimited contradiction. The trick of his rhetoric is soon learned: it consists in substituting for the obvious word and thought its diametrical antagonist. He praises wild mountains and winter forests for their domestic air; snow and ice for their warmth; villagers and woodchoppers for their urbanity, and the wilderness for resembling Rome and Paris. . . . It makes me nervous and wretched to read it.

A decade later Emerson was still complaining of his friend: "Always some weary captious paradox to fight you with . . . all his resources of wit and invention are lost to me." When he read *Walden* he probably squirmed at one sentence in the "Conclusion," realizing that the author's finger was pointed at him: "In this part of the world it is considered a ground for complaint if a man's writings admit of more than one interpretation." (358) But when Thoreau himself re-read his book shortly after publication, interestingly enough, he entered in his *Journal* a list of his faults, headed by: "Paradoxes,—saying just the opposite,—a style which may be imitated." (J. VII, 7–8) And yet, paradoxically, he kept on using them.

The truth of the matter is quite simple. Paradoxes, when indulged in indiscriminately, become a perverse and exasperating mannerism. Yet they can be very effective when made a disciplined and meaningful part of an author's style, as they are in *Walden*. There the first use of paradox is satirical, making the audience doubt the values of its own world, item by item, as Moldenhauer suggests; its second use is to make the narrator's world transcend the conventional world by subverting key terms in its language to new meanings. The *eiron* properly talks in riddles. He uses paradoxical language combined with verbal play to point up an actual paradox in life: that man is richest (in spiritual things) who is poorest (in material wealth). With it he can turn a cliché into an original aphorism: "How can you kill time without injuring eternity?" He can undermine what are presumed to be basic principles, such as man's need for human society: "I was no more lonely than the first spider in a new house."

For a book written in praise of the solitary life, *Walden* contains a surprising number of encounters between the narrator and representatives of society, sketched either with pretended realism or in undisguised caricature. These enliven the narrative and keep the presentation of its message from becoming solemn or didactic. They also provide one of the best ways of defining a concept such as solitude, so foreign to ordinary men as to seem an abstraction, by showing first of all what it is not. Once this has been accomplished in the first part of *Walden*, by showing the narrator participating to a limited extent in the gregarious life of men, Thoreau feels prepared to launch his quest for perfection. This is rendered largely by metaphors drawn from his experience of living alone in the woods.

Several unifying devices in *Walden* have now been pointed out: the character and speaking voice of the narrator, the transcendental patterns that give sequence to the chapters, the web of language woven by the two modes of wit and metaphor. Finally, there is an overall structure by which Thoreau achieves poetic unity: an intricate system of image-clusters that contains the book's inner meaning. Interpretation of the most significant of these will be undertaken in the chapters that follow.

2

Chrysalis

You think that I am impoverishing myself by withdrawing from men, but in my solitude I have woven for myself a silken web or *chrysalis,* and, nymph-like, shall ere long burst forth a more perfect creature, fitted for a higher society. (J, IX, 246)

The yearning for solitude runs all through Thoreau's writings. In *Walden* it is the subject of three chapters, centered in the one bearing that title, "Solitude." This is preceded by "Sounds" (Chapter 4), which leads him into it through harmony with nature, and is followed by "Visitors" (Chapter 6), those who threaten to impinge upon his privacy and win him back to society. Why Thoreau sought solitude was never more concisely put than in the restatement of purpose, quoted above, which he made late in life. His withdrawal was a preparation for rebirth, since it enabled him to complete his development from the nymph or pupa stage, the highest ever reached by most men. This remarkable metaphor, written down in his *Journal* many years after the experiment in living at the pond, shows the centrality of that episode to his career and sums up the major theme of *Walden* in a single sentence. It spans all the chapters from his initial rejection of a materialistic society to the spiritual economy of "Higher Laws," from his dying out of one world in "Solitude" to his fable of the bug that emerges into a new and perfect summer life at the end. The writing of the book was the weaving of his silken web. The conclusion was his metamorphosis, not into a butterfly, Christian symbol of the soul, but into "a strong and beautiful bug."

Withdrawal

"I have an immense appetite for solitude," Thoreau once said, "like an infant for sleep." The simile holds only for the overwhelming nature of the instinct. Children outgrow their need but Thoreau's was constant throughout his mature life. Just as it lasted more than ten years after he left Walden, so it had begun at least a decade before. In 1837 under the heading SOLITUDE (the very second entry in his *Journal*) he recorded at the age of twenty: "I seek a garret." (J, I, 3) The term used there, having a strictly literary reference, covers only part of Thoreau's desire for solitude, but an important practical part. Since the beginning of the Romantic period, half a century before, "garret" had come to symbolize the artist's solution to the problem of privacy and economic survival in a hostile world. As such it finds its way into *Walden*, in a satirical aside on the Englishman who went to India to make a fortune so he could afford to return home and become a poet: "He should have gone up garret at once." (59)

Thoreau himself, immediately after graduating from Harvard, had retired to the attic in his family's house so he could dedicate himself to study and writing. By the spring of 1840, with his first poem and essay accepted for publication, he felt himself fairly launched on a literary career. His next reference to the solitary life takes on a more complex tone:

> How shall I help myself? By withdrawing into the garret, and associating with spiders and mice, determining to meet myself face to face sooner or later. . . . The most positive life that history notices has been a constant retiring out of life, a wiping one's hands of it, seeing how mean it is, and having nothing to do with it. (J, I, 132–133)

Though literary implications are retained in the word "garret," the deeper motives of his later withdrawal to Walden are foreshadowed.

It is not surprising to find, about a year later, that he has shifted to a retreat in nature as better suited to the kind of solitude he desires: "I contemplate a hard and bare life in the woods." (J, I, 217) Then in April 1841:

> I only ask a clean seat. I will build my lodge on the southern slope of some hill, and take there the life the gods send me. Will

it not be employment enough to accept gratefully all that is yielded me between sun and sun? . . . If my jacket and trousers, my boots and shoes, are fit to worship God in, they will do. (J, I, 244)

By December of the same year he has chosen Walden Pond for his seat. The poetic sequence of the two *Journal* entries is clear from the similar phrasing (the only change being that the seasonal cycle is substituted for the daily):

> I want to go soon and live away by the pond, where I shall hear only the wind whispering among the reeds. It will be success if I shall have left myself behind. But my friends ask what I will do when I get there. Will it not be employment enough to watch the progress of the seasons? . . .
>
> I don't want to feel as if my life were a sojourn any longer. . . . It is time now that I begin to live. (J, I, 299)

The need for solitude, of a kind far different from mere literary privacy, was becoming insistent. But the great project had to be delayed for some time. At the end of April 1841 he had gone to live at Emerson's house for a two-year period, and this was followed by six months of tutoring on Staten Island. Neither of these experiments solved the problem of finding a suitable vocation, though 1841 and 1842 were crucial years for his literary career. He read voraciously in Emerson's library and wrote prolifically, both poetry and prose. But his failure to find a satisfactory outlet in the *Dial*, or a market in New York, turned him back to his dream of living at Walden. Now, also, that seemed the only solution to his economic needs as a non-selling author. Besides, both experiences in living with others had greatly increased his appetite for solitude, as he wrote to Emerson's wife.

These *Journal* entries over a four-year period, 1837–1841, reveal the remarkable evolution of one of Thoreau's major concerns. It begins, conventionally enough, with the creative artist's desire simply to be alone and free. Then it gradually expands to a quest for solitude much more profoundly motivated: to merge with the cycle of nature, to lose the World and find the Self, to live like an ascetic purifying himself for worship. It would be fascinating to follow the further development of his thoughts on solitude in the *Journal* prior to the Walden residence, but no entries survive between the spring of 1842 and the summer of 1845.

The gap can be bridged in a small way by passages in "A Winter Walk," which he published in the *Dial* for October 1843. This essay, written during the years when he was yearning for a solitary life at the pond, records his temporary escape from the trap of society by losing himself in the winter woods. "Here reign the simplicity and purity of a primitive age, and a health and hope far remote from towns and cities," he writes: "In this lonely glen . . . our lives are more serene and worthy to contemplate." The walk culminates at Walden Pond, though he conceals its name as a poet might that of his mistress:

> And now we descend again, to the brink of this woodland lake, which lies in a hollow of the hills. . . . It has not been idle, though sedentary, but, like Abu Musa, teaches that "sitting still at home is the heavenly way; the going out is the way of the world." . . . All trees direct the traveler to its brink, all paths seek it out, birds fly to it, quadrupeds flee to it, and the very ground inclines toward it. (V, 171, 174–175)

One sentence in the original draft of this paragraph, omitted from the published essay, not only identifies the pond but underscores the yearning for it that sustained him through the years of waiting: "The thought of Walden in the woods yonder makes me supple jointed and limber for the duties of the day. Sometimes I thirst for it."

A major practical problem was solved when in the fall of 1844 Emerson purchased some property on the shore of the pond and offered the use of it first to Alcott, then to Thoreau. By the spring of 1845 the latter was ready to yield to the lure of Walden and see if living there would appease his "immense appetite" for solitude. He had obviously mentioned his plans to his intimate friend, Ellery Channing, who replied on March 5, sharply but with a saving touch of humor:

> I see nothing for you in this earth but that field which I once christened "Briars"; go out upon that, build yourself a hut, and

there begin the grand process of devouring yourself alive. I see no alternative, no other hope for you. Eat yourself up; you will eat nobody else, nor anything else.

Before the month was over Thoreau obtained Emerson's permission to squat on his Walden acres (the "Briars"), borrowed an axe from Alcott, and began to build his cabin. By calculated simplicity in the act, and by dramatizing it in a unique book, Thoreau made his withdrawal one of the most famous in literary history.

If even a fellow transcendentalist felt there was something eccentric in this retreat to the woods, Concord villagers were convinced that it was perverse to the point of madness. His friends gradually came to understand the deeper purposes of his withdrawal, especially when clarified by the publication of *Walden* (1854). And, during the century following the English Romantic poets' retreat to the Lake Country, bookish people were increasingly aware of the tradition that literary men often have an affinity for nature both as subject and as a place of abode. It is on this more obvious level of significance that Thoreau's life at the pond and his book about it are usually understood.

The same note is struck in the opening paragraph of his chapter on "Solitude":

This is a delicious evening, when the whole body is one sense, and imbibes delight through every pore. I go and come with a strange liberty in Nature, a part of herself. As I walk along the stony shore of the pond in my shirt-sleeves, though it is cool as well as cloudy and windy, and I see nothing special to attract me, all the elements are unusually congenial to me. The bullfrogs trump to usher in the night, and the note of the whip-poor-will is borne on the rippling wind from over the water. Sympathy with the fluttering alder and poplar leaves almost takes away my breath; yet, like the lake, my serenity is rippled but not ruffled. These small waves raised by the evening wind are as remote from storm as the smooth reflecting surface. Though it is now dark, the wind still blows and roars in the wood, the waves still dash, and some creatures lull the rest with their notes. The repose is never complete. The wildest animals do not repose, but seek their prey now; the fox, and skunk, and rabbit, now roam the fields and woods without fear. They are Nature's watchmen,—links which connect the days of animated life. (143)

This is the kind of solitude that even urban readers can feel at home in, for instead of remoteness it has a quality of immediacy that draws them into participation. Because of the present tense and the total response of a first-person narrator whose whole body has become "one sense," readers are enabled to share his sympathy with the elements and identify with him as he comes and goes "with a strange liberty in Nature, a part of herself." The entire passage is a subtle blend of motion and stillness, the paradox being resolved in a single image comparing the narrator to the lake: "my serenity is rippled but not ruffled." Throughout, activity is related to communion with nature. Serenity is the fruit of it.

Wordsworth's well-known sonnet, "Evening on Calais Beach," makes an interesting analogue, and there is reason to believe that Thoreau had it in mind as a touchstone:

> It is a beauteous evening, calm and free,
> The holy time is quiet as a Nun
> Breathless with adoration; the broad sun
> Is sinking down in its tranquility;
> The gentleness of heaven broods o'er the Sea:
> Listen! the mighty Being is awake,
> And doth with his eternal motion make
> A sound like thunder—everlastingly. . . .

These verses are close to the *Walden* prose in theme and language. Here too is praise of nature for its beauty, "calm and free." Here is the ambiguity of a tranquil surface and the "eternal motion" of spirit thundering beneath. The chief difference is in tone, Wordsworth's being religious and Thoreau's sensuous. But the former's Nun at her evening adorations gives way at the end to a kind of pantheistic deity, the "mighty Being." And the latter's paean to nature is touched with awe in several phrases: "strange," "unusual," and a sympathy with poplar leaves that "takes away my breath." In overall effect they are not really far apart, though here the comparison ends, for Wordsworth's sestet moves off in another direction, less interesting to modern readers.

Thoreau's narrative purpose extends his evening song into the activities of night ("it is now dark"). Even then "repose" is not complete, for this is the time when predatory animals come out. As the narrator moves into this wilder nature the adverbs "now" and "still," repeated several times, make the temporal immediacy insistent and mitigate the feeling of remoteness and danger. Timorous readers can follow him as he finds kinship with the night animals who now roam the woods "without fear," since they are "links" with the daytime life when men are normally abroad. The *Journal* for 1850, when the book was still in progress, contains a highly relevant entry: "What shall we do with a man who is afraid of the woods, their solitude and darkness? What salvation is there for him? God is silent and mysterious." (J, II, 100) In the chapter on "Solitude" this topic is taken up and turned to wit:

> At night there was never a traveller passed my house, or knocked at my door, more than if I were the first or last man; . . . the black kernel of the night was never profaned by any human neighborhood. I believe that men are generally still a little afraid of the dark, though the witches are all hung, and Christianity and candles have been introduced. (144–145)

To come and go "with a strange liberty in nature" it was necessary to slip the noose of orthodoxy. To be truly at home there he must quit his home in society and live alone in the woods. Neither religion nor the other inventions of civilization could light his way into the dark and the wild.

Then, to avoid being too solemn about his dedication to solitude, Thoreau shifts from blasphemy to banter: "Men frequently say to me, 'I should think you would feel lonesome down there, and want to be nearer to folks, rainy and snowy days and nights especially.' " (147) This picks up one of those inquiries by his fellow villagers listed on the first page of *Walden* as being so "pertinent" they were the cause of his writing the book: "Some have asked . . . if I did not feel lonesome; if I was not afraid; and the like." (3) Now, in the chapter on "Solitude," he shows just how impertinent all such queries were by the extravagance of his own rhetorical questions and answers: "Why should I feel lonely? is not our planet in the Milky Way?" He has neighbors only a mile distant, he admits: "But for the most part it is as solitary where I live as on the prairies. It is as much Asia or Africa as New England. I have, as it were, my own sun and moon and stars, and a little world all to myself." (147, 144) The astronomical pun here on his own "world" is elaborated elsewhere:

> Where I lived was as far off as many a region viewed nightly by astronomers. We are wont to imagine rare and delectable places in some remote and more celestial corner of the system, behind the constellation of Cassiopeia's Chair, far from noise and disturbance. I discovered that my house actually had its site in such a withdrawn, but forever new and unprofaned, part of the universe . . . near to the Pleiades or the Hyades. . . . I was really there, or at an equal remoteness from the life which I had left behind, dwindled and twinkling with as fine a ray to my nearest neighbor. (97–98)

By this series of comparisons, in cosmic images of increasing extravagance, Thoreau has dramatized the distance of his retreat from all human habitation.

Actually his cabin was not in a very lonely place. It was only a mile and a half from Concord, a town of two thousand inhabitants. Within sight was the well-traveled highway to Lincoln, and across the pond was the Fitchburg Railroad. But the topography presented in *Walden* has only tenuous connections with Massachusetts. The pond, with the one-room hut on its shore, lies at the center of a symbolic landscape. On one side is the village, near enough so that he could hear the sound of church bells and the noise of "popguns" on militia days, but never delineated with any realistic detail. On the other "the view from my door . . . stretched away toward the prairies of the West." (97) It is as if no civilization existed to the westward of Concord, Massachusetts, and an untouched wilderness came right up to the village limits. In his essay "Walking," he actually makes such an extravagant claim: "I believe that the forest which I see in the western horizon stretches uninterruptedly toward the setting sun, and there are no towns or cities in it of enough consequence to disturb me." (V, 217–218) Such nearness to the wild and the primitive was essential to Thoreau's fable. The solitude at Walden Pond was less literal than created, a metaphor for a state of mind. How much he feels at home in these woods now is rendered by comparing himself to a long series of creatures and things in nature:

> I am no more lonely than the loon in the pond that laughs so loud, or than Walden Pond itself. . . . The sun is alone . . . God is alone. . . . I am no more lonely than a single mullein or dandelion in a pasture, or a bean leaf, or sorrel, or a horse-fly, or a humblebee. I am no more lonely than the Mill Brook, or a weathercock, or the north star, or the south wind, or an April shower, or a January thaw, or the first spider in a new house. (152)

The piling-up is an example of his technique for achieving emphasis by dramatic exaggeration. Beginning with the pond and ending with his own cabin this is his new domestic circle, a catalogue of the company he most enjoys.

As a matter of fact his list of companions-in-solitude is introduced with the playful paradox, "I have a great deal of company in my house; especially in the morning, when nobody calls." (151) The reverse situation forms the topic of an important linking paragraph early in the chapter on "Solitude." When the hermit returns to his cabin after a brief absence he discovers that "visitors have been there and left their cards," finding nobody at home. He then plays the game of boasting equally about his skill in evading visitors and in finding traces of them. The clues are mostly natural objects, of the sort that might have been left by elves and sprites: "a name in pencil on a yellow walnut leaf," "a willow wand woven into a ring." (143, 144) The narrator's seclusion is emphasized by this humorous dodging and spying on visitors instead of communicating with them. And the passage, by creating an air of the supernatural, prepares for the advent of unusual visitors later in the chapter, and again later in the book.

Visitors

One of the ways of dramatizing solitude is by contrasting it with society. The chapter on "Solitude" and its sequel "Visitors" are such a pair of polar opposites, in which the trivial offerings of social intercouse are set over against the rich rewards of the hermit's life. These two form part of a larger pattern of alternation between society and solitude that runs through half-a-dozen chapters, as has been shown. Emerson, and others, may have felt an equal pull toward the two ways of life, but Thoreau used this transcendental dualism only to emphasize his preference for being alone. In a letter to a friend, 21 May 1856, he explained his lack of sociability as something quite different from a positive dislike of people:

> As for the dispute about solitude and society any comparison is impertinent. . . . I love society so much that I swallowed it all at a gulp—i.e. all that came in my way. It is not that we love to be alone, but that we love to soar, and when we do soar, the company grows thinner and thinner till there is none at all.

It was only by "a very private *extacy*," he added, that he could hope to achieve the "translation" he yearned for. To return to the world of *Walden*, both the book and the place, when "Visitors" intrude from the social world he has left behind, they are treated with the same humorous evasion by which he escaped from more casual callers in "Solitude." The new chapter begins in irony:

> I think that I love society as much as most, and am ready enough to fasten myself like a bloodsucker for the time to any full-blooded man that comes in my way. I am naturally no hermit, but might possibly sit out the sturdiest frequenter of the bar-room, if my business called me thither. (155)

The conditional clause, tagged on at the end, sets the meaning right. It was some "private business," one remembers, that had already called him in the opposite direction, to Walden woods.

His more straightforward statement of preference in the preceding chapter makes an interesting comparison: "I find it wholesome to be alone the greater part of the time. To be in company, even with the best, is soon wearisome and dissipating." (150) This leads the way to a sharp satire on social life in the following paragraph:

> Society is commonly too cheap. We meet at very short intervals, not having had time to acquire any new value for each other. We meet at meals three times a day, and give each other a new taste of that old musty cheese that we are. We have had to agree on a certain set of rules, called etiquette and politeness, to make this frequent meeting tolerable and that we need not come to open war. We meet at the post-office, and at the sociable, and about the fireside every night; we live thick and are in each other's way. . . . It would be better if there were but one inhabitant to a square mile, as where I live. The value of a man is not in his skin, that we should touch him. (151)

The *Journal* is filled with tirades against society, but most of them, lacking the distinction of wit and metaphor, merely make the reader hostile to what he feels is Thoreau's ill temper, even perversity. As with most satirical passages in *Walden,* however, all the criticisms in the above passage are perceptive and are made acceptable by being good-humored. The monotony and routine of social life are pounded home by the initial reiteration, "We meet" and the like, in five successive sentences. The definition of "etiquette" as merely a thin veneer covering barbarism makes a surprise fillip at the center. "Cheap" at the start is rounded out with "value" at the end. If this little satire in "Solitude" begins with a direct statement of preference, it is quickly turned into a paradox: "I never found the companion that was so companionable as solitude." (150)

In the opening paragraphs of "Visitors" the same mode prevails: "I had three chairs in my house; one for solitude, two for friendship, three for society." (155) When there were larger numbers they had to stand up—"I have had twenty-five or thirty souls, with their bodies, at once under my roof." One inconvenience of such a small room, he adds, was the difficulty of getting at a sufficient distance from his guest for important conversation:

> You want room for your thoughts to get into sailing trim and run a course or two before they make their port. The bullet of your thought must have overcome its lateral and ricochet motion and fallen into its last and steady course before it reaches the ear of the hearer, else it may plow out again through the side of his head. . . . I have found it a singular luxury to talk across the pond to a companion on the opposite side. (156)

In a later chapter there is an anecdote of a fishing excursion with an elderly friend, the two of them sitting at opposite ends of the same boat. Few words passed between them, the man being deaf, but he occasionally hummed a psalm, which harmonized with Thoreau's philosophy: "Our intercourse was thus altogether one of unbroken harmony, far more pleasing to remember than if it had been carried on by speech." (193) For the most intimate society and the most thoughtful conversation, he concludes in "Visitors," we should not only be silent but so far apart bodily as to be out of hearing in any case. The most memorable rendering of this extravagant dictum occurred in his first book, *A Week*, as a double oxymoron: "As the truest society approaches always nearer to solitude, so the most excellent speech finally falls into Silence." (I, 418)

Ordinary visitors would probably have objected to the eccentric reception promised in this chapter, just as traditionalist readers have objected to Thoreau's mannerist prose. Such visitors did indeed come to Walden Pond but they did not find their way into the book. Those who were so immortalized were not members of any substantial society, and so would not have expected conventional treatment. The paragraph preparing for their advent is full of hints as to what they will be like. "I had withdrawn so far within the great ocean of solitude," says the hermit, "only the finest sediment was deposited around me." (159) The mere distance from town had "winnowed" his company, so that none came on trivial business. On the other hand, he adds, several came whom he would never have met save under the "favorable circumstances" of his woodland retreat.

The stage is now set. The first character to enter is a French Canadian woodchopper, who is described as "a true Homeric or Paphlagonian man." Half of Chapter 6, "Visitors," is devoted to him. "He interested me," says Thoreau, "because he was so quiet and solitary and so happy withal." (161–162) In his kinship with nature and his detachment from the institutions of civilization he seemed less a part of the social than of the natural world: "He was so genuine and unsophisticated that no introduction would serve to introduce him, more than if you introduced a woodchuck to your neighbor." (163) There was no danger that such a man would intrude on Thoreau's solitude. The same is true of the next visitor, who was even more offbeat, as the introductory sentence warns: "Far off as I lived, I was not exempted from that annual visitation which occurs . . . about the first of April." (167) There were half-wits from the almshouse and several kinds of April fools, whom he persuaded to "exercise all the wit they had . . . making wit the theme of our conversation." There was one in particular who talked quite openly about his deficiency in intellect:

He was a metaphysical puzzle to me. I have rarely met a fellow-man on such promising ground. . . . It seemed that from such a basis of truth and frankness as the poor weak-headed pauper had laid, our intercourse might go forward to something better than the intercourse of sages. (168)

Only a dull-witted reader would mistake these fictions for fact. They are followed by "Men of almost every degree of wit . . . some who had more wits than they knew what to do with," and the like. No intrusion here. Thoreau is left happily alone with the characters in his play:

The last three paragraphs of "Visitors" are crowded with brief mentions of numerous archetypes: people begging for help, a runaway slave who sorely needed it, but mostly the visionary or the thriftless. There are cranks of all sorts, "men of one idea, like a hen with one chicken," and "men of a thousand ideas . . . a sort of intellectual centipede that made you crawl all over"; saner types of the dull and conventional from many walks of life, including the prying and the meddlesome. (168–170) All become the victims of Thoreau's raillery and they exist solely for that purpose, being in no sense a representative cross-section of society. The chapter ends with a bare list of a half-dozen more cheering types, whom he welcomes, including "poets and philosophers." It is well-known that during his residence at the pond he had many visitors from among the intellectuals who made this part of New England famous in the 1840's, as well as from less distinguished neighbors and relatives in the village, but such identifiable people get short shrift in *Walden*.

Actual visitors would certainly have included those friends who helped Thoreau set up the frame of his house in May 1845. "No man was ever more honored in the character of his raisers than I," is his blanket reference in the book. (49) Who they were has long been known: Emerson, Alcott, and Channing; George and Burrill Curtis, former members of the Brook Farm utopia; Edmund Hosmer (Thoreau's ideal Concord farmer) and his sons John, Edmund, and Andrew—as identified by a contemporary. But in "Visitors" they are reduced to a phrase. Though several of them are given extended treatment in a later chapter, "Winter Visitors," it is only to be transformed there into symbolic characters. These four have been identified as Hosmer, Channing, Alcott, and Emerson—more by a process of eliminating rival candidates than from any realism in the portraits. There could be no better way to prove that *Walden* is not a literal autobiography than by a detailed comparison of actual visitors to the pond with their fictional counterparts in the book.

Thoreau begins Chapter 14, "Former Inhabitants; and Winter Visitors," quite typically, with an account of his unmolested solitude when there were none: "At this season I seldom had a visitor. When the snow lay deepest no wanderer ventured near my house for a week or fortnight at a time, but there I lived as snug as a meadow mouse." (291–292) Though the weather kept company from coming to him, it did not interfere with his going abroad "to keep an appointment with a beech tree, or a yellow birch, or an old acquaintance among the pines." (292) Then follows a long passage telling of his visit with an owl. So much for natural society. "For human society I was obliged to conjure up the former occupants of these woods," he begins a long prologue to his actual winter visitors. The next ten pages present a gallery of "characters"—former slaves, a veteran of Waterloo turned ditch digger, a potter, spinner of linen, fortune teller, and drunkard. Though based on originals, they are transformed by the conjurer's art into more-or-less mythical figures. These wraiths of "Former Inhabitants" are among the more colorful of those fictive people who enliven his story from time to time without damaging his solitude. "With such reminiscences I repeopled the woods and lulled myself asleep." (282–291) So ends his midwinter night's dream.

The "Winter Visitors" who actually made their way to snow-bound Walden cabin were, of course, his intimate friends. The first to come was "a long-headed farmer . . . one of the few of his vocation who are 'men on their farms.' " (294–295) The allusion is to Emerson's phrase, in the "American Scholar" address, defining one of the rare examples of integrity in a conformist age; and this self-reliant man has been identified as Edmund Hosmer. He appears frequently in Thoreau's *Journal,* as in an entry for July 1852, where he is described again as "long-headed," the most intelligent farmer in Concord, with the relevant comment added that he was "inclined to speculation in conversation—giving up any work to it for the time." (J, IV, 194) It is no surprise, then, to find him quitting his tasks and appearing at the hermit's door one winter afternoon to have "a social 'crack.' " The scene that follows is a vignette rather than the record of a visit:

> We talked of rude and simple times, when men sat about large fires in cold, bracing weather, with clear heads; and when other desserts failed, we tried our teeth on many a nut which wise squirrels have long since abandoned, for those which have the thickest shells are commonly empty. (295)

A longer and warmer account tells of the visit of "a poet," who came through "deepest snows and most dismal tempests," presumably more than once as the language implies:

> We made many a "bran new" theory of life over a thin dish of gruel, which combined the advantages of conviviality with the clear-headedness which philosophy requires. . . . We made that small house ring with boisterous mirth and resound with the murmur of much soberer talk, making amends then to Walden vale for the long silences. (295)

The puns and the laughter clearly point to his young friend Ellery Channing, companion of many walks, rather than to that other and more celebrated poet with whom Thoreau was intimate, the older and much more formal Emerson. The latter is dismissed in a sentence at the end of the chapter: "There was one other with whom I had 'solid seasons,' long to be remembered, at his house in the village, and who looked in upon me from time to time." (297–298) At least this faceless visitor is usually assumed to be Emerson, though neither of the "poets" is given enough personal characteristics to relate him convincingly to an original, the identities of both being established merely by informed guesses.

As a matter of fact, none of these three have left their own records of visits to Walden Pond to serve as corroboration. Hosmer was not a man of letters. Channing's curious book, *Thoreau the Poet-Naturalist*, though an intimate biography, is concerned with traits of personality and intellect rather than with narrative. Even under the promising heading of "Walks and Talks" he records not actual visits but imaginary meetings and conversations. Emerson's *Journals* contain more than a score of references to Thoreau, some quite detailed, but they also are restricted to analyses of character, philosophical outlook, and literary talents. There is no mention of him at all during the Walden years. Thus one of the principles that guided transcendentalists in their writings, to sublimate the factual and the personal, conspired to blank out the record and so preserve the solitude described in *Walden*. As actual visitors, on the other hand, they were certainly welcome intruders on Thoreau's privacy, especially during the winter-bound months at the pond.

Strangely enough it was Bronson Alcott, the most other-worldly of them all, who has left the only record of a visit to the

Walden hermit by one of the transcendental fellowship. According to the editor of his *Journals* he passed every Sunday evening during the winter of 1847 at Thoreau's cabin, their acquaintance ripening into friendship as a result of these long talks. Alcott's impressions of his visits will serve to gloss the fabulous evening described in *Walden*, but that fictional occasion must be presented first:

> I should not forget that during my last winter at the pond there was another welcome visitor. . . . One of the last of the philosophers, —Connecticut gave him to the world,—he peddled first her wares, afterwards, as he declares, his brains. . . . An Old Mortality, say rather an Immortality, with unwearied patience and faith making plain the image engraven in men's bodies, the God of whom they are but defaced and leaning monuments. . . . A blue-robed man, whose fittest roof is the overarching sky which reflects his serenity. I do not see how he can ever die; Nature cannot spare him. (295–297)

Though Thoreau begins with biographical details that identify his Concord guest beyond a cavil, the next sentences quickly bring about his metamorphosis into a transcendent being.

At this point, to anchor his floating portrait back to reality, he adopts the air of a factual reminiscence: "Of yore we had sauntered and talked, and effectually put the world behind us." (296–297) Surely enough Thoreau's *Journal* records such a walk and talk (not "of yore" but on a spring morning six years after the residence at the pond) that becomes a part of the visit described in *Walden*. Under date of 9 May 1853, he notes: "I have devoted most of my day to Mr. Alcott." Then after a paragraph about the pleasures of that day's conversation, he decides to continue it in imagination, saying to his absent friend, "Why should I not think aloud to you?" Clearly, what follows was drafted with the book in mind:

> Having each some shingles of thought well dried, we walk and whittle them, trying our knives, and admiring the clear yellowish grain of the pumpkin pine. We wade so gently and reverently, or

we pull together so smoothly, that the fishes of thought are not scared from the stream. (J, V, 130–131)

To fit this passage into their emblematic meeting on a winter evening in 1847, all Thoreau had to do was shift from present tense to past and change one verb, "walk" to "sat." (Except for this, it appears verbatim in *Walden*, p. 297.) Other parts of the *Journal* account were reworked for inclusion in the book or discarded as irrelevant. Most interesting of all is the entirely new passage created to conclude the *Walden* scene, extending the *Journal* draft from the fabulous to the supernatural:

There we worked, revising mythology, rounding a fable here and there, and building castles in the air for which earth offered no worthy foundation. Great Looker! Great Expecter! to converse with whom was a New England Night's Entertainment. Ah! such discourse we had, hermit and philosopher, and the old settler I have spoken of,—we three,—it expanded and racked my little house. (297)

The allusion at the end to "the old settler," a point of the first importance, will have to wait for clarification until the philosopher has rendered his own account of a visit to the hermit.

The many evenings Alcott spent at Walden cabin in the winter of 1847 are telescoped into two entries in his journal. The first, in February, parallels the high poetic praise Thoreau had given his friend, though each was writing in ignorance of the other's eulogy:

So vivid was my sense of escape from the senses while conversing with Henry today that the men, times, and occupations of coming years gave me a weary wish to be released from this scene and to pass into a state of noble companions and immortal labours. . . .

Thoreau is a walking Muse, winged at the anklets and rhyming her steps.

The other entry, dated 16 March 1847, suggests that besides "revising mythology" the two friends sometimes concerned themselves with more tangible writings: "This evening I pass with

Thoreau at his hermitage on Walden, and he reads me some passages from his MS volume which he is preparing to print some day entitled 'A Week on the Concord and Merrimack Rivers.'" What follows is an inside report on the progress Thoreau had made with that "private business" he went to Walden to transact.

Although Alcott may not have had many practical suggestions for revising the manuscript of *A Week*, he presumably gave the author the encouragement needed, if one can assume that he confided to Thoreau on this notable evening the substance of what he entered in his own *Journals:*

The book is purely American, fragrant with the lives of New England woods and streams, and could have been written nowhere else. It preserves to us whatever of the wild and mystic remains to us. . . . There is a toughness too, and a sinewy vigor, as of roots and the strength that comes of feeding on wild meats, and the moist lustres of the fishes in the bed below.

It has the merit, moreover, that somehow, despite all presumptions to the contrary, the sod and sap and fibre and flavour of New England have found at last a clear relation to the literature of other and classic lands . . . Egypt, India, Greece, England. . . .

Especially am I touched by this soundness, this aboriginal vigour, as if a man had once more come into Nature.

Such mutual appreciation and affectionate understanding must have proved heart-warming, especially in contrast to the strained idealism that usually marked transcendental friendships. Thoreau would have been particularly happy to read the last sentence entered in Alcott's *Journals* that night:

I came home at midnight through the woody snow-paths and slept with the pleasing dream that presently the press would place on my shelves a second beside my first volume, also written by my townsman, and give me two books to be proud of: Emerson's *Poems* and Thoreau's *Week.*

To be compared with Emerson, and favorably, was all the aspiring young author could have wished. But he did not need to look over his friend's shoulder to discover that he was held in such high estimation. Alcott was frequently comparing the two Concord writers he most admired, and on one occasion at least he expressed his thoughts orally to Thoreau, who recorded in his *Journal* for August 9, 1853: "Alcott spent the day with me yesterday. He spent the day before with Emerson. He observed that he had got his wine and now he had come after his venison. Such was the compliment he paid me." (J, V, 365) High among the practical rewards of solitude was that it "winnowed" the society Thoreau was exposed to. It could protect him from "wearisome and dissipating company." Better still, it could bring him communion with a self-reliant man of the soil, a convivial poet, and a blue-robed philosopher. His images for them reveal the joy he took in their company: nut-cracking around a roaring fire, making merry over a dish of gruel, whittling a pine shingle—the last being the traditional American symbol of the rustic philosopher. For one not desiring total seclusion such society-in-solitude was ideal. Thoreau's adoption of the term "hermit" was clearly figurative.

Only one thing was missing. "I sometimes expected the Visitor who never comes," he laments at the chapter's end. The capital letter suggests some kind of divinity, and so does the game of hide-and-seek Thoreau plays with this most mysterious visitor. One of his incarnations is "the old settler" who sometimes joined the "hermit and philosopher" when their discourse soared highest. The modifying clause, "[whom] I have spoken of," leads the reader back to the earlier chapter on "Solitude," which though mostly laid in summer has one paragraph that looks forward to "Winter Visitors":

> I have occasional visits in the long winter evenings, when the snow falls fast and the wind howls in the woods, from an old settler and original proprietor, who is reported to have dug Walden Pond, and stoned it, and fringed it with pine woods; who tells me stories of old time and new eternity; and between us we manage to pass a cheerful evening with social mirth and pleasant views of things, even without apples or cider,—a most wise and humorous friend, whom I love much. (152)

The "god" imaged here has been identified as Pan. But this description hardly fits the priapic follower in the retinue of Dionysus, nor even the shepherds' god of woods and pastures. When Thoreau actually had him in mind he was usually specific, as when referring to him in *A Week:*

In my Pantheon, Pan still reigns in his pristine glory, with his ruddy face, his flowing beard, and his shaggy body, his pipe and his crook, his nymph Echo, and his chosen daughter Iambe; for the great god Pan is not dead, as was rumored. No god ever dies. Perhaps of all the gods of New England and of ancient Greece, I am most constant at his shrine. (I, 65)

This does not sound like the "old settler" and creator of the pond. Besides, in *Walden* the nature-god aspect of Pan is fully taken care of in the personification immediately following, familiar in Romantic poetry:

An elderly dame, too, dwells in my neighborhood, invisible to most persons, in whose odorous herb garden I love to stroll sometimes, gathering simples and listening to her fables; for she has a genius of unequalled fertility, and her memory runs back farther than mythology. . . . A ruddy and lusty old dame, who delights in all weathers and seasons, and is likely to outlive all her children yet. (152–153)

The first visitor corresponds to Pan only in the sense of the Great All, as the Alexandrian mythologists came to symbolize him, but this is only another way of saying the universal god. Though Thoreau's is such a generalized figure of deity, his emphasis on aspects of the Creator and the Eternal One brings it closer to the transcendental version of the Christian God. Even the final phrase, "he is thought to be dead," does not necessarily refer to that story in Plutarch about the mysterious voice proclaiming "the great god Pan is dead" at the exact moment of Christ's birth. Many voices in the mid-nineteenth century were coming to say the same thing of Jehovah, and Emerson in the "Divinity School Address" (1838) had rebuked the orthodox church for talking about God "as if he were dead."

Thoreau is playfully evasive in describing the very best kind of company solitude offers him. To identify his gods more exactly would be to rob them of their poetry, as he does in this more prosaic *Journal* passage (7 September 1851):

We are surrounded by a rich and fertile mystery. May we not probe it, pry into it, employ ourselves about it, a little? To devote your life to the discovery of the divinity in nature or to the eating of oysters, would they not be attended with very different results? . . . My profession is to be always on the alert to find God in nature, to know his lurking-places, to attend all the oratorios, the operas, in nature. (J, II, 471–472)

"God" and "Nature" lack the suggestiveness of those symbolic figures in *Walden* who bring cheer to the closing pages of his chapter on "Solitude." But even though they are impressive figures, it should be remembered that they are only figures of speech. The heavenly way is not so simple that merely wishing to see God will make deity appear magically, as any yogi knows. It is not without significance that Thoreau, at the end of "Winter Visitors," invokes the discipline of patience from the *Vishnu Purana* when waiting for "the Visitor who never comes." And in an early essay, as quoted above, he had cited the example of Abu Musa, an island in the Persian Gulf: "sitting still at home is the heavenly way."

Solitude

After effectually getting rid of society in his introductory chapter on "Economy," Thoreau had begun exploring how to express adequately what he really lived for, what he sought in going to the woods. The self-exhortation in Chapter 2, "Where I Lived," is one of his most arresting directives for finding the affirmative way: "Let us spend one day as deliberately as Nature." (108) To the urban world, proud of having overcome nature, this would seem like arrant nonsense. At best it would only provoke a shrugging query, Why? A passage from the *Journal* for 1851, while *Walden* was in progress, will serve as a footnote to his cryptic sentence in the book: "The art of spending a day. If it is possible that we may be addressed, it behooves us to be attentive. If by watching all day and all night I may detect some trace of the Ineffable, then will it not be worth the while to watch?" (J, II, 471) The gloss, shifting from "Nature" to the "Ineffable," clarifies by reminding the reader that *Walden* cannot be understood except as a spiritual quest. Another *Journal* entry, ten years after Thoreau's residence at the pond, shows that the same quest was continuous with his life and was the basis of it. Writing in 1857 of his solitary walks, he creates an image of himself as the man of solitude that would have deserved a place of honor in his book had it been coined in time:

> This stillness, solitude, wildness of nature is a kind of thoroughwort, or boneset, to my intellect. This is what I go out to seek. It is as if I always met in those places some grand, serene, immortal, infinitely encouraging, though invisible, companion, and walked with him. . . . I suppose that this value, in my case, is equivalent to what others get by churchgoing and prayer. I come to my solitary woodland walk as the homesick go home. (J, IX, 209, 208)

Though he never finished the debate between society and solitude, the direction of Thoreau's life was steadily away from the world. He even wondered if there were not some inexorable law that kept one from having a deep sympathy for both man and nature. Justification for his own choice is made explicit in a *Journal* entry for 3 January 1853: "I love Nature partly *because* she is not man, but a retreat from him. . . . In her midst I can be glad with an entire gladness. If this world were all man, I could not stretch myself, I should lose all hope." (J, IV, 445) Certainly the one obvious movement in *Walden*, a book of intricate and subtle patterns otherwise, is the motion away from the world of men and ever deeper into the world of nature.

The "higher society" he found there is the subject of an important passage in his chapter on "Solitude":

> I have never felt lonesome, or in the least oppressed by a sense of solitude, but once, and that was a few weeks after I came to

the woods, when, for an hour, I doubted if the near neighborhood of man was not essential to a serene and healthy life. To be alone was something unpleasant. But I was at the same time conscious of a slight insanity in my mood, and seemed to foresee my recovery. In the midst of a gentle rain while these thoughts prevailed, I was suddenly sensible of such sweet and beneficent society in Nature, in the very pattering of the drops, and in every sound and sight around my house, an infinite and unaccountable friendliness all at once like an atmosphere sustaining me, as made the fancied advantages of human neighborhood insignificant, and I have never thought of them since. (146)

As Thoreau's communion with nature moves from sensuous to religious, the language becomes more formally rhetorical. His one experience of loneliness is rendered here by an elaborate construct of negatives emphasizing how exceptional it was, then reduced to the minimum duration of an hour, and finally dismissed as temporary insanity. This is for the deliberate purpose of contrast with his affirmation in the sentences immediately following. The society he finds in nature is expressed by superlatives, repetitions, and sentences swelling with paired modifiers, ending in an extreme re-statement.

The key to the new religious emphasis can be found in the phrase "a gentle rain." Its full meaning to Thoreau is spelled out in a late *Journal* account of a walk in "the April rain, which descendeth on all alike." There he tells of going along the woodland path "full of joy and expectation, seeing nothing but beauty, hearing nothing but music." It is a rain that suggests fairer weather than was ever known: "You feel the fertilizing influence of the rain in your mind. . . . You discover evidences of immortality not known to divines. You cease to die." (J, X, 262–263) It is clear from this that he was familiar with the medieval image of Christ as the spring rain, bringing new life to everything and every creature on earth.

In *Walden* the overt Christian allegory is replaced by a psalm-like passage in which the religious significance is not stated but merely suggested by adopting the mode of biblical poetry:

The gentle rain which waters my beans and keeps me in the house to-day is not drear and melancholy, but good for me too. Though it prevents my hoeing them, it is of far more worth than my hoeing. If it should continue so long as to cause the seeds to rot in the ground and destroy the potatoes in the low lands, it would still be good for the grass on the uplands, and, being good for the grass, it would be good for me. (145)

Once again there is a strong sense of affirmation achieved by the cumulative style, especially by the rhythmical reiteration and parallelism characteristic of the Psalms. If there were any doubt about the religious suggestiveness intended, it would be cleared up by the reference to the doctrine of Election at the end (though characteristically it is given a blasphemous twist): "Sometimes, when I compare myself with other men, it seems as if I were more favored by the gods than they. . . . I do not flatter myself, but if it be possible they flatter me." (145–146)

Such is the testament of one who has faith in the beneficence of nature, pagan though he be. Thoreau was well aware that this theme, expounded tediously by poets for half a century, was thick-set with clichés lying in wait for the unwary. Instead of skirting the danger he plunged in, trusting his verbal skill to save him from triteness. In the next to last paragraph of "Solitude" he lets go with his most exuberant paean to nature's capacity for sympathy, declaring that if any man should ever justly grieve, "all Nature would be affected, and the sun's brightness fade, and the winds would sigh humanely, and the clouds rain tears, and the woods shed their leaves and put on mourning in midsummer." (153) The personifications here are so outrageous as to be humorous. They may be taken as a virtuoso's parody of the Romantic style—a hunch that is confirmed by the sharp language of the context (quoted in my next paragraph). By this strategy he avoids sentimentality even while retaining the effect of sentiment.

Closely allied to the beneficence of nature is its healing power, a subject equally used up by mid-nineteenth century. It appears many times in Thoreau's *Journal*, not always with freshness. The idea was a necessary component of the nature theme in *Walden*, but to find an original way of expressing it seemed an insoluble problem. By a stroke of fancy, in the final paragraph of "Solitude," he hit upon the device of treating the hackneyed subject of nature's "medicines" in terms of the equally hackneyed advertisements for patent medicines. Instead of one of those "quack vials" claiming a universal cure, he recommends nature's own panacea, "morning air." For men who will not drink this at the fountainhead of the day, he suggests that it be bottled up and sold in the shops. Such prankishness does not inspire Thoreau's best writing, but by making a joke of nature-as-healer he gets across the idea of her restorative powers without falling into the Romantic convention. He rounds the passage off by rejecting Hygeia, "daughter of that old herb-doctor Æsculapius," and choosing instead as his tutelary goddess Hebe, "who had the power of restoring gods and men to the vigor of youth . . . and wherever she came it was spring." (154) It was new life, not a cure from sickness or melancholia, that Thoreau sought in nature. The chapter ends on a light and refreshing note.

Trance

One paragraph at the center of "Solitude"—in which Thoreau becomes a "spectator" of himself—remains to be examined. At first reading it seems totally unrelated to the rest of the chapter. But it has to do with one of the higher uses of solitude—how to meditate on nature until one finds a way beyond and through, to something that lies on the other side. The full significance of this crucial passage can be understood only by relating it to several others concerned with trancelike meditations and then, after adequate preparation, circling back to the "spectator" paragraph itself. Of his earliest visits to Walden Pond Thoreau recalls: "I have spent many an hour, when I was younger, floating over its surface as the zephyr willed . . . dreaming awake, until I was aroused by the boat touching the sand, and I arose to see what shore my fates had impelled me to." (213) The sheer idleness of such summer days was essential to his poetic youth, when he was rich, "if not in money, in sunny hours" to be spent lavishly. The trance in those days was purely sensuous.

Now in maturity, when he has moved out to the pond to live, his quest is more clearly defined. "As I sit at my window this summer afternoon,"—so he begins his search for serenity in Chapter 4, "Sounds," with a paragraph reminiscent of the opening one in "Solitude." He goes on to describe the scene framed before him: "a fish hawk dimples the glassy surface of the pond and brings up a fish; a mink steals out of the marsh before my door and seizes a frog by the shore; the sedge is bending under the weight of the reed-birds flitting hither and thither." Nature is not always congenial to contemplation—the hawk, the predatory mink, the restless birds. What peace it has to offer on this occasion is rudely interrupted; "and for the last half-hour I have heard the rattle of railroad cars, now dying away and then reviving like the beat of a partridge, conveying travellers from Boston to the country." (127) Comparing the noise of the train to a natural sound is only the beginning of his gradual build-up of irony which justifies his ten-page digression on the railroad, concluding with a satire on the cattle cars going to the city: "So is your pastoral life whirled past and away." (135) The reverse happens when commercial berry-pickers come to invade the rural quiet. It is one of the taxes we pay for having a railroad, he lamented late in life: "Almost all our improvements, so called, tend to convert the country into the town." (J, XIV, 57) Similarly ironical is his remark in "Sounds" that he is "related to society by this link," the only use he made of the train tracks being as a short cut in his walks.

All this high-jinks about the Fitchburg Railroad, one of the best-known passages in *Walden*, serves two purposes. Negatively, in contrast with the peace of nature, it is a satire on the destructiveness of industrialism. But its chief purpose is affirmative: to dramatize the point that solitude can be achieved by an effort of the will even if all efforts of the legs fail. "Now that the cars are gone by and all the restless world with them . . . I am more alone than ever." (136) Even in mid-nineteenth century New England it was all but impossible to get far enough away to be absolutely alone. The nearness of the railroad was a calculated risk for one who deliberately chose the experiment of seeking "a primitive and frontier life, though in the midst of an outward civilization." (12) To create his own solitude was part of the task he set himself.

In spite of all intrusions of machines and men, the days at Walden were largely peaceful, and occasionally he achieved an ideal serenity. Declaring that there were times when he could not afford to sacrifice the "bloom of the present moment" to any work, in the bean-field or at his study desk, he records a classic example of his experience of trance. The casualness of his description makes it seem almost too easy of attainment, until one remembers the long preparatory disciplines that comprise the first hundred pages of *Walden:*

Sometimes, in a summer morning, having taken my accustomed bath, I sat in my sunny doorway from sunrise till noon, rapt in a revery, amidst the pines and hickories and sumachs, in undisturbed solitude and stillness, while the birds sang around or flitted noiseless through the house, until by the sun falling in at my west window, or the noise of some traveller's wagon on the distant highway, I was reminded of the lapse of time. I grew in those seasons like corn in the night, and they were far better than any work of the hands would have been. They were not time subtracted from my life, but so much over and above my usual allowance. I realized what the Orientals mean by contemplation and the forsaking of works. (123–124)

The reference here to the Orientals—"contemplation and the forsaking of works"—is a clue to the meaning of this passage that launches his chapter on "Sounds," and to much else in *Walden.* It must be followed out in detail. Thoreau had begun his reading of the great "bibles" of India early, probably in the library at Emerson's house where he lived from 1841 to 1843, and the *Journal* is full of quotations and comment. A general reference, 1 September 1841, shows how he was applying them to the conduct of life: "One may discover the root of a Hindoo religion in his own private history, when, in the silent intervals of the day or the night, he does sometimes inflict on himself like austerities with a stern satisfaction." (J, I, 279) He does not specify the nature of these austerities, but those he practised at

Walden Pond were certainly Hindu-like and they gave him the satisfaction he sought. Actually Thoreau liked to think of himself as a yogi. Writing to a friend in 1849, between quotations from the *Harivansa* (an Oriental classic he was reading at the time), he affirmed that he was one, though in a qualified sense only:

"Free in this world, as the birds in the air, disengaged from every kind of chains, those who have practised the *yoga* gather in Brahma the certain fruit of their works."

Depend upon it that rude and careless as I am, I would fain practise the *yoga* faithfully.

"The yogin, absorbed in contemplation, contributes in his degree to creation: he breathes a divine perfume, he hears wonderful things."...

To some extent, and at rare intervals, even I am a yogin.

Such a statement cannot be ignored, though it need not be taken literally. Thoreau's withdrawal to Walden deliberately stopped far short of the yogi's complete abstraction from the world. Unlike the yogi he undertook no rigid system of disciplines, no total renunciation of the body, and no self-torture. He had satirized these harsher practices in the first chapter of *Walden*. (4–5) Even so, the leading authority on Oriental influences in American literature, after quoting the passage in "Sounds" from which this inquiry took off, declares: "The Hindu Yogi wrapt in his contemplations is not a far cry from the picture Thoreau gives of himself, sitting in his sunny doorway lost in reverie.... To draw nice distinctions here between Oriental contemplation in general and the technical processes of the Yoga is to quibble."

In his wide reading of Hindu scriptures Thoreau found one book which made the goal and even the practices of the yogi sufficiently liberalized to include him. The *Bhagvat-Geeta* mediates between the extreme asceticism of yoga, as expounded in Vedantic literature, and the Sankhya philosophy, "the way of works." He had read separate treatises on the two "ways," but the *Geeta* was the bible that came closest to his needs. Emerson had discovered it in the spring of 1845, just as the Walden experiment was taking shape, and shortly afterward, presumably, Thoreau caught fire from his enthusiasm. In *A Week* (1849), which was drafted by 1847, he gives it more space and higher praise than any other book. At the beginning of several pages of quotations he cites the specific teaching of Krishna ("the Forsaking of Works") which he says at the end of the trance in *Walden* he now understands. But the reason he admires the *Bhagvat-Geeta*, according to his earlier book, is that it "assigns their due rank respectively to Action and Contemplation."

Finding the proper balance between the two was one of the major problems in Thoreau's life. As he put it in *A Week:* "How can I communicate with the gods, who am a pencil-maker on the earth, and not be insane?" The solution offered in the *Geeta*—let the motive to action be in the deed itself so that the mind will not be distracted by concern with results—was much to his purpose: "He is both a Yogee and a Sannyasee who performeth that which he hath to do *independent* of the fruits thereof." This reconciles the two-way pull a good man feels—sometimes to remain in the world and do his duty; at other times, when he feels so called, to enter upon a life of contemplation by himself. The combination of sanity and sublimity in the *Bhagvat-Geeta* gave direction to the dialectic of *Walden:* the ignorant man is one who measures the meaning of his life in terms of the success or failure of his actions; the wise man seeks deliverance from this bondage by withdrawal into solitude and the practice of austerities.

This teaching of the *Geeta*, that one should not renounce action itself but "all longing for the fruit of action," is perfectly exemplified in "The Bean-Field" (Chapter 7). Thoreau's pretended display of economic success in his experiment there—a page from his account book showing a profit of $8.71½ for his summer's labor (180)—is of course a satire on the profit motive in agriculture. It leads to his sharp judgment that "the farmer leads the meanest of lives," concerned only with the dollar value of his crops. The whole purpose of this chapter is to show the solitary worker in the Walden bean-field as leading just the opposite kind of life. It concludes with an ideal that makes mock of the prudential rule for good husbandry laid down in the Bible: "The true husbandman will cease from anxiety . . . and finish his labor with every day, relinquishing all claim to the produce of his fields, and sacrificing in his mind not only his first but his last fruits also." (184) In its extreme unworldliness this illustrates the principle of his Hindu bible for achieving inner peace, the prerequisite for contemplation.

The actual discipline of yoga was used by Thoreau in a deliberately loose way, simply as the ascetic gesture of one deeply drawn to the Oriental scriptures. Yet he could find many passages in the *Bhagvat-Geeta* congenial to his temper and his approach to life. The way of the yogi certainly fits the austere program at Walden: "The *Yogee* constantly exerciseth the spirit in private. He is recluse, of a subdued mind and spirit. . . . He planteth his own seat firmly on the spot that is undefiled. . . . There he, whose business is the restraining of his passions, should sit." And the following passage makes a valuable gloss on the meditative trance in "Sounds"—not the occasion itself, but the disciplined preparation for it and the mystical goal aimed at:

> A man being endued with a purified understanding, having humbled his spirit by resolution, and abandoned the objects of the sense organs . . . who worshippeth with discrmination, eateth with moderation,and is humble of speech, of body, and of mind; who prefereth the devotion of meditation, and who constantly placeth his confidence in dispassion; who is freed from ostentation . . . and in all things temperate, is formed for being *Brahm*. . . . He at length is absorbed in my nature.

The whole philosophy of yoga was centered on renouncing the sinful world, escaping from this life of pain, and freeing the soul at last from the prison of its body. Thoreau was not Hindu enough to desire the total eclipse of his ego by absorption into Brahma, though one contemporary suggested the possibility. What he really wanted was a discipline by which he could live in the spirit without forsaking the world, despite its materialism. Yoga appealed to him chiefly because of the direction of its emphasis, that the life of contemplation is a higher road than the life of action. He read the Hindu scriptures not for their metaphysics but as a source of metaphor.

In *Walden* his one specific reference to the *Bhagvat-Geeta* makes brilliant use of it as the gateway to a vision—the kind of trance most congenial to western literary tradition. It follows a long section on the ice-cutters at Walden Pond and the shipping by Yankee clippers of its frozen "pure sea-green water" to Madras, Bombay, and Calcutta—concluding with the suggestive phrase that their sweltering inhabitants may now "drink at my well." Though in "The Pond in Winter" (Chapter 16), he says he must forego the daily baths he took there in summer, he is content with a symbolic one:

> In the morning I bathe my intellect in the stupendous and cosmogonal philosophy of the Bhagvat-Geeta. . . . I lay down the book and go to my well for water, and lo! there I meet the servant of the Bramin, priest of Brahma and Vishnu and Indra, who still sits in his temple on the Ganges reading the Vedas, or dwells at the root of a tree with his crust and water jug. I meet his servant come to draw water for his master, and our buckets as it were grate together in the same well. The pure Walden water is mingled with the sacred water of the Ganges. (328–329)

In *A Week*, appropriately for a book about a student who is exploring new worlds, the *Bhagvat-Geeta* was drawn on for voluminous quotations interspersed with comments on the appeal of its doctrines to a modern reader. In *Walden* it is absorbed into the text, or used imaginatively for taking off into an extended metaphor, as here. Thoreau puts aside his book of philosophy and creates a dream-fable that expresses, better than any argument about theology could do, the kinship he feels. His concluding image—the "pure" Walden water mingled with the "sacred" Ganges—sums up perfectly this American poet's relation to his Hindu bible.

This long preparation should be of aid in understanding that enigmatic "spectator" paragraph lying at the center of "Solitude." It must now be given in full:

> With thinking we may be beside ourselves in a sane sense. By a conscious effort of the mind we can stand aloof from actions and their consequences; and all things, good and bad, go by us like a

torrent. We are not wholly involved in Nature. I may be either the driftwood in the stream, or Indra in the sky looking down on it. I *may* be affected by a theatrical exhibition; on the other hand, I *may not* be affected by an actual event which appears to concern me much more. I only know myself as a human entity; the scene, so to speak, of thoughts and affections; and am sensible of a certain doubleness by which I can stand as remote from myself as from another. However intense my experience, I am conscious of the presence and criticism of a part of me, which, as it were, is not a part of me, but spectator, sharing no experience, but taking note of it; and that it is no more I than it is you. When the play, it may be the tragedy, of life is over, the spectator goes his way. It was a kind of fiction, a work of the imagination only, so far as he was concerned. This doubleness may easily make us poor neighbors and friends sometimes. (149–150)

The opening pun performs a double function. It takes out of the mouths of his fellow villagers their ready objection, that any one who can think himself into "doubleness," so as to become a spectator of his own actions, is "beside himself" in the sense of being insane—a point that is rounded off at the end by his apology for being such a thinker and hence a bad neighbor. More importantly, it gives a light touch to the philosophical abstractions he is about to tackle: the relation of subject to object, as a problem in perception, and the dilemma of appearance and reality.

These propositions, to be sure, are among the oldest in philosophy. Thoreau could have invoked many Western theorizers, from Plato on down, but he chose to go to the source for all concepts related to Maya. What cues this paragraph to the Orient is its brief sentence referring to Indra, in which the power of this primal Hindu god to interchange perceiver and perceived, at will, is claimed by the narrator too. There follows immediately his discourse on Illusion, but made concrete in a sequence of images drawn from the theater. The most recent student of Oriental influences on Thoreau has suspected a similarity here to one of the myths of Vishnu. "This game of the divine playing hide-and-seek with himself illustrates that he [Vishnu] plays out the part or role of all his creations," he suggests. "In effect, man must realize that in dying to his body he wakes up into his true Self, into the illusive spectator. Then the veil of *maya* falls from his eyes." But instead of following up this shrewd hunch, he tries without success to find a source in the *Bhagvat-Geeta*.

It is not in this small bible but in a large tome on Hindu mythology, the *Vishnu Purana*, that one must look for analogues of the spectator passage. Thoreau read this volume during the years when he was revising *Walden*—actually adding the paragraph in question—and he took down many pages of quotations from it in one of his commonplace books. Among several dealing with the interrelations of subject and object, creator and his creation, two may be cited:

> Those who have not practised devotion, conceive erroneously of the nature of the world, . . . judge of it as an object of perception only, [and] are lost in the ocean of spiritual ignorance. But they who know true wisdom, and whose minds are pure, behold the world as one with divine knowledge, and as one with thee, oh god.

> Until all acts, which are the cause of notions of individuality, are discontinued, spirit is one thing and the universe is another, to those who contemplate objects as distinct and various; but that is called true knowledge, or knowledge of Brahma, which recognizes no distinctions, which contemplates only simple existence, which is undefinable by word, and is to be discovered only in one's own spirit. . . . By him who knows this, all the existing world, fixed or movable, is to be regarded as identical with himself, as proceeding alike from Vishnu, assuming a universal form.

Even in the theoretical parts of his paragraph Thoreau is less abstruse than the *Vishnu Purana*. But he wanted to make his point even clearer and more concrete. Being immersed at this same period in a famous Hindu play, Kalidassa's *Sacontala*, he decided to dramatize his philosophical idea by putting it in terms of the stage. Of course, one does not have to go to India to find the theater used as a metaphor for illusion, but there is good reason to suspect that the inspiration for Thoreau's striking imagery came from his reading of *Sacontala* or from Horace Wilson's long introduction to a collection of classic Indian dramas, in which he discussed techniques, scenic apparatus, and other aspects of theatrical entertainment.

The spectator passage has very real relations to Thoreau's wide reading in Hindu literature and is another example of the imaginative use he made of ideas gleaned from that source. It is also further proof of how, in *Walden* at least, he absorbed his erudition and turned it into writing that is entirely original. The spectator here who is watching the action of his own life is merged with the god who has created it in the first place as a play. And since Thoreau at this very moment was in the process of writing a book that was a kind of autobiography of the action aspect of this "spectator," the passage becomes a fable of the creation of *Walden*—which can be described as "a kind of fiction, a work of the imagination only," if the thesis of the present study is valid. On the practical level it is now clear how this paragraph fits in with a retreat to solitude as the ideal situation for a creative artist. But its relationships with the whole concept of solitude in Chapter 5, and throughout the book, are much more intricate and subtle. That "doubleness" described here is a sort of trancelike state ("it is no more I than it is you"), arrived at by disciplined meditation ("a conscious effort of the mind"). It separates the spectator from society ("makes us poor neighbors and friends"), and even divorces him partially from the natural world ("we are not wholly involved in Nature"). What had begun as a simple retreat to the woods to find solitude for writing has become involved in probing the meaning of nature, of reality itself, and through that a search for God and the discovery of Self. His long exploration has just begun. Unable or unwilling to lose that Self in Brahma, like a true yogi, Thoreau takes the poet's path through nature. His way differs from that of the transcendentalists, but his goal, like theirs, lies beyond it.

3
Maya

It is a remarkable fact that *Walden,* though generally thought of as a book about nature, does not have any chapter entitled "Nature" nor a single section dealing with it directly as subject. There is, of course, much about the natural world, increasing in fullness of representation as the civilized world fades and the narrative of Thoreau's experiment in economy is completed. His woodland retreat is described in profuse detail—plants and animals, trees and flowers, pond, pasture, sky, seasons—to create the *mise en scène.* But nature was not his goal, only a means to that goal. *Walden* was designed as a poem, not a transcendental thesis like Emerson's early booklet *Nature.* For Thoreau's general ideas about the meaning of nature and its significance for man, one must go to the *Journal.* There he will find a great deal of theorizing (in particular, a running debate between two rival concepts) that is indispensable to an understanding of nature as "the way" for his *Walden* quest.

When Thoreau left Concord and went to the woods, he walked straight into a paradox. Is nature out *there,* a reality, or is it only a symbol? The dilemma, like the kindred one discussed in the last chapter, again goes back to Plato, and beyond to those early expounders of philosophic idealism in India. Eventually Thoreau found the Hindu concept of Maya more useful to him as a poet than any of the formulations of Western philosophers. According to Maya, when men see trees it is because trees *are* there, though they are not the Real. By such reasoning Maya accounts for all phenomena and is accepted as the modus operandi of the universe, even though concealing the eternal Reality of Brahma. In discussing the influence of this Oriental doctrine on American transcendentalists, Arthur Christy has given a helpful definition: "Maya registers man's finiteness and sets the limit to his knowledge. It is the name of the dividing force, the finitising principle, and that which measures out the immeasurable and creates form in the formless." It was this balance between the actual and the ideal, with a shade of emphasis on the former, that gave Maya its special appeal for Thoreau. But as a matter of fact his interest in this idea (Is nature a reality or only a symbol?) had taken its start early in his career from a source no farther away than the other end of his native village.

Emerson's *Nature* was the classic American attempt to make a modern reconciliation of these two traditional ways of looking at the world, though weighted heavily on the idealistic side. This essay, read by Thoreau when a college student, provoked his first interest in the man who was to become a kind of mentor during his apprentice period. A few years later, as their relationship matured, Emerson hung his young protégé on the other horn of the Romantic dilemma by asking him to make a review article for the *Dial* out of a sheaf of scientific surveys of the state. It was published in the July 1842 issue as "Natural History of Massachusetts." Pedestrian as these pamphlets were they had a double appeal for Thoreau. They dealt with the local scene, to which he was dedicated, and their instrument for seeing was science, on which the young poet placed so much hope. They were only factual catalogues, of course, but his enthusiasm transmuted them into a lively essay. "Entomology extends the limits of being in a new direction," he wrote, by inviting us to "take an insect view" of the world. Of the motions of the serpent, "They make our hands and feet, the wings of the bird, and the fins of the fish seem very superfluous, as if Nature had only indulged her fancy in making them." This style holds up throughout. Thoreau's review makes good reading as a literary essay and it is as such, rather than as a contribution to science, that it claims attention. He concluded with an apology for the unavoidable dullness of such surveys, saying that we should not complain if the pioneer raises no flowers with his first crop. In this context he added a sentence that has been taken as prophetic: "Let us not underrate the value of a fact; it will one day flower in a truth." (V, 107, 123, 129–130)

Appearance and Reality

Thoreau's juxtaposing of fact and truth here shows him grappling with a major problem in the Romantic interpretation of nature. The solution of it comprised his whole artistic endeavor, according to one of his most astute critics: the need for "striking and maintaining the delicate balance between object and reflection, [between] minute observation and generalized concept." The history of this struggle, as recorded in the *Journal*, is fascinating. The earliest notation of his interest occurs in an entry for 8 December 1837, praising Goethe for "giving an exact description of objects as they appear to him . . . even the reflections of the author do not interfere with his descriptions." (J, I, 15) Commenting thus on his reading of the *Italiänische Reise*, with its climactic visit in 1786 at Padua to the oldest botanical garden in Europe, Thoreau is harking back to the launching of the great debate between science and poetry by Goethe, prime exemplar of the literary artist throughout the Romantic period.

Emerson, Thoreau's model nearer home, had found his own awakening at the Jardin des Plantes a half century later. Nature ordered and encompassed by the mind, as he saw it displayed there, had suggested to him that man could merge with the universe, that the religion of the future might be a natural rather than a revealed one. These "facts" observed in Paris had flowered in *Nature* (1836), a manifesto of "truths" that is usually taken as the starting point of American transcendentalism. "In the woods, we return to reason and faith," Emerson proclaimed, following up with his most extravagant metaphor:

> Standing on the bare ground,—my head bathed by the blithe air and uplifted into infinite space,—all mean egotism vanishes. I become a transparent eye-ball; I am nothing; I see all; the currents of the Universal Being circulate through me; I am part or parcel of God.

Though there is no reference to this transcendental essay in any of Thoreau's writings, he well knew the appeal of such heady idealisms, as can be discovered from suggestive entries in the *Journal* here and there. For example, in April 1852 he lamented: "Once I was part and parcel of Nature; now I am observant of her." (J, III, 378) The echo of Emerson is obvious enough, but there is a significant shift of emphasis. When Thoreau freed himself from his mentor's influence, as he usually did, his insight became quite different. A *Journal* passage as early as 1839 shows him moving off in another direction, one that could lead to *Walden* just as surely as the other could not. Under the rubric of THE POET he wrote:

> Nature will not speak through but along with him. His voice will not proceed from her midst, but, breathing on her, will make her the expression of his thought. He then poetizes when he takes a fact out of nature into spirit. . . . His thought is one world, hers another. He is another Nature,—Nature's brother. . . . Each publishes the other's truth. (J, I, 74–75)

He tried to solve the Romantic riddle in "Natural History of Massachusetts" by inspecting nature through a microscope while simultaneously using traditional typology to make man's experience in it intelligible. Twelve years later, in his one great book, "he had for a breathless moment held the two in solution, fused and yet still kept separate," he and nature publishing each other's truths, thus making *Walden* one of the supreme achievements of Romantic Naturalism—as Perry Miller has phrased it—fit to be placed beside *The Prelude*. Actually, Wordsworth's long-awaited poem appeared opportunely in 1850 and Thoreau, though his budget allowed few purchases, immediately added it to his library.

From "Tintern Abbey," published at the turn of the century, he had long ago learned that a "wise passivity" in the presence of nature is superior to studied observation. Now from the same pen came a poetic autobiography, centered not on nature but on the artist's imaginative response to it, that he must have found curiously analogous to his own "growth of a poet's mind" then in progress. In Book Twelfth of *The Prelude* there is a passage especially close to the central idea of *Walden:*

> O Soul of Nature! excellent and fair!
> That didst rejoice with me, with whom I, too,
> Rejoiced through early youth, . . . Powers on whom
> I daily waited, now all eye and now
> All ear; but never long without the heart
> Employed, and man's unfolding intellect. . . .

But Wordsworth then goes on to speak of "A twofold frame of body and of mind," and of the battle he waged to overcome the tyranny of the senses. There came a time in his life when that despot "the bodily eye" held his mind "in absolute dominion," and made him "Insensible"

> . . . to the moods
> Of time and season, to the moral power,
> The affections and the spirit of the place.

It was only by a long effort of the will and by recapturing the imaginative power he had known early in life that he could shake off at last this habit of observing "meagre novelties" and stand in nature's presence, once again, "A sensitive being, a *creative* soul."

Looking back now to Thoreau's *Journal* lament in 1852, one sees clearly that he had Wordsworth in mind as well as Emerson. But he differed from Wordsworth too, as the full context will show: "How few valuable observations can we make in youth! What if there were united the susceptibility of youth with the discrimination of age? Once I was part and parcel of Nature; now I am observant of her." (J, III, 378) The difference from Emerson turns on a single word: even in youth Thoreau felt himself merged only with nature, not with God. What distinguishes him from both poets is his effort to maintain a delicate balance between two opposing approaches to nature.

These several comparisons, especially with Wordsworth and Goethe, help to locate Thoreau's proper place in the history of Romanticism. But it will be far more instructive to follow his own explorations, in journal and essay, of those ideas about nature that lie behind *Walden* and are essential to an understanding of its meaning. Since Thoreau took his start from Emerson, the present inquiry must begin with a brief account of *Nature.* The heart of it may be found in the chapter called "Idealism," where Emerson sets up the traditional dilemma by saying: "A noble doubt perpetually suggests itself . . . whether nature outwardly exists." Knowing the instinctive belief of common sense in the absolute existence of the external world, he marshals against it all available witnesses. The first two categories of evidence have special reference to Thoreau: the various angles from which reality can be perceived and the uses to which it is put by the poet, who "conforms things to his thoughts" instead of conforming his thoughts to things as the ordinary man does. The other witnesses were most important for Emerson—science, philosophy, religion, and ethics, in that order. Their testimony, taken all together, is conclusive for him:

> Culture inverts the vulgar views of nature, and brings the mind to call that apparent which it uses to call real, and that real which it uses to call visionary. . . . The advantage of the ideal theory over the popular faith is this, that it presents the world in precisely that view which is most desirable to the mind.

The two remaining sections of his essay define "that view." Nature is the "apparition" of God. So to man it is the symbol of that universal spirit he was soon to call the Oversoul, of which the individual soul can hopefully become "part and parcel."

It is Emerson's emphasis on the religious and ethical uses of nature, as the incarnation of God, that differentiates him from his supposed disciple. There is some tendency to accept the idea of nature as symbol in Thoreau's early writings, to be sure, and it even remains fairly strong in *A Week* (1849). But as he was composing *Walden* he was moving steadily away from Emerson's idea—that the literary artist who perceives nature from the correct angle of vision need only record what he sees and automatically his writing will be symbolic. Thoreau came to believe that the poet must create the symbols that go into his work, though he draws on nature as a reservoir. This is exactly what he was doing as he revised and rewrote his masterpiece, adding new levels of meaning to the previously observed and described realities, so as to raise them to the status of symbols. He had shifted from ethical to esthetic uses of nature.

Emerson was somewhat slow in recognizing their divergence. In his *Journals* he wrote with pride of the young man he liked to think of as a disciple: "Henry said that the other world was all his art; that his pencils would draw no other." He was apparently not aware that this meant art, rather than transcendental philosophy, was coming to be the direction of Thoreau's development, though the shift was not sudden and was never complete. In his own *Journal* Thoreau sets the emphasis right: "He is the richest who has most use for nature as *raw material* of tropes and symbols with which to describe his life." (J, V, 135; my italics) This concept finds its way into *Walden*, where he declares that his labors in the bean-field are "only for the sake of tropes and expression, to serve a parable-maker." (179) Two more *Journal* passages will help to underscore this artistic orientation. In 1852 he writes: "My thought is a part of the meaning of the world, and hence I use a part of the world as a symbol to express my thought." (J, IV, 410) The next year he puts his belief in the form of a rhetorical question: "Is it not as language that all natural objects affect the poet?" (J, V, 359) All these points in his maturing esthetic creed were noted down in the years when *Walden* was undergoing its final revision, and they are responsible for the special way in which nature functions in that book.

Yet on occasion Thoreau could adopt the viewpoint of Idealism in a way Emerson would have approved. A *Journal* entry in the spring of 1852, for example, seems straight out of Plato. The sight of the sucker floating in the river at this season "affects me singularly," he writes, "realizing my *idea* of a fish":

I see it for what it is,—not an actual terrene fish, but the fair symbol of a divine idea, the design of an artist. Its color and form, its gills and fins and scales, are perfectly beautiful, because they completely express to my mind what they were intended to express. . . . I am serene and satisfied when the birds fly and the fishes swim as in fable . . . when the events of the day have a mythological character, and the most trivial is symbolical. (J, III, 437–438)

But at other times he inclines to the opposite position. Late in life, confessing in the *Journal* his preference for the ideal over the real in friendship, he declares on the other hand that he is "not so ready to perceive the illusion that is in Nature," having experienced so much actual joyful intercourse with her. "Yet, strictly speaking, the same must be true of nature and of man," he concludes: "our ideal is the only real." (J, XI, 282)

As a literary artist Thoreau takes advantage of both sides of this dilemma. In *A Week* the transcendental position is argued in a long and significant section: "We need pray for no higher heaven than the pure senses can furnish, a *purely* sensuous life"; he begins paradoxically: "May we not *see* God? Are we to be put off and amused in this life, as it were with a mere allegory? Is not Nature, rightly read, that of which she is commonly taken to be the symbol merely?" (I, 408) To get through to this transcendent Reality would be harder than for a new Columbus to discover another New World, he admits. So he puts the case in soberer language: "But there is only necessary a moment's sanity and sound senses, to teach us that there is a nature beyond the ordinary, in which we have only some vague pre-emption right and western reserve as yet. We live on the outskirts of that region." (I, 409)

For his next metaphor he turns to science, relying on the contemporary hope that this is *the* way to the truth. He begins by referring to a prediction of Copernicus, "reasoning long and patiently about the matter," that was confirmed a century after his death by Galileo through the newly invented telescope. Then his own poetic use of astronomy:

I am not without hope that we may, even here and now, obtain some accurate information concerning that OTHER WORLD which the instinct of mankind has so long predicted. Indeed, all that we call science, as well as all that we call poetry, is a particle of such information, accurate as far as it goes, though it be but to the confines of the truth. . . . Surely, we are provided with senses as well fitted to penetrate the spaces of the real, the substantial, the eternal, as these outward are to penetrate the material universe. (I, 412)

The "real" and the "substantial" here, it should be remembered, are transcendental terms for the spiritual or essential world in contrast with that known to the physical senses. He adds, for emphasis, that the cosmos of astronomy is but the "outward and visible type" of the "immaterial starry system."

In the midst of this Western argument about reality and appearance, ranging from the Greeks to modern science, Thoreau sets an image from the Orient. He merely says, without further identification, that he is quoting a Hindu sage: "As a dancer, having exhibited herself to the spectator, desists from the dance, so does Nature desist, having manifested herself to soul." (I, 409) The source of this mystical utterance is identified in Thoreau's notebook. It is drawn from the *Sankhya Karika*, a rendering in verse of the leading tenets of the Sankhya philosophy, the object of which is to free the soul from the body and attain knowledge of "the real nature of all that is." The dancer here has been identified as the personification of Maya-Shakti, the creative activity of Brahma, and the spectator as the Atman, the soul or true Self residing in every person. Through the dance he perceives that the external world is illusory. If he could free himself entirely from the tyranny of the senses, his view of nature would be "*purely* sensuous." This finds a faint echo in *Walden*, where Thoreau is observing the activities of those animals who are his chief links to nature in the winter months: "all the motions of a squirrel, even in the most solitary recesses of the forest, imply spectators as much as those of a dancing girl." (302) But the problems of philosophic idealism do not come to the surface in his chapter on "Winter Animals."

Indeed they are argued only once in *Walden*, whose proper mode is that of poetry. Early in this book, when Thoreau is seeking images to express what he really lived for, he states the case with equal persuasiveness for both sides. He begins by espousing idealism (using the term "reality" in its transcendental sense):

Shams and delusions are esteemed for soundest truths, while reality is fabulous. If men would steadily observe realities only, and not allow themselves to be deluded, life, to compare it with such things as we know, would be like a fairy tale and the Arabian Nights' Entertainments. . . . I perceive that we inhabitants of New England live this mean life that we do because our vision does not penetrate the surface of things. We think that that *is* which *appears* to be. . . . God himself culminates in the present moment, and will never be more divine in the lapse of all the ages. And we are enabled to apprehend at all what is sublime and noble only by the perpetual instilling and drenching of the reality that surrounds us. The universe constantly and obediently answers to our conceptions. . . . Let us spend our lives in conceiving then. (106–108)

This is a kind of extension of the "prospect" envisaged on the last page of *Nature*, when men at last come to look at the world with new eyes. But Emerson put the words there in the mouth of his "Orphic bard," as he often did when making an extravagant statement: "Nature is not fixed but fluid. Spirit alters, moulds, makes it. . . . Build therefore your own world. As fast as you conform your life to the pure idea in your mind, *that* will unfold its great proportions." Thoreau takes full responsibility for his own extreme position, instead of shouldering it off on a poetic "double." What is more important, he emphasizes the esthetic basis of it. In this, and in much of his phrasing, he seems closer to the modern concept that the poet quite simply creates his own world than to Emersonian transcendentalism. "The artist changes the direction of Nature and makes her grow according to his idea," he noted in his *Journal* the month after *Walden* was published. (J, VII, 10)

Thoreau's great advantage as a writer was that the philosopher and moralist in him never took the pen away from the artist—at least for long. Immediately following his most abstract treatment of Idealism in *Walden*, quoted above, there comes a paragraph in praise of objective reality (the term this time having its common-sense meaning):

Let us settle ourselves, and work and wedge our feet downward through the mud and slush of opinion, and prejudice, and tradition, and delusion, and appearance . . . through poetry and philosophy and religion, till we come to a hard bottom and rocks in place, which we can call *reality*, and say, This is, and no mistake. . . . If you stand right fronting and face to face to a fact, you will see the sun glimmer on both its surfaces, as if it were a cimeter, and feel its sweet edge dividing you through the heart and marrow, and so you will happily conclude your mortal career. Be it life or death, we crave only reality. (108–109)

The poet needs the actual world to make his images concrete, just as his vision must look beyond it, or through it. Yet perhaps the "reality" Thoreau is talking about in these two passages is that of neither the materialist nor the transcendentalist but of the artist in his dual function. In the first passage he is so conceiving facts as to make them flower into truths. In the second he is deflowering transcendent truths in order to rediscover their factual bases.

As he continues his pursuit of this evasive "reality" its two aspects become more and more fused, and the esthetic nature of his quest becomes clearer. The newly opening American West, as the place where men supposedly grapple with raw life in a way that the cultured East does not, gave him a fresh image for reality in his first book:

The frontiers are not east or west, north or south; but wherever a man *fronts* a fact, though that fact be his neighbor, there is an unsettled wilderness between him and Canada, between him and the setting sun, or, farther still, between him and *it*. Let him build himself a log house with the bark on where he is, *fronting* IT, and wage there an Old French war for seven or seventy years, with Indians and Rangers, or whatever else may come between him and the reality, and save his scalp if he can. (I, 323–324)

Implicit throughout *Walden* also is the assumption that the hermit has come to grips with reality in his mind more successfully than Concord farmers in their barnyards. And from his cabin door he can envision the prairies and the Western wilderness without any need of going there in a covered wagon. The poet fixes and unfixes the limits of his world, as he puts it in a *Journal* entry for 1853: "The boundaries of the actual are no more fixed and rigid than the elasticity of our imaginations." (J, V, 203)

As early as *A Week*, in the "frontier" passage just quoted, he suggests that the geography of realism can be an interior matter. Yet in the very next chapter he locates it outside, once more in the actual world:

When I visit again some haunt of my youth, I am glad to find that nature wears so well. The landscape is indeed something real, and solid, and sincere, and I have not put my foot through it yet. There is a pleasant tract on the bank of the Concord, called Conantum, which I have in my mind. . . . When my thoughts are sensible of change, I love to see and sit on rocks which I *have* known, and pry into their moss, and see unchangeableness so established. I not yet gray on rocks forever gray, I no longer green under the evergreens. (I, 374)

Here only the objects in the world are stable and real, the subject shifts and changes. These paradoxes of the poet would have been applauded by Wallace Stevens in this century and by Emily Dickinson among Thoreau's contemporaries, but hardly by Emerson.

In the *Journal* several years later, when he returns to this metaphor for testing reality and appearance, he resolves the dilemma in an image of the poet as bond servant to earth for his sustenance:

I long for wildness, a nature which I cannot put my foot through, woods where the wood thrush forever sings, where the hours are early morning ones, and there is dew on the grass, and the day is forever unproved, where I might have a fertile unknown for a soil about me. I would go after the cows, I would watch the flocks of Admetus there forever, only for my board and clothes. A New Hampshire everlasting and unfallen. (J, V, 293)

The allusion is to the servitude of Apollo, when he was temporarily banished from heaven by Zeus and forced to tend the flocks of the King of Pherae. While watching them he would play his lyre, and even the savage beasts of the forest were charmed by his divine music.

This is Thoreau's favorite image for the poet, likening himself to the god of light and song. It appears often in his writings, once in *Walden*, where it is related to the problem of remaining a poet even while adjusting to the realities of the world—specifically, making a living with the minimum of distraction from his true business. "While my acquaintances went unhesitatingly into trade or the professions," he says, "I thought often and seriously of picking huckleberries . . . ranging the hills all summer . . . so, to keep the flocks of Admetus." (77) By choosing to work in the natural rather than the commercial world, as with his labor in the bean-field, he hopes to find sustenance for his body and at the same time "tropes to serve a parable-maker one day." By studying nature in a very special way, according to a *Journal* passage in 1852, he hopes to make its facts flower into poetry:

How much, what infinite, leisure it requires, as of a lifetime, to appreciate a single phenomenon! You must camp down beside it as for life, having reached your land of promise, and give yourself wholly to it. It must stand for the whole world to you, symbolical of all things. . . . Unless the humming of a gnat is as the music of the spheres, and the music of the spheres is as the humming of a gnat, they are naught to me. It is not communications to serve for a history,—which are science,—but the great story itself, that cheers and satisfies us. (J, IV, 433–434)

Scientist vs. Poet

Thoreau gave new zest to his pursuit of nature's meaning by changing the counters in his game, substituting the personified scientist and poet for the abstractions, appearance and reality, that have previously served as contenders. This was a definite advantage, since his ultimate purpose was not to prove a thesis in philosophy but to discriminate two modes of perception, the scientific and the poetic. The point of the game is not which side is going to win—a foregone conclusion—but to make the play of one against the other an opportunity for sharpening his definitions of meaning and value. For a poet in the Romantic period, Thoreau certainly gives science all the odds, at least at the start of his career. In a *Journal* entry for 1840 he declares: "The eye that can appreciate the naked and absolute beauty of a scientific truth, is far rarer than that which discerns moral beauty." (LJ, 182) True, the comparison is not specifically with poetry but it is on the level of esthetics. Two years later his praise is higher still, in the last paragraph of his "Natural History of Massachusetts": "The true man of science will know nature better by his finer organization; he will smell, taste, see, hear, feel, better than other men. His will be a deeper and finer experience." (V, 131) Again the poet is not named, but since he, too, must perceive the world through his senses, the scientist's "finer organization" is held up as something to be emulated or otherwise made use of.

By the end of the 1840's, when Thoreau comes to rework his ideas on science for a small essay in the *Week*, his high hopes have begun to fade. It is clearly the descriptive purpose of contemporary science that disappoints him—the endless counting, measuring, classifying. "There is wanting constant and accurate observation with enough of theory to direct and discipline it," he says. "But, above all, there is wanting genius." This is what he has in mind in all of the criticisms that follow. Neither here nor anywhere else, of course, does Thoreau have anything important to say about science as such; only what it means to him. As a consequence, the most notable point in this his longest deliverance on the subject is his casual aside: "The poet uses the results of science and philosophy, and generalizes their widest deductions." (I, 388, 387)

One of the most profitable ways in which he had been using science was by emulating its method of close observation. But for the poet, he came to believe, this was a curse as well as a boon. There is a very significant comment in the *Journal* for 1851, the period of the regestation of *Walden:*

I fear that the character of my knowledge is from year to year becoming more distinct and scientific; that, in exchange for views as wide as heaven's cope, I am being narrowed down to the field of the microscope. I see details, not wholes nor the shadow of the whole. (J, II, 406)

The "whole" and the "shadow" here are presumably nature as spectacle and nature as spirit. But his lament that he has lost them through too much attention to particulars is lightened by his rhyming in prose ("cope . . . scope").

Similarly, a few years later, he tempers his attack on science by his verbal play about its overemphasis on vision:

> One might say that all views through a telescope or microscope were purely visionary, for it is only by his eye and not by any other sense—not by his whole man—that the beholder is there where he is presumed to be. It is a disruptive mode of viewing as far as the beholder is concerned. (J, VII, 61)

"The age is ocular," Emerson had declared somewhat pontifically in an early essay, and Thoreau in his *Journal* for 1840 devotes a paragraph of exuberant punning to the idea, not of vision in the scientific sense but of visionary in its common-sense meaning:

> The eye does the least drudgery of any of the senses. It oftenest escapes to a higher employment. . . . I attach some superiority even priority to this sense. It is the oldest servant in the soul's household —it images what it imagines—it ideates what it idealizes. Through it idolatry crept in—which is a kind of *religion*. . . . We *see* truth— We are children of *light*.

After all this play he concludes with the serious point he had to make: "The body of science will not be complete till every sense has thus ruled our thought and language, and action, in its turn." (LJ, 165–166) This would constitute the "whole man" he had defined as the only true beholder of nature—the poet rather than the scientist.

In the *Journal* throughout the 1850's there is a running series of comparisons between scientist and poet, increasingly unfavorable to the former as Thoreau's own pages ironically become filled more and more with detailed observations of nature. Men of science draw mere outlines or "pencil sketches," for example, whereas poets make use of the "wealth of color." (J, III, 301) Again, the scientific description differs from the poetic as "photographs from paintings," he declares, though this comparison is too favorable to the former: "All science is only a makeshift, a means to an end which is never attained." (J, XIV, 117) The strictly personal nature of this debate is shown by an extreme statement made in the crucial year of 1852:

> It is impossible for the same person to see things from the poet's point of view and that of the man of science. The poet's second love may be science, not his first,—when use has worn off the bloom. I realize that men may be born to a condition of mind at which others arrive in middle age by the decay of their poetic faculties. (J, III, 311)

Such exaggeration reveals nothing about the scientist, but a great deal about Thoreau's fear at this period that his poetic youth was lost beyond recall—a fear that was dispelled only with his successful rewriting of *Walden* as his "one book of poetry." It was during the same crisis that he responded with such fury to the printed questionnaire of the Association for the Advancement of Science. To describe his specialty to those who "do not believe in a science which deals with the higher law," he complains, would make him ridiculous in the eyes of the world. So he replies, in the privacy of his own *Journal*, "The fact is I am a mystic, a transcendentalist, and a natural philosopher to boot." (J, V, 4) None of these labels really describe Thoreau accurately. The statement has meaning only as an extravagant protest against what he was not—not a scientific observer but a seer-sayer.

When you are concerned that objects in nature should signify something to you, "that they be another sacred scripture and revelation to you, helping to redeem your life," he says, then you must get rid of your botany:

> It is only when we forget all our learning that we begin to know. I do not get nearer by a hair's breadth to any natural object so long as I presume that I have an introduction to it from some learned

man. To conceive of it with a total apprehension I must for the thousandth time approach it as something totally strange. (J, XII, 371)

Nature does not make her report to him who approaches her "consciously as an observer," Thoreau argues, but to one who goes forth in "the fullness of life." (J, IV, 174) Late in life he attempts a more balanced view:

As it is important to consider Nature from the point of view of science, remembering the nomenclature and system of men, and so, if possible, go a step further in that direction, so it is equally important often to ignore or forget all that men presume that they know, and take an original and unprejudiced view of Nature, letting her make what impression she will on you, as the first men, and all children and natural men still do. (J, XIII, 168–169)

The trouble with these ideas is that none of them are original themselves. Even the way they are expressed is hackneyed. They are part of the Romantic cult of awe, innocence, and primitivism, reiterated for a half-century as constituting the proper poetic approach to nature. He could not find his way to *Walden* by following a tradition that had already reached dead end.

When Thoreau talks about art instead of ideas he usually finds something original to say and a bright new way of saying it. Writing of the observer from the esthetic point of view, he says:

There is no such thing as pure *objective* observation. Your observation, to be interesting, *i.e.* to be significant, must be *subjective*. The sum of what the writer of whatever class has to report is simply some human experience, whether he be a poet or philosopher or man of science. The man of most science is the man most alive, whose life is the greatest event. Senses that take cognizance of outward things merely are of no avail. . . . No mere willful activity whatever, whether in writing verses or collecting statistics, will produce true poetry or science. (J, VI, 236–237)

This is shooting far beyond the descriptive scientists of the nineteenth century; it is fascinatingly prognostic of the great theorists of the twentieth, from Freud to Heisenberg, whose writings are so important for poetry as well as for science. Again, speaking of nature as a source of the poet's language:

> If I am overflowing with life, am rich in experience for which I lack expression, then nature will be my language full of poetry,—all nature will *fable,* and every natural phenomenon be a myth. The man of science, who is not seeking for expression but for a fact to be expressed merely, studies nature as a dead language. I pray for such inward experience as will make nature significant. (J, V, 135)

The concern with literary expression here is something quite different from the philosophical thesis on "Language" in Emerson's *Nature.* It suggests Thoreau's kinship with a whole school of modern poetry whose first great spokesman was Yeats—an ardent admirer of *Walden,* by the way.

This theorizing about techniques gave Thoreau confidence that his prophecy in "Natural History of Massachusetts," made so long ago, might at last be brought to fulfillment: "Let us not underrate the value of a fact; it will one day flower in a truth." Now a decade later, in 1852, he confides to his *Journal:*

> I have a commonplace-book for facts and another for poetry, but I find it difficult always to preserve the vague distinction which I had in my mind, for the most interesting and beautiful facts are so much the more poetry and that is their success. They are *translated* from earth to heaven. I see that if my facts were sufficiently vital and significant,—perhaps transmuted more into the substance of the human mind,—I should need but one book of poetry to contain them all. (J, III, 311)

There can be no doubt that the "one book of poetry" referred to here is *Walden.* Its rich factual content has accounted for its appeal to the general reader. But, as the present study is attempting to show, its facts are translated by metaphor into a quest for heaven, "and that is their success."

Two more *Journal* passages at this period clearly refer to the crisis in his esthetic development at the time of rewriting *Walden,* and specifically to the new kind of book he is making it into. The first follows a reference to Emerson and may have been prompted by some discussion with him:

A fact truly and absolutely stated is taken out of the region of common sense and acquires a mythologic or universal significance. Say it and have done with it. Express it without expressing yourself. See not with the eye of science, which is barren, nor of youthful poetry, which is impotent. . . . What was *enthusiasm* in the young man must become *temperament* in the mature man. Without excitement, heat, or passion, he will survey the world which excited the youth and threw him off his balance. As all things are significant, so all words should be significant. . . . As you *see,* so at length will you *say*. (J, III, 85–86)

The writer here is discussing with himself the relation of perception to expression, the thought-thing-word sequence that lies at the basis of literary creation. And the kind of writer he is becoming, as he transforms *Walden* from the expository early drafts to the poetic final version, is sufficiently evidenced by his desire to take his facts not only out of the personal world but out of the region of common sense, then elevate them into myth.

The second *Journal* passage is actually stated as taking off from a transcendental debate with a friend. The incident briefly referred to is a walk with the poet Ellery Channing who, watching Thoreau scribbling observations of nature in his field book on the spot, remarked rather petulantly that he was welcome to all the facts he wanted: "*I* am universal; I have nothing to do with the particular and definite." That evening, as Thoreau transferred his rough notes to the *Journal,* galled by the accusation of being limited like a scientist, he continued the dialogue as though his friend were there to hear and to be persuaded by his rejoinder:

I, too, would fain set down something beside facts. Facts should only be as the frame to my pictures; they should be material to the mythology which I am writing; . . . facts to tell who I am, and where I have been or what I have thought. . . . My facts shall be falsehoods to the common sense. I would so state facts that they shall be significant, shall be myths or mythologic. Facts which the mind perceived, thoughts which the body thought,—with these I deal. (J, III, 99)

Here is the most revealing statement Thoreau ever made about the kind of book he was creating in *Walden*—"the mythology which I am writing"—set down unequivocally in his *Journal*, 9 November 1851, yet previously unnoticed. Facts about himself which would be "falsehoods to the common sense," that is, an autobiographic fiction. It was to be the myth of Henry Thoreau as poet and seeker, a quest for heaven on earth. And there is even an unexpected new dimension, the metaphysical mode of fusing thought and feeling, which takes him one step toward explaining how facts can be so mythologized. They are to be facts felt by the mind and thought by the body—"with these I deal."

Modes of Perceiving

It is all very well to generalize about translating the facts of nature and of one's own life into symbol, fable, and myth. But the all-important question is, How? Thoreau did not shirk the task of experimenting with his new techniques of perception and expression, then defining them. Naturally enough some of his explorations to discover the best angle of vision for the poet are related to his rejection of the scientist's method of meticulous observation of nature. In a series of *Journal* entries he argues with himself the general principles of perception:

I must walk more with free senses. It is as bad to *study* stars and clouds as flowers and stones. I must let my senses wander as my thoughts, my eyes see without looking. Carlyle said that how to observe was to look, but I say that it is rather to see, and the more you look the less you will observe. I have the habit of attention to such excess that my senses get no rest, but suffer from a constant strain. Be not preoccupied with looking. Go not to the object; let it come to you. . . . What I need is not to look at all, but a true sauntering of the eye. (J, IV, 351)

On another occasion walking at the "true hour for sauntering," twilight, he refers to "that favorable frame of mind described by De Quincey, open to great impressions, [when] you see those rare sights with the unconscious side of the eye, which you could not see by a direct gaze before." (J, V, 254) This idea recurs several times, and is set forth clearly in the *Journal* for 23 March 1853:

> Man cannot afford to be a naturalist, to look at Nature directly, but only with the side of his eye. He must look through and beyond her. To look at her is fatal as to look at the head of Medusa. It turns the man of science to stone. I feel that I am dissipated by so many observations. I should be the magnet in the midst of all this dust and filings. (J, V, 45)

In a word, man as poet must draw nature to himself and assimilate it to his needs, not as scientist be drawn into it and lost in its materiality.

Thoreau felt the need of coining new terms to express what he hoped would be a new perspective on nature. But he was also aware of its relation to a long tradition. The references above to De Quincey and Carlyle, favorable and unfavorable, are rounded out by one more, this time a reference to the first promulgator of the doctrine of "wise passivity." A *Journal* passage on the greater openness to impressions of nature enjoyed by woodchoppers as compared with scientists, because the latter do not spend enough of their "unconscious life" there, concludes significantly: "(*Mem.* Wordsworth's observations on relaxed attention.)" (J, III, 123) In what sense, then, is Thoreau proposing an original approach, one that goes beyond his heritage from Romanticism? His new terms suggest the quality of the difference, "the side of the eye" and "a true sauntering of the eye." The Wordsworthian doctrine was concerned only that poets should attain the proper psychological state of receptivity. Thoreau, on the other hand, is trying to work out new techniques for seeing, moving in the direction of Impressionism and Symbolism. One of his last comparisons between scientist and poet raises the issue: "Sometimes I would rather get a transient glimpse or side view of a thing than stand fronting to it," he says. "I do not care to front it and scrutinize it, for I know that the thing that really concerns me is not there, but in my relation to that. *That* is a mere reflecting surface." Not only the scientist but the average man makes the mistake of looking at the phenomena that excite his attention as if they were independent of him, Thoreau declares, whereas the important fact is their effect on him. "With regard to such objects, I find that it is not they themselves (with which the men of science deal) that concern me," he concludes; "the point of interest is somewhere *between* me and them (*i.e.* the objects)." (J, X, 164–165) Where, indeed, is "*between* me and them" unless it is the point where subject and object meet, and hopefully fuse?

Toward the close of his life Thoreau came to realize, somewhat sadly, that the ends he was seeking in nature were not compatible with scientific ends. His emphasis on the relationship between perceiver and thing perceived was legitimate for the poet but increasingly rejected by scientists. Thoreau, like other transcendentalists, stuck to the pre-Newtonian conviction that the perceiver is central. He is the instrument specifically created to see, just as the reason objects exist in nature is for the purpose of being perceived by man. "Wherever I sat," he declares in *Walden,* "the landscape radiated from me accordingly." (90) The perceiving poet is not detached and objective, as science demands. He is impersonal only in the sense that he stands symbolically for all men; actually, the meanings of facts come to him subjectively. One can now venture an interpretation of a cryptic passage in the *Journal* for 1857:

> What is the relation between a bird and the ear that appreciates its melody, to whom, perchance, it is more charming and significant than to any else? Certainly they are intimately related, and the one was made for the other. It is a natural fact. If I were to discover that a certain kind of stone by the pond-shore was affected, say partially disintegrated, by a particular natural sound, as of a bird or insect, I see that one could not be completely described without describing the other. I am that rock by the pond-side. (J, IX, 274–275)

The purpose here is to argue that he becomes part and parcel of nature by the very process of observing and participating; the perceiver is merged with the thing perceived. But this does not mean that he ruled out objective observation. Down through the composition of *Walden*, despite Thoreau's growing awareness of the split between his poetic and scientific selves, he manages to keep them in equilibrium, however precarious, and that is one of the secrets of his book's success.

Nature itself varies the spectacle presented to man's eyes by changes in the amount and quality of light, one of the chief elements of perception. The practical man, who thinks of objects as having a fixed and absolute existence in nature, merely chooses the time and place affording the clearest observation. But the artist takes advantage of every difference in the weather, season, and time of day or night. Thoreau, describing how the atmosphere "paints and glasses everything," shows himself aware of how manifold these changes are. "I cannot well conceive of greater variety than it produces by its changes from hour to hour of every day," he says: "It is a new glass placed over the picture every hour." (J, III, 291) The alert perceiver can thus become a spectator at many scenes of nature's show without need of inventing new techniques—simply by being present at the right time and place.

Thoreau is constantly pointing out what goes unnoticed by the average person, having only scorn for the fair-weather friends of nature. One never sees the true beauty of flowers unless he takes a walk in the pouring rain, he declares. One does not really perceive what coldness is until he staggers for miles in the face of a biting nor'-easter; then he knows that a drop of a few more degrees would wipe out the human race. He goes forth in all kinds of weather: pre-dawn fog, snowstorm, glowing Indian summer, sun drenched July in the meadow. He journeys to all kinds of places: the wind-swept cliffs of Cape Cod, the fly-swarming wilderness of Maine, deserted farms near Walden, and the middle of Beck Stow's swamp on the outskirts of Concord. Caught in a spring rain under a large tree, he spends half a day happily studying the insects in its bark. He records his observations at all times and seasons: moonlight and blackest night, winter sunset, teeming noon, a drizzly morning in April. His *Journal* is filled not only with the multitudinous details but also with the infinite variety of nature's spectacle.

Atmospheric conditions that changed the picture, and so in a sense recreated the world, were particularly interesting to Thoreau. When he looks across the pond on a spring day the opposite shore is made "more remote and indistinct by a bluish mistiness" which he finds exciting. (J, III, 429) A heavy morning fog enveloping the river and its adjacent farms turns them into a "stupendous pageant." (J, IV, 255) The haze of dog days in August transforms a familiar meadow for him:

> It has an indescribable beauty to my eye now, which it could not have in a clear day. The haze has the effect both of a wash or varnish and of a harmonizing tint. It destroys the idea of definite distance which distinctness suggests. . . . It is as if you had painted a meadow . . . then washed it over with some gum like a map and tinted the paper a fine misty blue. (J, VI, 454)

He forgot for the moment his source for this fanciful idea. Just a few months before he had copied down from Gilpin's "Art of Sketching Landscape" his instructions for tingeing "with some light horizon hue" one's India ink sketch: "By washing this tint over your *whole drawing*, you lay a foundation for harmony."

During the early 1850's Thoreau read several books by William Gilpin, noting that the "Essay on Picturesque Beauty" was the key to all his writings. The *Journal* of this period contains a running debate on this subject. It is of considerable length but rather fumbling and inconclusive. He takes issue with Gilpin for saying of the painter, " 'the very essence of his art requires' that he select the Picturesque for the sake of composition, variety, light and shade, and coloring." Then comes the objection, rather obscurely put: "But he is superficial. He goes not below the surface to account for the effect of form and color, etc." Fifty pages later the grounds of his disagreement are clarified, rather surprisingly: "Gilpin talked as if there was some food for the soul in mere physical light and shadow, as if, without the suggestion of a moral, they could give a man pleasure or pain!" (J, VI, 53–57, 103)

Thoreau was rejecting an early Romantic cliché only to fall into a mid-Victorian one. But it was highly uncharacteristic of him to think of art, or nature, as morally significant. And he could not rid himself of the appeal of the picturesque so easily. During this same period, for example, he became fascinated by the effects of moonlight, and filled his *Journal* with observations on the subject. These were gathered into an essay near the end of his life and published posthumously as "Night and Moonlight." During a walk under the full moon he begins promisingly, "On all sides novelties present themselves," shadows becoming more conspicuous than the objects that cast them. But the reader's expectations of something new on the optics of illusion are soon dashed, and the reason is suggested by a single sentence: "The whole landscape is more variegated and picturesque than by day." (V, 326–327) What follows is one of the poorest essays he ever wrote, imitative of an outworn Romantic mode.

Although Thoreau did not add anything original to the concept of the picturesque, he did learn something of value from Gilpin. The latter's formula for painting distant mountains is copied down with approval in the *Journal*: "unless you make them exceed their *real* or *proportional* size, they have no effect." The conclusion Thoreau drew from this was of great value to him in his writing: "Thus it is only by emphasis and exaggeration that real effects are described." (J, IV, 339) His immediate application of it to a mountain landscape, playing with the color change wrought by distance rather than with the problem of size, is more fanciful than effective: "I wish to see the earth translated, the green passing into blue. How this heaven intervenes and tinges our more distant prospects!" (J, IV, 351) In *A Week* he had written: "The most stupendous scenery ceases to be sublime when it becomes distinct, or in other words limited, and the imagination is no longer encouraged to exaggerate it." (I, 202) The principle of exaggeration for effect is put to brilliant use in *Walden*, for example, by describing this simple New England pond as "God's Drop" and "a lower heaven," in order to translate it into a symbol of perfection. (96, 215) It has been previously shown how he applied the technique of extravagance, probably borrowed from Carlyle, to his satire on society. It is interesting now to discover his source for using exaggeration in the description of nature, a parallel component of his style.

Nature has other ways of transforming itself, for example by snow and ice and reflections in the water. After a midwinter storm he notes in the *Journal*: "It is like the beginning of the world. There is nothing hackneyed where a new snow can come and cover all the landscape. . . . The world is not only new to the eye, but is still as at creation." (J, VII, 123–124) Who has not felt the same thrill of discovery, as if he were the first to have done so? Nature's white version of itself does indeed escape from the familiar and hackneyed, but Thoreau's language describing this miracle is not quite so successful. Far more original is the climax of his ten-page description of the myriad new forms created by nature, working "with such luxuriance and fury," in a January ice storm. Not only is the world transformed for eye, and ear, but it is transfigured too:

> The bells are particularly sweet this morning. I hear more, methinks, than ever before. How much more religion in their sound, than they ever call men together to! Men obey their call and go to the stove-warmed church, though God exhibits himself to the walker in a frosted bush to-day, as much as in a burning one to Moses of old. (J, IV, 443)

The idea of nature as Revelation is a trite one, of course, but the expression of it here is fresh enough to have deserved a place in *Walden*.

More closely concerned with the techniques of perception are his many comments on nature as reflected in river and pond. Looking at the shoreline bushes as he sails up the Concord, he finds that they appear in the reflection as they would if actually viewed from that point on the surface from which they are reflected to his eye:

> Hence, too, we are struck by the prevalence of sky or light in the reflection . . . for in the reflection the sky comes up to the very shore

or edge and appears to extend under it, while, the substance being seen from a more elevated point, the actual horizon is perhaps many miles distant over the fields and hills. In the reflection you have an infinite number of eyes to see for you and report the aspect of things each from its point of view. (J, XI, 213)

The problem becomes more complicated as the perceiver maneuvers his own position. Looking across the pond at the opposite hillside he compares the substance with its reflection in the water, as he looks at each of them from different angles and from different levels of the hill he is standing on. Like a true experimenter he raises all the hypotheses that might lead to some new discovery. "Is the reflection of a hillside," he asks himself for example, "such an aspect of it as can be obtained by the eye directed to the hill itself from *any* single point of view?" (my italics) His conclusion takes nature as an imitator-of-itself and turns it into an exemplar of the artist as "imitator" of nature: "The reflection is never a true copy or repetition of its substance, but a new composition, and this may be the source of its novelty and attractiveness." (J, X, 96–97)

A broader application of his study of reflections may be found in a passage that contrasts the imaginative perceiver with the practical observer, using a barrage of seemingly frivolous puns to make a serious point about his own methods as a writer:

I think that most men, as farmers, hunters, fishers, etc., walk along a river's bank, or paddle along its stream, without seeing the reflections. Their minds are not abstracted from the surface, from surfaces generally. It is only a reflecting mind that sees reflections. I am aware often that I have been occupied with shallow and commonplace thoughts, looking for something superficial, when I did not see the most glorious reflections, though exactly in the line of my vision. If the fisherman was looking at the reflection, he would not know when he had a nibble! I know from my own experience that he may cast his line right over the most elysian landscape and sky, and not *catch* the slightest notion of them. You must be in an abstract mood to see reflections however distinct. I was even startled by the sight of that reflected red oak as if it were a black water-spirit.

When we are enough abstracted, the opaque earth itself reflects images to us; *i.e.*, we are imaginative, see visions, etc. (J, X, 156–157)

The most interesting of Thoreau's observations are those in which the perceiver plays the most active part, looking at nature from all possible angles of vision. In a series of notations, he experiments like a landscape painter of a more modern school than the picturesque. Going across Bartonia Meadow toward a low rising ground just west of Walden one bright October afternoon, he notices "the top of the maple swamp just appearing over the sheeny russet edge of the hill." At the distance of about three hundred yards it is apparently only a narrow strip of intense scarlet, orange, and yellow. But, the *Journal* continues, "As I advance, lowering the edge of the hill, which makes the firm foreground or lower frame to the picture, the depth of this brilliant grove revealed steadily increased, suggesting that the whole of the concealed valley is filled with such color." (J, X, 71) He thought well enough of this to incorporate it into "Autumnal Tints," one of the best of his late essays.

On another occasion he records the distant view from several levels as he ascends Round Hill, before arriving at his conclusion:

The prospect is often best from two thirds the way up a hill, where, looking directly down at the parts of the landscape—the fields and barns—nearest the base, you get the sense of height best, and see how the land slopes up to where you stand. From the top, commonly, you overlook all this, and get a sense of *distance* merely. (J, III, 384)

More experimental still are the two contrasting reports, just before sunset, of slanting rays as they penetrate Ebby Hubbard's pine wood. Having seen them from the sunny side on one afternoon he comes around to the opposite side at the same hour two days later to observe the difference:

Then I saw the lit sides of the tree stems all aglow with their lichens, and observed their black shadows behind. Now I see chiefly the dark stems massed together, and it is the warm sunlight that is reduced to a pencil of light; *i.e.*, then light was the rule and shadow the exception, now shadow the rule and light the exception. (J, X, 160)

Such observations were not the result of whim, but were part of a deliberate program for discovering new ways of looking at the world. If proof were needed, it could be found in such a notation as the following: "(*Mem.* Try this experiment again, *i.e.* look not toward nor from the sun but athwart this line.)" (J, III, 394–395) This memorandum refers to a preceding paragraph recording what he sees at 8 A.M. boating on the Concord: when he looks northwest (upstream) the water is dark, when southeast (downstream) it is silvery bright; by looking "athwart" next time he expects to see "the medium between the dark and light above mentioned."

A more elaborate experiment in color perception relates to the dwarf andromeda. Walking around a small pond near Walden on the afternoon of 17 April 1852, he mistakes the shrubs along shore for sweet gale because of their grayish brown color. Then, realizing that from every position he has been seeing the sun reflected from the surface of the leaves, he moves around to the one angle (facing due west) from which he can discover that they are indeed the andromeda: "from this position alone I saw, as it were, *through* the leaves which the opposite sun lit up, giving to the whole . . . the mellowest, the ripest, red imbrowned color." Varying his position vertically by walking up the hill, he finds that the light is once more reflected upward from the surfaces and that the warm "*Indian* red color" is lost. The conclusion is another self-reminder: "Let me look again at a different hour of the day, and see if it is really so. It is a very interesting piece of magic." On 19 April he returns to verify. His joy is recorded in the *Journal*:

The thing that pleases me most within these three days is the discovery of the andromeda phenomenon. It makes all those parts of the country where it grows more attractive and elysian to me. It is a natural magic. These little leaves are the stained windows in the cathedral of my world. At sight of any redness I am excited like a cow. . . . How sweet is the perception of a new natural fact! suggesting what worlds remain to be unveiled. (J, III, 430–431, 441–442)

As he says in another connection, we get only transient and partial glimpses of this world's beauty unless we are alert and responsive: "It is only necessary to behold . . . the least fact or phenomenon, however familiar, from a point a hair's breadth aside from our habitual path or routine, to be overcome, enchanted by its beauty and significance." (J, VIII, 44)

Thoreau was quick to take advantage of all possibilities for a different angle of vision. When winter rain puts a crust of ice on the deep snow firm enough to bear his weight, he is out early the next morning traversing a familiar route to make comparisons. "It is pleasant to walk over the fields raised a foot or more above their summer level," he reports to his *Journal*, "and the prospect is altogether new." (J, III, 288) There was no end to the experiments he conceived of. In an entry for 16 June 1840 he makes the striking proposal: "Would it not be a luxury to stand up to one's chin in some retired swamp for a whole summer's day, scenting the sweet-fern and bilberry blows, and lulled by the minstrelsy of gnats and mosquitoes?" Some years later this was transcribed into *A Week,* followed by such a vivid account of what could be seen and heard from the stance of a "leopard frog" as to make one suspect that he actually carried out the suggestion, though probably not as a day-long experiment.

On another occasion he uses the eye trick later made famous by Impressionist painters. Looking at the pitch pines of Fair Haven Hill above the pond on a spring afternoon, he notes: "The reflections grow more distinct every moment. At last the outline of the hill is as distinct below as above." Then the new technique: "By partly closing my eyes and looking through my eyelashes, the wood end appears thus:—" followed by a pencil sketch in his *Journal.* Shifting to a maple grove he records: "At this season the reflections of deciduous trees are more picturesque and remarkable than when they are in leaf, because, the branches being seen, they make with their reflections a more wonderful rhyme. It is not mere mass or outline corresponding to outline, but a kind of geometrical figure. The maples look thus"—then another sketch. (J, III, 402–403)

The starting point for much of this, as for many of Thoreau's ideas, can be found in the early writings of Emerson. One of the evidences brought forward in *Nature* to prove that the "meaning" of objective reality is dependent on the subjective viewer was demonstrating how the world can be changed by slight alterations in the observer's position—seeing the shore from a ship, the earth from a balloon, one's own village street from a moving coach. "Turn the eyes upside down, by looking at the landscape through your legs," he said in the chapter on Idealism, "and how agreeable is the picture, though you have seen it any time these twenty years." When one reads the following passage in Thoreau's *Journal*, he seems at first blush a mere dutiful disciple carrying out the master's suggestion: "I look between my legs up the river across Fair Haven. Subverting the head, we refer things to the heavens; the sky becomes the ground of the picture." But Emerson's use of this stunt was philosophical, Thoreau's esthetic. Like a true experimenter he makes observations from this posture by morning light and then by afternoon light, for comparative purposes. His conclusion is clearly that of the artist:

> The prospect is thus actually a constantly varying mirage, answering to the condition of our perceptive faculties and our fluctuating imaginations. If we incline our heads never so little, the most familiar things begin to put on some new aspect. If we invert our heads completely our desecrated wood-lot appears far off, incredible, elysian, unprofaned by us. (J, III, 333, 291)

Emerson was not slow to recognize his own ideas in other people's writings. As early as 1841 he noted in his *Journals*: "I told Henry Thoreau that his freedom is in the form, but he does not disclose new matter. I am very familiar with all his thoughts, —they are my own quite originally drest." This has often been quoted as proof that Thoreau was an imitative thinker, which in a philosophical sense he was. But the last three words ("quite originally drest"), which are usually overlooked, make the important point that his originality lay in his expression. Thoreau himself remarked late in life, "I do not in the least care where I get my ideas, or what suggests them." (J, VIII, 135) Much less well known than Emerson's early journal comment is the one recorded nearly a quarter-century later, showing his final recognition of the basic difference between them. As literary executor, going through the writings of his dead friend in 1863 to select the best for posthumous publication, he made a very revealing comparison: "In reading Henry Thoreau's journal . . . I find the same thought, the same spirit that is in me, but he takes a step beyond and illustrates by excellent images that which I should have conveyed in a sleepy generality." This is virtually a confession, in the privacy of his own *Journals*, that Thoreau is the poet while he is something else—philosopher, ethical thinker, transcendentalist. If the difference was recognizable from a comparison of their journals, how much more so from a comparison of *Walden* with the *Essays*. But Emerson has left no significant comment on the masterpiece of his friend, possibly because it appeared after the rift in their relationship had become serious. Possibly he counted it a fault in his former protégé that he was just a poet and nothing more. Certainly, he did not treat Thoreau as a literary artist in his final public pronouncement, the funeral address, later reprinted so often that it gave a wrong direction to his reputation for almost a century.

The poetic use to which Thoreau put Emerson's ideas—and therefore the difference between them—can be illustrated perfectly by tracing from *Nature* (1836) to *Walden* (1854) this very device of looking at the landscape between one's legs. In the former its purpose was to argue the case for philosophic idealism. In the latter it is one of the techniques for translating the pond into a symbol. From this new angle of vision, by diverting his attention from the landscape as such, Thoreau can focus on the glassy surface of the water which now seems to have a heaven below as well as a heaven above it:

When you invert your head, it [the surface] looks like a thread of finest gossamer stretched across the valley, and gleaming against the distant pine woods, separating one stratum of the atmosphere from another. You would think you could walk dry under it to the opposite hills, and that the swallows which skim over might perch on it. Indeed, they sometimes dive below the line, as it were by mistake, and are undeceived. . . . It is like molten glass cooled but not congealed, and the few motes in it are pure and beautiful like the imperfections in glass. . . . Not a fish can leap nor an insect fall but it is thus reported in circling dimples, in lines of beauty, as it were the constant welling up of its fountain, the gentle pulsing of its life. (207–209)

Some of the finest images and most significant symbolic meanings in *Walden* follow immediately after this experiment, as will appear in a later chapter.

Thoreau had been reasoning for some time that all these special effects—from looking at nature in reflections, out of the side of the eye, inverted between the legs—had to do with optics, the relation of light and vision. "Man's eye is so placed as to look straight forward on a level best, or rather down than up," he wrote in his *Journal* in 1852: "His eye demands the sober colors of the earth for its daily diet. He does not look up at a great angle but with an effort." (J, III, 387) So he was ready, a year or two later, to participate in an interesting three-way transcendental debate, which took place characteristically without any friendly give-and-take. Channing (a cousin of the poet) simply made a point to Emerson who passed it on with implied sanction to Thoreau who recorded it in his *Journal* along with his rebuttal:

R. W. E. told me that W. H. Channing conjectured that the landscape looked fairer when we turned our heads, because we beheld it with nerves of the eye unused before. Perhaps this reason is worth more for suggestion than explanation. It occurs to me that the reflection of objects in still water is in a similar manner fairer than the substance, and yet we do not employ unused nerves to behold it. Is it not that we let much more light into our eyes,—which in the usual position are shaded by the brows,—in the first case by turning them more to the sky, and in the case of the reflections by having the sky placed under our feet? *i.e.* in both cases we see terrestrial objects with the sky or heavens for a background or field. Accordingly they are not dark and terrene, but lit and elysian. (J, VI, 17)

Thoreau's serious interest in the esthetics of perception was clearly shared by some of the fellowship, who presumably were making their little experiments here and there just as he was, without much regard to the conventions of public behavior. What must the Concord villager have thought when he saw these confessed transcendentalists in such strange postures—standing with faces frozen in one direction while they cocked their eyes to this side or that, bending themselves in an undignified U-shape to look at the world upside down? Unaware of the esthetic ends they were pursuing, he probably thought they were practicing some outlandish discipline like yoga. Or, rather, not knowing in all likelihood what that was, he undoubtedly thought they were slightly mad. Thoreau was one of the most eccentric of them, in the ordinary meaning of that word. Also in the root sense, removing himself from the center of transcendentalism as well as from village orthodoxies. But his concern with esthetic theory was soberly in earnest, and he excelled them all in the practical application of it to his writings.

Despite his elaborate experiments with angles of perception, hoping he could develop techniques that would help him bring thing-thought-and-word together, Thoreau was not naïve enough to believe he could trap nature with a bag of tricks. He keeps reminding himself of the essentially ungraspable quality of the external world. In the autumn of 1850, for example, he tries to describe a quite commonplace landscape with such simple directness and accuracy that he can "possess" it. Admitting his failure, he returns to the same scene in a *Journal* revision three months later, 14 February 1851, and makes a second valiant attempt:

One afternoon in the fall, November 21st, I saw Fair Haven Pond with its island and meadow; between the island and the shore, a strip of perfectly smooth water in the lee of the island; and two hawks sailing over it; and something more I saw which cannot easily be described, which made me say to myself that the landscape could not be improved. I did not see how it could be improved. Yet I do not know what these things can be; I begin to see such objects only when I leave off understanding them, and afterwards remember that I did not appreciate them before. But I get no further than this. How adapted these forms and colors to our eyes, a meadow and its islands! What are these things? Yet the hawks and the ducks keep so aloof, and nature is so reserved! (J, II, 160–161; cf. 107)

The point is that no description, however fine-meshed, can ever snare nature. What the writer gets is not the object but his perception of it, something quite different. "The poet must bring to Nature the smooth mirror in which she is to be reflected," he notes two years later: "He must be something superior to her, something more than natural." (J, V, 183–184) Art is superior to nature as imagination is to fact. In this way it is "more than natural." It gives us not a literal imitation but nature "reflected." It will be remembered that Thoreau said of the reflection of a landscape in water, it is not a copy or repetition "but a new composition, and this may be the source of its novelty." Every artist holds up this kind of mirror to nature and so recreates the world.

According to transcendental doctrine, since "man is a god in ruins," all men are potentially poets and creators if they could only realize their true natures. This idea finds its way indirectly into Thoreau's *Journal* once:

How novel and original must be each new man's view of the universe! For though the world is so old, and so many books have been written, each object appears wholly undescribed to our experience, each field of thought wholly unexplored. The whole world is an America, a *new World*. (J, III, 384)

But normally he is too tough-minded for such idealisms. He is convinced that most people are incapable of having new worlds revealed to them and even resent it when a poet tries to present them with his own, since "they do not wish to take a new view in any case." (J, IX, 495) The poet himself has only moments of such creative perception, when all his faculties are receptive to some new discovery or revelation. The first of a series of notations on this point occurs in a late *Journal* entry. "Many an object is not seen, though it falls within the range of our visual ray, because it does not come within the range of our intellectual ray, *i.e.*, we are not looking for it," he writes on 2 July 1857. "So, in the largest sense, we find only the world we are looking for." (J, IX, 466) Sixteen months later the topic is picked up again just as if three hundred pages had not intervened, this continuity being all the evidence one needs that Thoreau's *Journal* is not a diary but a writer's workbook:

> Objects are concealed from our view not so much because they are out of the course of our visual ray (continued) as because there is no intention of the mind and eye toward them. We do not realize how far and widely, or how near and narrowly, we are to look. The greater part of the phenomena of nature are for this reason concealed to us all our lives. (J, XI, 285)

The passage is used verbatim in "Autumnal Tints" (1862), with a surprising new sentence added in the middle: "For there is no power to see in the eye itself, any more than in any other jelly." This fine late essay then extends the topic at considerable length:

> There is just as much beauty visible to us in the landscape as we are prepared to appreciate,—not a grain more. The actual objects which one man will see from a particular hilltop are just as different from those which another will see as the beholders are different. The scarlet oak must, in a sense, be in your eye when you go forth. We cannot see anything until we are possessed with the idea of it, take it into our heads,—and then we can hardly see anything else. (V, 285–286)

To avoid too much solemnity in discussing an abstract idea, Thoreau then gives a witty turn to the hackneyed illustration of the subjective interpretations of objective reality by several different observers of the same scene. "Take a New England selectman, and set him on the highest of our hills, and tell him to look . . .

using a spy-glass, if he likes," the anecdote begins. "What, probably, will he *spy*?—what will he *select* to look at?" The answer is that he will see that some of his neighbors' properties should be assessed at a higher value for taxation. "Now take Julius Caesar, or Emanuel Swedenborg, or a Fiji-Islander, and set him up there," he continues. When they compare notes afterward, what each has seen will be as different as Rome is from heaven and hell, and as both are from a jungle paradise. No devout transcendentalist would have treated either the doctrine of philosophic idealism or a "saint" such as Swedenborg so lightly. (V, 286–287)

Thoreau's essay concludes with an elaborate conceit of the hunter of wild game as symbol for the poet pursuing beauty in nature:

> The sportsman trains himself, dresses, and watches unweariedly, and loads and primes for his particular game. He prays for it, and offers sacrifices, and so he gets it. After due and long preparation, schooling his eye and hand, dreaming awake and asleep, with gun and paddle and boat, he goes out after meadow-hens, which most of his townsmen never saw nor dreamed of, and paddles for miles against a head wind, and wades in water up to his knees, being out all day without his dinner, and *therefore* he gets them. He had them half-way into his bag when he started, and has only to shove them down. The true sportsman can shoot you almost any of his game from his windows: what else has he windows or eyes for? It comes and perches at last on the barrel of his gun; but the rest of the world never see it *with the feathers on.* (V, 287–288)

A seventeenth-century metaphysical poet would have rested his image there. Being a mid-nineteenth-century one, Thoreau felt it necessary to spell out the analogy, but he does not ruin the conceit. One can even be grateful for the tag: "And so it is with him that shoots at beauty; though he wait till the sky falls, he will not bag any, if he does not already know its seasons and haunts, and the color of its wing,—if he has not dreamed of it, so that he can *anticipate* it." (V, 287) This passage was written too late to be used anywhere but in a posthumous essay. But it throws an invaluable backward light on *Walden*, where the figure of the hunter (along with the fisher and the woodsman) plays a role that is closely and significantly related to the poet, as will be seen in a later chapter. Far better than by abstractions and argument, Thoreau uses such emblematic figures to illustrate his theory of perception and the poet's techniques for translating nature into words.

4

Bog-trotter

Nature contributes in important ways to the poetic meaning of *Walden*, but all philosophizing about it is quite properly excluded. As a shaping artist, conscious of the flaws in his first book, Thoreau took care to keep his "machinery" from obtruding as he composed what was to prove his masterpiece. The formulation of esthetic theory and rules for putting it into practice—quite as much as the usual problems of working out a structure, a style, and so on—should be confined to the workshop, he now realized. They should be invisible in the book. The same held for the main body of nature material he had gathered. "Journalist" and thinker, as well as poet, Thoreau felt the need not only to record his observations in great detail but also to reckon with the rival philosophies of Real and Ideal, and to experiment with new techniques for perceiving the external world. The proper place for all three, however, was the *Journal* (as the preceding chapter has shown). The resulting skills alone should function in the finished creation, in order to turn perceptions into expression.

Nature is everywhere in *Walden*, as background and as orientation. It rises to special significance in the central chapter on "Ponds" and the final one on "Spring." These will be analyzed later. But it is also focused in two groups of chapters. One of these has already been discussed, the trio centered on "Solitude" in the first half of the book, where the withdrawing hermit learns to be at home in nature. The other is a triad (Chapters 10 to 12) in the second half, with its apex in "Higher Laws," structured on the theme of man's long and arduous struggle upward toward the divine, out of nature and his own nature. Thoreau's impossibly lofty aspiration here is flanked by two chapters concerned with the lower laws of life on this earth. The one that precedes "Higher Laws" tells of a degraded Irishman at "Baker Farm," whose life has sunk to the level of the brute. The one that follows it, "Brute Neighbors," deals with the wildlife in Walden woods and is one of his most successful probings of nature. The animals prove a better point of departure for Thoreau's spiritual education than the bog-trotter, since they are less "bestial." He has fallen far below his human potential, but they have risen to the highest level of theirs by growing wild according to their nature. By studying both, Thoreau hopes to find out something about nature, and even more about himself. Threading his way through all three chapters and tying them together is the protean figure of the narrator, exploring for the meanings of wildness and virtue in the natural world, and in the human world too.

Those who give *Walden* only a surface reading may well feel that "Baker Farm," brief though it is, has been put together too casually to have any unity. If the great book is simply the exposition of a thesis, as many maintain, then the argument of this tenth chapter is the contrast between John Field's drudging life there and Thoreau's own successful experiment in living by the shore of Walden Pond. But the episode of his visit occupies only the central third of this six-page chapter, and the opening and closing pages seem irrelevant, wayward, and fanciful in the extreme. Thoreau could write fine sentences, such readers would admit, but he was a typical transcendental rambler who never could construct organized wholes.

Since this is one traditional way of approaching *Walden,* as an essay in social criticism, it may be adopted temporarily. One readily admits that the ostensible subject of "Baker Farm," as indicated in the title itself, is this visit to John Field. (226–229) He is described as a "hard-working, but shiftless" Irish laborer; his wife staring forlornly "with the never absent mop in one hand, and yet no effects of it visible anywhere"; his infant child a "poor starveling brat" and his son doing a man's work toiling at the father's side, "bogging" for a neighboring farmer at slave wages. Yet for all their labor they live in misery and squalor. They have neither enough to eat nor to wear; their one-room hut is dilapidated; the roof leaks; the dirt floor is shared by chickens; even the well is broken.

The comparison of their desperate situation with Thoreau's happy one is implicit, and is even cued by a sentence that introduces the description of Baker Farm: "I thought of living there [myself] before I went to Walden." Readers who have come this far in the book will immediately recall the opening of Chapter 2, where he told of surveying the country on all sides for the possible site of a house and of how he bought "in imagination" any number of farms (presumably including Baker Farm), before deciding to settle on Emerson's acres at Walden Pond. (90) Then he gave a detailed account of "Where I Lived, and What I Lived For"—a memorable picture fixed in the reader's mind. That one purpose of Chapter 10 will be a comparison between his way of life and John Field's is made explicit: "I tried to help him with my experience." Thoreau tells him of his "tight, clean" cabin, built with his own hands at a cost no greater than the annual rent of this "ruined" hut. He also earns his own living, though he looks like "a loafer"; but "as I did not work hard, I did not have to eat hard." He had simplified his life by reducing his needs to a minimum. His work load is light because his bill for food and clothing is light, and vice versa. "I could," he boasts, "in an hour or two, without labor, but as a recreation . . . earn enough money to support me a week." (228) Thus, most of his time is left free, for enjoyment and adventure.

John Field's life is just the opposite. That his plight is meant to serve as a kind of travesty of the Walden way, hence not a subject for serious criticism, is revealed by Thoreau's bantering word play as he reads him a lesson in economy. Because Field makes the initial mistake of indulging himself in the cash luxuries of tea, coffee, butter, and beef, "he had to work hard to pay for them, and when he had worked hard he had to eat hard again to repair the waste of his system." This leaves no energy for repairing his hut, much less for building a house of his own, so that he has to continue drudging as a serf for a low wage to pay a high rent. He is on an endless treadmill and knows not how to get off. Thoreau says ironically that he tried to reason with him "as if he were a philosopher, or desired to be one," but to no avail. When he holds up to the Fields the ideal of living with freedom and joy—if they would live simply "they might all go a-huckleberrying in the summer for their amusement"—they only heave a sigh, wondering if they have capital enough to try such a complex thing as a simple life. (228)

At this point the only metaphor in this prosaic episode is inserted, wrapped in a triple pun: "It was sailing by dead reckoning to them, and they saw not clearly how to make their port so." (228–229) They are already settled at "Fair Haven," though they have made a foul harbor of their hut; their way of life is more dead than alive; and where they are in the world is at best a calculated guess. All this is implied by Thoreau's word play. And the reason for their plight is rendered in the single image, "dead reckoning." This is an elemental method of determining by log and compass where you are when at sea, especially useful for ships in a fog, but less a "true reckoning" than one determined by astronomical observations would be. In a word, the Fields are incapable of scientific calculations (that is, reason) as to their course in life. Similarly when he concludes: Poor John Field! "living . . . alas! without arithmetic, and failing so." (229) He undoubtedly means here not only budget bookkeeping, such as he wittily displayed ledger-fashion in the earlier account of his own "Economy," but a balancing of outgo against income in the real values of life.

Such is the "argument" of this chapter, presented logically and factually, as if it were the case history of a family who are solving incorrectly the basic problem of acquiring the necessaries of life that formed the staple of his long introductory chapter—shelter, food, and clothing. But as a solution to the economic problems of mankind, *Walden* itself is fatally vulnerable, as a whole as well as in its parts. As such it has been attacked by numerous critics, from Lowell on down, who have totally misconceived its intent. Thoreau began his experiment with capital, they have pointed out, including an education and enough money to build his house; he had well-placed friends to help him, such as Emerson, whose land he was allowed to squat on; he supplemented his meager diet with full dinners at his family's house in the village; he was a bachelor who had declined to take on the responsibility of wife and children. Since John Field had none of these advantages, they could argue, the economic lesson of "Baker Farm" is invalidated. But Thoreau was careful to answer in advance all such criticism, for the whole book as well as for this chapter. "I desire to speak . . . as one not interested in the success or failure of the present economical and social arrangements," he said near the beginning of *Walden*. (62) Again, "My purpose in going to Walden Pond was not to live cheaply nor to live dearly there." (21) And finally, "I would not have any one adopt *my* mode of living on any account," but "find out and pursue *his own* way." (78–79) Clearly the comparative economy of Field and Thoreau is only the pretended subject of this chapter.

If the real significance of "Baker Farm" is to be grasped, it must be approached differently. The best way to begin is where the author began, with the two introductory pages, on the assumption that he was artist enough to make every part of his chapter relevant. The opening paragraph is an evocation of the woods as a place for worship, even as the huckleberry thickets could serve the Fields as a place for entertainment. The narrating "I" tells of pine groves "like temples" for the Druids, cedar trees above Flint's Pond "fit to stand before Valhalla," a perfect hemlock rising "like a pagoda" in the midst of the forest. But clichés lie in wait everywhere to ambush this kind of writing, hackneyed for a half-century by Thoreau's day. He escapes by the freshness of occasional images (the toadstools are "round tables of the swamp gods"); better still by shifting from metaphor to hyperbole ("the wild-holly berries make the beholder forget his home with their beauty"); and most effective of all by slipping into the role of naturalist in the last half of the paragraph. "Instead of calling on some scholar," he says, "I paid many a visit to particular trees," and what follows proves he was writing with his eye on the natural world rather than on literary tradition. The phrasing in his description of a dozen trees is precise enough to seem scientific to the general reader, even while seeming poetic to the scientist (the "lichen-painted" boles of beech trees, the "silver sparkle" of their grain when split). The role of naturalist is but one of Thoreau's disguises. At the end of his list he concludes: "These were the shrines I visited both summer and winter." (224) This generalized account of former rambles, though lacking in stylistic distinction, has at least set a tone of religious wonder and imaged the narrator as a saunterer on the plane of beauty.

The second paragraph begins in surprise, as the fictive "I" tells of a rare experience: "Once it chanced that I stood in the very abutment of a rainbow's arch." It tinged the whole scene around, he says, and "dazzled" him (even as he had been "dazzled," and tempted, by "wild forbidden fruits, too fair for mortal taste" in the previous paragraph). "It was a lake of rainbow light, in which, for a short while, I lived like a dolphin." (224) This has a double quality of the fabulous, calling for close analysis, since it is a principal clue to the chapter's meaning. For part of his effect Thoreau was depending on the popular belief that the experience of actually standing in a rainbow is an impossibility, since it is thought to be an optical illusion that will always appear directly ahead of the observer. But it is possible, though the experience is rare enough to suggest the miraculous. The usual rainbow does appear far away and sky-spanning, formed by the double refraction and dispersion of the sun's rays in falling drops of rain. Hence the legend of a pot of gold at its foot, because of the supposed impossibility of getting there to disprove it. But as any confirmed rambler knows, he can on rare occasions walk right into a much smaller rainbow in the woods, caused by the diffraction of light through a single drop of water hanging from leaf or limb, or he can stand in the abutment of one formed by the spray of a waterfall. In his *Journal*, Thoreau twice describes an actual experience of standing in the abutment of a full-sized rainbow. In 1851, returning to town from bathing at Walden Pond, he was caught in the rain just as the sun was setting. Seeing "a celestial light on all the land," he realized he was standing in the very edge of the shower where the sun's rays shone through the falling rain: "We were, in fact, in a rainbow and it was here its arch rested on the earth." Just one year later he records a similar experience: "Sometimes we are completely within it [a rainbow], enveloped by it, and experience the realization of the child's wish." (J, II, 382–383; IV, 288) So the incident he reports in *Walden* is not fabulous, though the rainbow itself is central to several fables, as will be seen.

The sudden appearance of a dolphin on land, however, cannot be acounted for in naturalistic terms. He seems like a fish out of water, though of course he is not a fish at all but a mammal that has gone to sea and sports in the waves, just as the earthbound narrator is for the moment dancing in the rainbow's vapory atmosphere "like a dolphin." As an attributive adjective, or a simile, the dolphin implies beauty and joy. "His delights were dolphin-like," Thoreau could have read in Shakespeare's *Antony and Cleopatra*. The name "dolphin" is also popularly applied to several fishes, not only the playful porpoise but the dorado or golden fish, celebrated for its beautiful colors, since it undergoes rapid changes of hue when taken out of water and on the point of death. As such it appears in several of Thoreau's favorite authors, in George Herbert's *Temple* and notably in Byron's *Childe Harold*: "Parting day dies like the dolphin, whom each pang imbues with a new colour . . . The last still loveliest." The inaccuracy in marine biology is unimportant to the literary man who can transform a dolphin into the rainbow fish, when it is dying.

This poetic meaning seems implied in the paradoxical sentence at the end of Thoreau's own brief transfiguration: "If it had lasted longer it might have tinged my employments and [my] life." Here is the two-way pull of being translated into immortality, yet wanting to cling to the mortal life a while longer. Such an interpretation is supported by the much older history of the dolphin, with which he was certainly familiar also. In classical mythology the dolphin, strongest and swiftest of fish, is often shown rescuing drowned men and bearing their souls across the sea to the other world. Christian art picked up this myth, portraying the dolphin more frequently than any other fish, generally to symbolize the soul guided to resurrection and salvation by Christ. That Thoreau was aware of this twofold tradition, pagan and Christian, is borne out by the next experience recounted in this second paragraph: "As I walked on the railroad causeway, I used to wonder at the halo of light around my shadow, and would fain fancy myself one of the elect"—the doctrine of Election applying in heaven, not on earth. A link with the John Field episode of "Baker Farm," incidentally, is made by his allusion to the folk saying that Irishmen had no such halo about them; only natives were so distinguished. There follows Thoreau's account of a similar phenomenon in *The Autobiography of Benvenuto Cellini*, in which he is careful to say that "in the case of an excitable imagination like Cellini's, it would be basis enough for superstition." Then he adds: "But are they not indeed distinguished who are conscious that they are regarded at all?"—that is, by some special sign or recognition. (225) The imagery of rainbow-dolphin-halo is thus brought back to earth, to railroad causeway and shanty Irish, though the introduction has already built up a mood of wonder to precede the factual event promised by the title, a visit to Baker Farm.

As Thoreau begins his journey there, he tells us, it was on "one of those afternoons . . . in which many events may happen"—striking the note of expectation again. (225) The promise is fulfilled in the very next sentences, telling of a sudden thunder shower that made him take shelter under a tree, then run for the nearest hut. The passage is lifted up into poetic suggestiveness by a few unobtrusive rhymes scattered at irregular but recognizable intervals throughout the prose. And the concluding sentence is a comic echo of the rainbow-halo image of himself as one singled out for distinction: "The gods must be proud, thought I, with such forked flashes to rout a poor unarmed fisherman." The passage is surrounded by fragments of an actual poem, written by his friend Ellery Channing, who had once lived in a cabin at Baker Farm and had celebrated it in mediocre verse. The opening quotation is a pastiche of hackneyed phrases: "mossy fruit trees," "ruddy brook," "gliding musquash," and "mercurial trout." How much fresher Thoreau's lilting prose sentence that follows, establishing the narrator as a kind of Puck figure: "I 'hooked' the apples, leaped the brook, and scared the musquash and the trout." The closing quotation from Channing's poem brings the narrative down from the suggestive to the prosaic: "here a poet builded" in years now past, but with the present tenant the hut is falling to "destruction." (226)

This same contrast between the evocative and the mundane is carried out in Thoreau's choice of proper names for his anecdote from the local places and people available to him. He had chosen to go a-fishing at "Fair Haven" and his way led through "Pleasant Meadow." But a storm interrupted his plans, forcing him to pay a visit to "John Field" at "Baker Farm." It does not destroy the meaning of this word game to discover that there was an actual Irish laborer named Field living at nearby Lincoln during the period. There were undoubtedly other Irishmen, with names like Patrick Flynn and Michael O'Casey, he could have used. What is notable is Thoreau's choice of John *Field*, to symbolize a man of the earth, earthy. And so with the place names he chose from the actual topography of Concord township, to suggest the commonplace and the poetic. It is also notable that the visit is made to happen by accident (a thunderstorm) rather than by design, thus fulfilling the transcendental doctrine of a natural, even organic, form for his narrative. It also avoids what would have been the didacticism of an economic lesson drawn from a deliberately planned visit to serve as the contrast between Thoreau's way of life and that of his neighbor.

In the episode of the visit proper there are no scenes evoking wonder, and the imagery gives way to language that is bare and factual. All is stated rather than suggested, with great economy and precision of phrasing to render the degradation of John Field's life, so that the manner is appropriate to the matter. But as soon as the narrator leaves this tumbled-down hut, the language lifts just as the clouds do: "The shower was now over, and a rainbow above the eastern woods promised a fair evening." With its first reappearance, this is the bow of the covenant, God's promise of a renewed earth after the flood, and a new life for mankind. The fisherman is now in great haste to resume his interrupted expedition, but it immediately rises to a new plane of meaning: "I ran down the hill toward the reddening west, with the rainbow over my shoulder, and some faint tinkling sounds borne to my ear through the cleansed air, from I know not what quarter." The glory is such that all motion is arrested for a moment, while his Good Genius seemed to say: "Go fish and hunt far and wide day by day,—farther and wider. . . . Remember thy creator in the days of thy youth. Rise free from care before the dawn, and seek adventures." (230) The world is again filled with the music of the spheres and with many-hued color, from sunrise to sunset, and a rainbow arching the sky between—a kind of epiphany.

Although the well-known exhortation—"Remember thy creator"—buried in the passage just quoted from *Walden* has been readily identified as coming from Ecclesiastes, no one has bothered to examine its context there for other parallels. The close student of Thoreau will be alerted when he reads:

> Rejoice, O young man, in thy youth; and let thy heart cheer thee in the days of thy youth; and walk in the ways of thine heart, and in the sight of thine eyes. . . .
>
> Remember now thy Creator in the days of thy youth, while the evil days come not, nor the years draw nigh, when thou shalt say, I have no pleasure in them;
>
> While the sun, or the light, or the moon, or the stars, be not darkened, nor the clouds return after the rain.

Echoes from all these verses permeate the "Baker Farm" paragraph. The joyful youth walking in the ways of his heart is imaged in two sentences: "Let the noon find thee by other lakes, and the night overtake thee everywhere at home. . . . rest thee by many brooks and hearth-sides without misgiving." (230) His heedlessness of the dark storms that trouble those no longer young is rendered in a vignette: "Let the thunder rumble; what if it threaten ruin to farmers' crops? that is not its errand to thee. Take shelter under the cloud, while they flee to carts and sheds." (230)

Thoreau was far from adopting the general viewpoint of Ecclesiastes—its gentle cynicism based on the vanity of a life ambushed by death, with the oft-quoted injunction "to eat, and to drink, and to be merry." *Walden* suggests this only tangentially, with its accent on youth (being alive, awake) set over against a clustering imagery of darkness and decay. But the biblical language that colors this part of his chapter all comes from the Old Testament's most unorthodox book. The passage begins as the narrator wonders whether fishing is not a trivial thing for one "who had been sent to school and college." (230) But the preacher of "vanities" had already admonished him that "much study is a weariness of the flesh." Finally, a pervasive text in Ecclesiastes furnishes the "moral" for the whole John Field episode: "What profit hath a man of all his labour which he taketh under the sun? . . . For whom do I labour, and bereave my soul of good?" At the end of the passage under consideration Thoreau says: "Let not to get a living be thy trade, but thy sport." (230) This apothegm, borrowed from the gentle cynic, is presumably directed back up the hill to the ruined hut and wasted life he has just left behind.

At any rate it acts as a kind of magic invocation to bring Field back into the story, in a kind of epilogue, after an absence of three paragraphs. With a change of mind, he has decided to join in the fishing at Fair Haven Pond. But he does not even know how to fish. Trying to "catch perch with shiners" for bait—that is, using a "derivative old country mode in this primitive new country"—he gets only a few bites while the narrator is catching a fair string. "Poor John Field! . . . he said it was his luck; but when we changed seats in the boat luck changed seats too." The Goddess of Fortune has singled out Thoreau for distinction, just as the rainbow-dolphin-halo had, but none of these things fall to the lot of Field. Such earthbound mortals are "not to rise in this world," the chapter concludes, "till their wading webbed bog-trotting feet get *talaria* to their heels." (231) Thoreau's whole meaning is thus delivered in one stroke in the final sentence—which is also the last appearance of the rainbow, though as a submerged image.

Talaria were the winged sandals, symbolizing the faculty of swift and unimpeded flight through space, worn by several minor deities in Greek mythology. One of them was Hermes, son of Zeus and messenger of the gods, always represented in art as a vigorous youth. He was also protector of travelers and rogues, god of science and invention, and above all patron of the arts of life. This reads almost like a list of John Field's specific lacks, and a list of the traits that are attributable to Thoreau—that is, to his fictive projection as the "I" of *Walden*. The other famous wearer of *talaria* was Iris, also a messenger of the gods, usually pictured as a radiant maiden borne on golden wings. In her chief function she was goddess of the rainbow, the path she used in her flights from heaven to earth. It is the same path Thoreau uses in "Baker Farm" for his symbolic flight from earth *toward* heaven.

It will be instructive now to compare this chapter with the *Journal* account of Thoreau's visit to John Field, for he actually made one in August 1845, shortly after moving to the pond. Containing only about half of the two central pages of "Baker Farm," it is confined to a brief description of the degraded Irish family, and Field's complaint about his hard plight; it even omits the long discussion of economics in which Thoreau drives home his lesson about simplicity. What there is of it, however, he transcribed almost verbatim into his book. He was artist enough to recognize and utilize the impact of the precise details in his *Journal* account: "the wrinkled and sibyl-like, crone-like infant"; the wife "with round, greasy face and bare breast"; the chickens which, "like members of the family, stalked about the room, too much humanized to roast well." (J, I, 383–384) But what is notably missing is the rainbow-dolphin-talaria imagery—the introductory and concluding pages that comprise two-thirds of the chapter's substance and all of its meaning. Those who think of *Walden* as a pastiche, scissored from the *Journal*, might argue that the imagery is mere decoration borrowed from the realm of poetry and added to the autobiographical experience to give it color. But those who learn to read *Walden* as a poem would say that the chapter was conceived as part of a quest for meaning to be rendered by an image cluster. If so, then the factual episode was borrowed from the *Journal* merely to serve as a counterweight to the aspiring imagery. There is a vast difference between the two methods: one for an expository essay, the other for a work of art. Here, indeed, is an example of how the facts from his commonplace book are turned into poetry: "They are *translated* from earth to heaven." (J, III, 311) By such techniques the magical "world" of *Walden* is created.

So a rainbow colors the whole chapter and images its meaning. The economic lesson of Field's involuntary poverty set over against Thoreau's voluntary poverty is only an illustrative episode. The real theme is a contrast between the elevated and the degraded life, between freedom through imagination and serfdom through stupidity, between a poet's desire to soar into the life of the spirit and a clod's resignation to being bogged down in squalid materialism. The pun was intended, for Field could have been made a rail-splitter or milkman or general hired hand. He is portrayed instead as a bogger, at heart as well as by trade, stuck in the mire of his miserable life. On the contrary, Thoreau is always presented as a vigorous and radiant youth (a fusion of Hermes and Iris): leaping the brook en route to Baker Farm, running down the hill to Fair Haven when he leaves it, and in the last sentence taking off on winged heels into the aspiring "Higher Laws" that follow in Chapter 11. But in a preceding sentence, "Grow wild according to thy nature," he has already prepared for his return to earth by an enigmatic link to Chapter 12, in which he compares his own yearning for wildness with the actual life of his "Brute Neighbors."

One final proof of the larger meaning of "Baker Farm" can be found in the next-to-last of its concluding paragraphs. There the comparison is extended from John Field to most men, who "come tamely home at night" from their drudging labors and pine their lives away. "We should come home from far, from adventures, and perils, and discoveries every day," Thoreau says, "with new experience and character." Thus he unites the fabulous and the pragmatic. This chapter may seem like a fishy story to the literal-minded, but in it the angler of Walden Pond has managed to catch a form and a meaning by using metaphors for bait.

5
Talaria

The Natural Man

Returning from his expedition to Fair Haven, the narrator walks straight into the next chapter with his pole and string of fish over his shoulder. But a sudden encounter in the evening woods brings the story to a halt and transforms "Higher Laws" into a meditation. "I caught a glimpse of a woodchuck stealing across my path," Thoreau says, "and was strongly tempted to seize and devour him raw." His impulse came not from hunger but from "a strange thrill of savage delight . . . for that wildness which he represented." (232) This introduces one of the two opposing themes of the chapter. The duality is made explicit midway in the first paragraph: "I found in myself, and still find, an instinct toward a higher, or, as it is named, spiritual life, as do most men, and another toward a primitive rank and savage one, and I reverence them both." (232) Thoreau's emphasis on wildness here and throughout the book takes its start from a century old tradition, as an extension of the Romantic cult of nature-animal-child-peasant-primitive. In this sense it should not puzzle readers as it seems to have done. By using an abstraction, he has freed himself from particularizations, such as Cooper's Indians and Wordsworth's rustics, which tend to be unconvincing. In this way he can deal with the quality, the essence, of wildness. "Grow wild according to *thy* nature," was his exhortation in the preceding chapter. (230, my italics) Then, as need arises, he can make the idea concrete in a hunter or woodchopper, in himself, in his brute neighbors, and so on. Herein lies his originality. With it, by the end of *Walden*, he has added a new dimension to the literature of nature.

Thus Chapter 11 begins not with the tail end of a fishing story but with a celebration of the fisher as a type of those who, "spending their lives in the fields and woods, [are] in a peculiar sense a part of Nature themselves." (233) They penetrate deeper "than philosophers or poets even," because they participate in its "wildness." Hunters and woodsmen of all sorts are assimilated to this type of simple, solitary, happy, natural man. They pop up everywhere in Thoreau's writings. When they appear in his *Journal* and his posthumous books, they are merely described in relation to daily experiences. But in *Walden*, though they also appear as literal figures, they function chiefly as an integral part of an image pattern. This is because his lesser writings are a designing of facts drawn from some particular adventures he has actually had. But *Walden* is the designing of an adventure in pursuit of *the* fact. At the beginning of "Higher Laws" this quest is launched by transforming fishermen, hunters, and woodchoppers into symbols.

The last named take the reader back to Chapter 6 where a Canadian woodchopper, the most memorable of Thoreau's "Visitors," furnishes his most elaborate description of the archetypal man-in-nature. He is clearly superior to John Field in that he combines sport with getting his living, making a pastime of his trade. He has such "an exuberance of animal spirits" that he overflows with good humor and contentment. More important, he is one of those natural men who, with their instinctive skill and first-hand knowledge of facts, are able to do much more than they know how to articulate, so that the Canadian woodchopper at first presents something of an enigma: "I did not know whether he was as wise as Shakespeare or as simply ignorant as a child." (164) After several anecdotes illustrating his natural talents and his educational limitations, Thoreau concludes that he was "so primitive and immersed in his animal life . . . the intellectual and what is called spiritual man in him were slumbering as in an infant." (166, 162–163) His final rank in the *Walden* scale-of-being can be guessed from the suggestive words that introduce him: "He had so suitable and poetic a name that I am sorry I cannot print it here." (159) Though this follows the book's rule of not naming recognizable living persons, it also piques the curiosity. In a *Journal* entry for 1845 one discovers that the model was

Alek Therien, a "character" well known around Concord. Since *therion* is Greek for "animal," it is a reasonable inference that Thoreau buried a learned pun here for contemporary readers who knew their classics as well as the village original, and for later readers who could retrieve this information—Alexander (the Great) Animal. In the text as published, his wildness is sufficiently indicated by the fact that he actually ate woodchucks with relish—though not raw.

When at the beginning of his book Thoreau spoke of going to Walden Pond for the advantages of living "a primitive and frontier life," it must be remembered that he added "in the midst of an outward civilization." (12) Though he keeps his Homer open on the table (111), he also wants to experience "an unconscious life" in nature, like the woodsmen, because they are more intimately acquainted with it than naturalists who approach nature with "expectation," that is, with too many preconceptions. He has much to learn from woodchoppers, hunters, and fishermen. He likes to think of them as legendary survivors of a time now deep in history, descendants of the Indians still chopping, hunting, and fishing in Walden woods. "There is a period in the history of the individual, as of the race," he says in Chapter 11, "when the hunters are the 'best men,' as the Algonquins called them." (235) Such was the period of Thoreau's youth, when rod and gun were his introduction to field and stream, "one of the best parts of my education." (234) But this is merely the "embryo" stage of man's development: "If he has the seeds of a better life in him, he distinguishes his proper objects, as a poet or naturalist it may be, and leaves the gun and fish-pole behind." (235) Thoreau does not want to *be* an Indian or a woodsman but to be *like* them so as to educate his "animal man," then develop a life far beyond theirs as seer and sayer. He wants to see and understand nature as well as live in it. He wants to forget himself there only in order to find his Self, then to express that experience in poetry. If Field represents the vegetable stage, Therien stands for the animal stage, and both must be transcended by one who aspires to live in the spirit.

Sometimes the "I" of Walden is an actual woodchopper or

fisherman (though not a hunter, as will be seen), sharing the life of these woodsmen in a small way. But even when his accounts of these activities begin on the literal level, they are quickly translated to the poetic. In the spring when he is cutting down trees to make studs and rafters for his house, what makes the vignette memorable is not the work of the woodchopper but the "fragrance [of] the green pine boughs" on which he sat to eat his lunch. (47) In the fall, digging up old stumps for kindling, he is "prospecting [for] a great treasure" and he mined the fat pine roots "as if [he] had struck on a vein of gold, deep into the earth." (278) The pickerel, caught during the winter through holes cut in the ice, are "fabulous fishes . . . foreign as Arabia to our Concord life"; they seem "like flowers and precious stones" of a "quite dazzling and transcendent beauty." (314, 315) Digging for fish bait one summer day, he discovers the ground nut, "the ancient . . . diet of the hunter tribe," which seems like nature's promise to feed her children once again at some future period "when the reign of poetry commences here." (264, 265) In *A Week,* describing an old fisherman who was the real "Walton of this stream," Thoreau said: "His fishing was not a sport, nor solely a means of subsistence, but a sort of solemn sacrament and withdrawal from the world, just as the aged read their Bibles." (I, 22–23) So the environs of Walden Pond become a sacred grove to Thoreau. When they are laid waste by the encroachments of civilization—railroad, ice-cutters, or sawmills—the muse departs. (276)

This pattern of images is so pervasive in his "unroofed" book as to give a special significance to the hunters, fishers, and woodchoppers. But actual woodsmen, for all their admirable simplicity and naturalness, live in a limited physical world. They are only the embryos out of which may develop the poetic woodsman called for by the complex world of *Walden.* They are incapable of that excess of doing and being which is required by a transcendent adventure after *the* fact: "They know nothing about the hook of hooks with which to angle for the pond itself." (236) The transformation is made explicit near the end of his prologue to "Higher Laws." His advice to young men is that they should strive to make themselves, "though sportsmen only at first, if possible, mighty hunters at last, so that they shall not find game large enough for them in this or any vegetable wilderness,—hunters as well as fishers of men." (234) The phrasing immediately suggests two great biblical archetypes. The first is from the Old Testament: Nimrod, great-grandson of Noah, the "strong and valiant one" who founded Babylonia. He was "a mighty hunter before the Lord" and has become the symbolic hunter in Western tradition. The second, from the New Testament, is one of the most familiar of Christian symbols. It was used by Jesus as he drew two of his disciples away from their mundane calling: "Come ye after me, and I will make you to become fishers of men."

As with all Thoreau's allusions to the Bible, these are transmuted to new meanings. Hunter and fisher for him become archetypes of those who praise God and serve men. In their conventional sense both may seem foreign to Thoreau, because of the popular image of him as a recluse who withdrew from the church, rejected all philanthropic enterprises, and satirized most of what comprised religion for his contemporaries. Yet concern for praising and serving is central to much of his writing, though not rendered in Christian terms. At the end of his long introductory chapter he had struck one of the keynotes of *Walden:* the only "memorable praise of God" is to enjoy "the gift of life." (87) And in an early *Journal* entry he had made the dedication of his career as a writer: "I would fain communicate the wealth of my life to men, would really give them what is most precious in my gift." (J, I, 350) Hunter and fisher, as Thoreau uses them, are Christian symbols only by indirection. He does not intend any evangelical meaning of "hunters and fishers of men" as those dedicated to saving souls for Christ. They are poetic names for the author of a new scripture, whose mission was to hunt and fish for the human condition, for the true nature of man buried under a material civilization.

Some of the symbolic meanings Thoreau intended are detailed in a remarkable passage in the *Journal* for 1 January 1854:

The great game for mighty hunters as soon as the first snow falls is Purity. . . . Did this great snow come to reveal the track merely of some timorous hare, or of the Great Hare, whose track no hunter has seen? . . . Are there not hunters who seek for something higher than foxes, with judgment more discriminating than the senses of foxhounds, who rally to a nobler music than that of the hunting-horn? As there is contention among the fisherman who shall be the first to reach the pond as soon as the ice will bear, in spite of the cold, as the hunters are forward to take the field as soon as the first snow has fallen, so the observer, or he who would make the most of his life for discipline, must be abroad early and late, in spite of cold and wet, in pursuit of nobler game, whose traces are then most distinct. A life which, pursued, does not earth itself, does not burrow downward but upward, which takes not to the trees but to the heavens as its home, which the hunter pursues with winged thoughts and aspirations—these the dogs that tree it,—rallying his pack with the bugle notes of undying faith, and returns with some worthier trophy than a fox's tail, a life which we seek, not to destroy it, but to save our own. Is the great snow of use to the hunter only, and not to the saint, or him who is earnestly building up a life? Do the Indian and hunter only need snow-shoes, while the saint sits indoors in embroidered slippers? (J, VI, 44–45)

This elaborate conceit makes the perfect gloss for the *Walden* passage on "hunters and fishers of men." The mighty hunter is here defined as "he who would make the most out of his life for discipline"; his quarry flees to its home in heaven, and he pursues it "with winged thoughts and aspirations." These ideals extend the meaning of the paragraph in "Higher Laws," and the passage that dramatizes them in hunting imagery would have deserved inclusion in that chapter—which was being written and revised in 1853–1854, one of the last in the book to be completed.

Whatever the reason for its omission, it serves as a valuable commentary on the opening pages of this chapter and on what Thoreau's Good Genius advised him at the end of the preceding chapter, "Baker Farm," in lieu of actual fishing at Fair Haven: "Go fish and hunt far and wide day by day,—farther and wider." (230) The genuine excess and extravagance of his new economy is controlled and brought to focus by Thoreau's new names as hunter and fisher. So the relevance of these terms to *Walden* can be extended by their derived meanings. "Hunter" has come to stand for anyone who is a seeker, and this book is above all things a quest. Hunting supplied a memorable image, "to drive life into a corner," in the chapter describing where he lived and what he lived for. (101) The "fisher" is one who is angling for some hidden thing below the surface. This image was given a new direction at the end of the same chapter where, having fished in the stream of time only to find it shallow, he resolved to "fish in the sky, whose bottom is pebbly with stars." (109)

The Disciplined Man

The structural pattern of "Higher Laws" is just such an ascent from earth to heaven. According to Thoreau, there is only one true direction for man's development: from wildness to virtue. He must accept and understand his savage self before he can transcend it and aspire toward the divine. If he tries to find a shortcut, by denying the animal in him and asserting his higher nature, he lands in the limbo of civilization—where men ignore the natural world and forget the soul, engrossed in the pursuit of abstractions or sunk in the sty of materialism. So, Thoreau went to the woods to work his way up from the jungle of nature to the higher laws of the spirit. His first step upward was to renounce the life of the literal woodsman. "With every year I am less a fisherman," he says; "at present I am no fisherman at all." (236) Whenever his activities later in the book seem to contradict this, a close reading shows that he is enacting a symbolic role. Hunting he had rejected even earlier: "I . . . sold my gun before I went to the woods." (234) The reason he gives forms the transition to his second attempt to rise above nature. He sets himself the ideal of abstaining from all animal food, since to eat flesh necessarily involves slaughtering, whether by hunter or butcher.

The plea for vegetarianism that follows has proved a stumbling block to readers. Getting to heaven by a reformed diet strikes the modern critic as the aberrant dream of food cranks, and Thoreau is linked with them in the only extended analysis of the passage so far attempted. In an essay whose title betrays the bias, "Transcendental Grocery Bills," this critic maintains there was nothing original in the dietetic experiments at Walden Pond since they corresponded to the programs of numerous reformers during the 1840's. The one chiefly cited, by a cousin of Bronson Alcott, did indeed outline a diet that would reduce grocery bills similar to Thoreau's deflation of the food problem in his "Economy," as has been pointed out. But the sources of his wit differed from the sources of his imagery. The current fad of vegetarianism gave timeliness to any discussion of it, of course, and he was quick to take advantage of this, beginning the passage in "Higher Laws" with an appeal to the general reader: "Like many of my contemporaries, I had rarely for many years used animal food." (237) But the treatment of food in this chapter is symbolical, just as it has been in most religions. To conclude that Thoreau was too "homespun" to go to such remote sources as classical, Christian, and Hindu writers for his program of austerity, as this critic does, is to forget his erudition and ignore his rich borrowings from ancient tradition. These are the very authorities whose works will clarify the most baffling chapter in *Walden;* and they do so by showing that diet was only one of many disciplines by which he aspired to spiritual perfection.

A brief tour around Thoreau's library will provide a sample of the learning that lies below the surface of *Walden.* He was the best Latin and Greek scholar among the New England literary figures of his day, according to a specialist in the classics. He was more deeply read in the Oriental scriptures than any of the other transcendentalists, according to an authority on the intellectual backgrounds of both Emerson and Thoreau. He was conversant with the chief monuments of Western philosophy, Greek mythology, and the Bible; and he ranged widely in the literature of England and Europe from the Renaissance down to his own day. It is to his credit as an artist that none of this erudition was used for display, at least in his best work. Since his reading was assimilated to his creative needs, his writing remains original and indigenous. Hence the style of *Walden* can be deceptively simple, in the American tradition (inaugurated by Franklin) of the natural as opposed to the bookish writer. But the experienced reader learns to see through this homespun disguise to the body of learning buried beneath.

In 1841, Thoreau recorded his intention to read several books, including Iamblicus' *Life of Pythagoras* and Porphyry's treatise on *Abstinence from Animal Food*. That he did so is proved by passages from them copied down in his commonplace book at some time between this date and the Walden residence, 1845–1847. As to the first of these, there were several reasons why Thoreau should have been drawn to Pythagoras. He was the "father" of Plato; he believed that the soul was divine; and he advocated the study of nature as a way of life that led to the truth. Regarded by some as a son of Apollo, he was actually worshipped by one elderly priest as that god incarnate. The general appeal of this is obvious, and even the last particular has a parallel: Thoreau also identified himself with Apollo frequently in his writings, once indirectly in *Walden*. (48) Moreover, admitting to his divine origin, Pythagoras had said that he came into the world "for the purpose of remedying and benefiting mankind, and that on this account he had assumed a human form." As a kind of prefiguration of Christ he was doubly attractive to one who was searching for a surrogate to the Christian God. More specifically to the purpose of his book, Thoreau could have read in Iamblicus' biography: "He imitated in his diet the frugal simplicity of the most ancient times. . . . He was also adorned by piety and disciplines, by a mode of living transcendently good, by firmness of soul, and by a body in due subjection to the mandates of reason."

Central to *Walden* is the strenuous apprenticeship required of candidates before Pythagoras would admit them as disciples:

> He ordered his familiars to abstain from all animals, and farther still from certain foods, which are hostile to the reasoning power. . . . He likewise enjoined them continence of speech, and perfect silence. . . . he ordered them to abstain from wine, to be sparing

in their food, to sleep little, and to have an unstudied contempt of, and hostility to glory, wealth, and the like.

They were to avoid luxury and disease, ignorance and discord. They were to cultivate temperance and fortitude, freedom from the passions, friendship and love, including justice to animals "as their familiars and friends." He instituted laws regulating eating, the preparation of food, the use of medicines, the proper relation of labor to repose, and almost every aspect of their lives. All this—to purify the soul and prepare for the contemplative life of philosophers—parallels the program of living set forth in *Walden*. More specifically, the regimen outlined for a typical day among Pythagoreans called for them to begin with solitude, in order to harmonize the soul and the reasoning power; then discussion of science and divine doctrines, to discipline the mind; then exercise for bodily health, baths, and so on. If one substitutes "meditation" for "discussion," this sounds like a typical day at Walden Pond.

Like all the transcendentalists, Thoreau read chiefly for confirmation and turned the page when he did not find it. For example, though he was drawn to the recluse aspect of monasticism, he had no use for the communal. So, referring to those associations set up by Pythagoras called the *Coenobitae*, the anchorite in his cabin exploited this famous name in order to make a jibe at the luckless brotherhood of poor fishermen who dawdled beside Walden Pond, calling them the "ancient sect of Cenobites," depending on the current English pronunciation (see-no-bites) for his broad pun. (193) Again, he rejected all the esoteric mysteries in Pythagoras and bypassed his complex theory of numbers. In *Walden* the single direct reference to the master is a piece of irreverent wit, aimed specifically at his dietary laws: "I am by nature a Pythagorean, so far as beans are concerned." (179) Since the unnamed reason for their prohibition by the ancient Greek was that they caused flatulency, readers today can enjoy the joke on Thoreau's Concord neighbors to whom he sold his beans in exchange for rice—the fitting dish for one "who loved so well the philosophy of India." (67) Thoreau uses his source with discrimination. He skips the irrelevant, manipulates details to suit his needs, then appropriates the general principle of austerity without becoming derivative. A summary sentence in Iamblicus, copied down by Thoreau in his commonplace book—"In short Pythagoras ordered them to be attentive to order and method as long as they lived"—points to the center of interest for the author of *Walden*. Pythagoras offered "a way" which was of value as an example of discipline, even though it was not followed as an exact model.

The other Neoplatonic writer to influence Thoreau was the master under whom Iamblicus had studied. Porphyry held especial attractions for a transcendental rebel. He was one of the violent contenders against Christianity in the crucial third century, dying just before Constantine swung the empire to the new religion; he was also one of the great "rediscoverers" of the long neglected Plato, as well as a champion of the old paganism. Porphyry's treatise on *Abstinence from Animal Food* contained much to interest Thoreau, and for the reader of "Higher Laws" it is an indispensable key. It even provides an explanation for the seemingly abrupt shift from the hunter-fisher section in this chapter to the one on dietary laws. Porphyry held that men should behave "innoxiously and reverentially towards brutes, as if they were of a kindred nature with us," citing the belief of Pythagoras that they actually have souls. Killing animals for sport "through insolent wantonness, and for the sake of luxury" in eating, he taught, is degrading because it "renders us insensible to pity." Hence "if all men conceived rightly" they would abstain from eating flesh, and "there would be no need of fowlers, or hunters, or fishermen."

This humanitarian argument is transposed into *Walden* as one reason for Thoreau's vegetarianism, with even the phrasing echoed: "No humane being, past the thoughtless age of boyhood, will wantonly murder any creature which holds its life by the same tenure that he does." Pushing his advantage, he appeals to the tender sensibilities of animal-lovers (the phil-otheric) by assuring them, in a fancy piece of word play, "that my sympathies do not always make the usual phil-*anthropic* distinctions." (235)

Then at the end of his own treatise on abstaining from animal food he reverses himself in order to deny any "squeamish" faddism, declaring: "I could sometimes eat a fried rat with a good relish," the pun (India relish or chutney?) being intended for its shock value. (240) In between are set forth his real reasons for advocating a strict diet.

Thoreau was acquainted with other classical ascetics, but Porphyry offers the closest parallels to the whole austerity program in *Walden.* This Neoplatonist also knew that the discipline he proposed was so extreme it would appeal to only a limited audience. His famous treatise was actually addressed to a single recalcitrant disciple. And of all his writing he said:

> For it is not directed to those . . . who lead an active life [athletes, soldiers, politicians]. But I write to the man who considers what he is, whence he came, and whither he ought to tend, and who, in what pertains to nutriment, and other necessary concerns, is different from those who propose to themselves other kinds of life, [such as the man] who endeavors to obtain sleep through the whole of life. . . .
>
> To the man, however, who once suspects the enchantment attending our journey through the present life, and belonging to the place in which we dwell . . . to this man addressing ourselves . . . it is requisite to advise the use of a drink sober and without wine, food of an attenuated nature, and almost approaching to fasting; a house lucid, and participating of a subtle air and wind, and to urge him to be strenuously excited by solitude and thought, and to prepare for himself a small and hard bed.

Even the casual reader will recognize here a kind of paradigm for *Walden.* There are many parallels. The epigraph Thoreau chose for his title page (taken from his own second chapter) was the famous image of himself as "chanticleer in the morning, standing on his roost, if only to wake my neighbors up." On the first page he says his words are "particularly addressed to poor students," and even with them he urges that none should "stretch the seams in putting on the coat." Throughout the book he keeps up a running attack against those who are asleep, finally limiting his audience to the few who are really awake and aware of life's possibilities. To them, he offers the anticipation of high adventures, in a journey of enchantment around Concord. The house and diet, the identification with a locale, the dedication to a life of the spirit—all are similar to the program quoted above. It seems clear that the way of life proposed for philosophers by Porphyry, in its simplicity and austerity, offered a model for the Walden experiment.

Over and beyond mere abstention from animal meat, Porphyry held up the ultimate ideal of ascetics. "If it were possible, we should abstain from all food," he declared; "I wish, indeed, that our nature was not so corruptible, and that it were possible we could live . . . even without the nutriment derived from fruits. O that, as Homer says, we were not in want either of meat or drink, that we might be truly immortal!" Thoreau turns this extreme asceticism into a memorable piece of wit. "There is a certain class of unbelievers who sometimes ask me . . . if I think that I can live on vegetable food alone," he says in reference to his own economy. His reply, cited before as an example of his stylistic device of extravagance, was: "I am accustomed to answer such, that I can live on board nails." (72) Both Porphyry and Thoreau, being concerned with this world also, returned from such flights to formulate workable programs for mortals. The "wise and temperate man," said Porphyry, "granting to nature what is necessary . . . will reject whatever exceeds this, as only contributing to pleasure":

> The pleasure, however, which is produced through luxury, does not even approach to that which is experienced by him who lives with frugality. For such a one has great pleasure in thinking how little he requires. . . . [He does not] desire to possess silver tables and couches, and to have ointments and cooks, splendid vessels and garments, and suppers remarkable for their sumptuousness and variety. . . . The multitude, [on the other hand] though their possessions are abundant, incessantly labour to obtain more, as if they were in want.

This is the theme song of "Economy": the advantages of frugality over luxury in all walks of life. Thoreau's boasting about the greater joys of *his way*, the life of simplicity and austerity, is part of his satire on the contemporary gospel of materialism, the economy of abundance.

Porphyry's definition of the spiritual goal of his discipline may at first strike the reader as going far beyond *Walden*. We must divest ourselves of "everything material and mortal [that may] impede our purification," he wrote. "For the reascent of the soul is not to any thing else than to true being itself. . . . But intellect is truly-existing being; so that the end is to live according to intellect." Then he concluded, "our contest is for immortality, and an association with divinity, from which we are prevented through an association with the body." Thoreau's aim was higher than is usually thought, however. He also wanted to live "according to intellect," though he was far from rejecting the sensuous life. In the chapter on "Solitude," as pointed out before, he speaks of a visit from God on a winter evening, but it is cast in the form of a fable. Finally, in this central triad of chapters, his theme is the attempted ascent to purity and perfection, though not in Porphyry's terms. The latter made his meaning clear by going a step further than Thoreau ever went:

> Both inward, therefore, and external purity pertain to a divine man, who earnestly endeavors to be liberated from the passions of the soul, and who abstains from such food as excites the passions, and is fed with divine wisdom. . . . For he who thus mortifies his body will receive every possible good, through being sufficient to himself, and an assimilation to divinity.

There is a world of difference, however, between "assimilation to divinity" and mere "association" with it. Thoreau never subscribed to the Emersonian doctrine of the Oversoul, of which the individual soul was part and parcel; consequently his self-reliance was not God-reliance. He was not enough of a mystic to seek merger with the divine, and he was far from rejecting his mortal part altogether. He certainly stopped short of Porphyry, who at one point in his life, hating his body as the fetters of mortality, resolved to destroy himself and was prevented from doing so only by his master Plotinus. Thoreau was content to exclaim, at the high point of his most aspiring chapter, "The wonder is . . .

how you and I can live this slimy, beastly life, eating and drinking." (241) Usually when he speaks of the divine life he equates it with the poetic life, and by immortality he seems to mean the immortality of man's spirit as it flowers in art. The central statement of his reason for austerity in diet makes clear his difference from Porphyry: "I believe that every man who has ever been in earnest to preserve his *higher or poetic faculties* in the best condition has been particularly inclined to abstain from animal food, and from much food of any kind." (237, my italics)

Walden owes much to the classical ascetics, but it rises above its sources by giving modern meaning to the old arguments and by rendering them in a new mode of wit and metaphor. For example, when Porphyry specifically applied to food his rejection of everything superfluous, he was setting up a doctrine of literal asceticism: "Reason [does not] endeavor to receive much pleasure in eating, nor, through satiety, to be filled with much indolence; nor by rendering [the body's] burden more gross, to become somnolent." In "Higher Laws" Thoreau turns the argument for abstemiousness into a subtle play between the glutton and the gourmet. "The gross feeder is a man in the larva state," he says, "and there are whole nations . . . without fancy or imagination, whose vast abdomens betray them." For the opposite he draws on the traditional symbol of the soul, the butterfly, but transforms it into an image of the poet: a soaring thing of beauty nourished by nectar, in contrast to the "voracious caterpillar." (237–238)

In general, the emphasis on plainness of diet in *Walden* has been taken as proof that its author simply did not care for food and so deserves no credit for disciplining his appetites. But there is plenty of evidence that Thoreau had a palate, though it was that of a special kind of gourmet, savoring the dishes of nature's larder rather than of culinary art. In his writings he is forever tasting wild fruits, like acorns and ground nuts, or testing the subtle flavors of different kinds of grasses. Of his favorite huckleberries he declares in *Walden* that city folk who have never picked them do not know their real taste: "The ambrosial and essential part of the fruit is lost with the bloom which is rubbed off in the market cart. . . . If you would know the flavor of huckleberries, ask the cow-boy or the partridge." (192) Then, imperceptibly, he slips from the role of a natural into that of a spiritual epicure. When in the past he had eaten flesh and fish, "they seemed not to have fed me essentially." But now he is thrilled to remember "that some berries which I had eaten on a hillside had fed my genius." (241) The *Journal* original of this *Walden* passage, 11 July 1852, elaborates the point in an interesting way:

> What is called genius is the abundance of life or health, so that whatever addresses the senses, as the flavor of these berries, . . . intoxicates with a healthy intoxication. . . . I am thrilled to think that I owe a perception to the commonly gross sense of taste, that I have been inspired through the palate, that these berries have fed my brain. After I had been eating these simple, wholesome, ambrosial fruits on this high hillside, I found my senses whetted, I was young again, and whether I stood or sat I was not the same creature. (J, IV, 218–219)

He has been born again to a new life, though the transformation is given in poetic rather than spiritual terms.

Thoreau's handling of food reaches a high point with bread and wine which he treats sacramentally, though in a far-from-orthodox way. In late summer of 1853 he writes in the *Journal:*

> The fields and hills are a table constantly spread. Wines of all kinds and qualities, of noblest vintage, are bottled up in the skins of countless berries, for the taste of men and animals. To men they seem offered not so much for food as for sociality, that they may picnic with Nature,—diet drinks, cordials, wines. We pluck and eat in remembrance of Her. It is a sacrament, a communion. The not-forbidden fruits, which no serpent tempts us to taste. Slight and innocent savors, which relate us to Nature, make us her guests and entitle us to her regard and protection. It is a Saturnalia, and we quaff her wines at every turn. (J, V, 330–331)

Natural religion is presented here in language so clearly sacrilegious it would have offended a contemporary audience, so he chose the previous berry passage for transcribing into *Walden.*

The sacramental treatment of bread is much more indirect. In 1848, reflecting on his recent experiment at the pond, he wrote to a friend with *double-entendre:* "Let each man, then, earn at least a crumb of bread for his body before he dies, and know the taste of it,—that it is identical with the bread of life, and that they both go down at one swallow." In the book this is translated into the problem of finding food for the body that "will not offend the imagination," with the injunction that "they should both sit down at the same table." (238) Bread becomes the symbol for such a clean and simple diet as will meet this test. Lovingly and at length he elaborates the ritual of preparing and partaking it. He cooks it by a recipe from the Elder Cato. He breaks it in transcendental fellowship with the occasional guest at his frugal table. (68–69, 157) Alone he eats it, washed down with pure water from the pond, as a pagan version of the Eucharist.

The chief use of food in *Walden* is clearly metaphorical. The imagery drawn from it makes a pattern throughout the book, reaching from his initial statement of purpose—"I wanted to live deep and suck out all the marrow of life"—(101) to the "Conclusion" (Chapter 18) in which he sums up—"It is life near the bone where it is sweetest." (362) The same duality is applied to drink. In "Baker Farm" he had tried to persuade John Field to give up coffee and tea for water as a matter of basic economy. Now, in "Higher Laws," the argument is poetical: "think of dashing the hopes of a morning with a cup of warm coffee, or of an evening with a dish of tea!" (240) Drinking brings up drunkenness and Thoreau, who "would fain keep sober always," declares that "water is the only drink for a wise man," preferable to wine which is "not so noble a liquor." This invokes the familiar transcendental distinction between intoxication and inspiration, as in Emerson's "Bacchus," published while his former disciple was at Walden:

> Bring me wine, but wine which never grew
> In the belly of the grape.

Fifteen years later Emily Dickinson was to parody this by expressing her joy of living in terms of a cosmic spree:

Inebriate of Air—am I—
And Debauchee of Dew—

Midway between them in chronology and in seriousness, Thoreau added a fillip to the same theme by saying, "Of all ebriosity, who does not prefer to be intoxicated by the air he breathes?" (240)

The contrast between nourishment for the spirit and for the body is brought to a conclusion that would have seemed a contradiction in terms to an anti-epicure like Porphyry: "He who distinguishes the true savor of his food can never be a glutton." (241) Thoreau glories in the occasions when he has been "inspired through the palate," and conversely in those when he has found "inexpressible satisfaction from his food in which appetite had no share." He cites *The Great Learning* of Confucius to support him: "The soul not being mistress of herself," according to Thseng-tseu, "one eats, and one does not know the savor of food." This comes, significantly, from a chapter on the duty of self-perfection, to be achieved by purifying oneself of all passions so the soul may be filled with probity and justice. The context shows how Thoreau found in the Orientals what neither Neoplatonists nor Christians could give him: precisely that balance between a proper sensuousness and complete freedom from sensuality which was his ideal.

The sequence in "Higher Laws" continues with an indictment of his Calvinist fathers that gives a new twist to their Scriptures, so that he could get on with writing his own: "A puritan may go to his brown-bread crust with as gross an appetite as ever an alderman to his turtle. Not that food which entereth into the mouth defileth a man, but the appetite with which it is eaten." (241) Thoreau could bedevil the Bible as ingeniously as the Great Apostate himself. The verse he deliberately scrambled should read: "Not that which goeth into the mouth defileth a man; but that which cometh out of the mouth, this defileth a man"—that is, the evil thoughts and deeds that proceed from a corrupt heart. This was Christ's rebuke to the Pharisees who complained that his disciples transgressed religious tradition because "they wash not their hands when they eat bread." The shift of meaning made by a transcendental devil "quoting" Scripture here may seem slight, but it is crucial to an understanding of *Walden.* The full biblical context, placed in conjunction with that of "Higher Laws," brands Thoreau's puritan as pharisaical for following the letter rather than the spirit of Christian precepts against sensuality. His own definition is central to his new scripture: "It is neither the quality nor the quantity [of food], but the devotion to sensual savors; when that which is eaten is not a viand to sustain our animal, or inspire our spiritual life, but food for the worms that possess us." (241) In a word, the physical as well as the higher appetites can be satisfied without sinking into sensuality. The exploration of this transcendental paradox leads to Thoreau's final ascent into the higher laws, through chastity, one of the most misunderstood sections in the book and yet one of the most important.

Higher Laws

"Chastity is the flowering of man," he declares, "and what are called Genius, Heroism, Holiness, and the like, are but various fruits which succeed it." (243) Critics have tended to pass over this statement in embarrassed silence, while to offset it biographers have tried arduously to uncover some small flame of sexual love among the ashes of Thoreau's neutral behavior toward women (as set forth in the biographical section at the beginning of this study). Those determined to find an autobiographical motivation for the passage in "Higher Laws" will leap at one piece of evidence. This is the letter to Harrison Blake in September 1852, at the very time the section on chastity was being written for inclusion in *Walden:* "I send you the thoughts on chastity & sensuality with diffidence and shame, not knowing how far I speak to the condition of men generally, or how far I betray my peculiar defects." But what follows is an essay, not a confession. It is a curious example of Victorian prudery, a steady evasion of sex as a reality that is epitomized by his falling back on the conventional language of flowers instead of discussing it forthrightly. The only personal note to be discovered in its ten pages is in a pair of sentences at the end: "The intercourse of the sexes, I have dreamed, is incredibly beautiful, too fair to be remembered. I have had thoughts about it, but they are among the most fleeting and irrecoverable in my experience." This essay is indeed embarrassing, not because it proves Thoreau was "unnatural" in his person but because on this occasion he was false in his writing. Hence it is an unrewarding document for the literary analyst of *Walden*.

The question of chastity in Thoreau's life, interesting as it may be in its own right, belongs to his biographers. Motivation, even when it can be established, is seldom helpful to the literary critic, who is concerned with rendered meanings, with the effects of a work of art rather than with its causes. There were undoubtedly many virginal bachelors in his day, as in every age, but only one of them wrote *Walden*. The meaning of the section on chastity there can be discovered only by close reading of that text to see how it functions in the whole context of "Higher Laws."

The best way to begin is with a sharp second look at the key sentence: "Chastity is the flowering of man; and what are called Genius, Heroism, Holiness, and the like, are but various fruits which succeed it." It should be noted here that chastity is not a negative virtue (a resistance to deflowering) but an affirmative one (a "flowering"), and that it is emphasized only with regard to poets and saints, the spiritual heroes Thoreau admired. That he means the term partly in its strict sense, as abstinence from all sexual intercourse, is proved by the preceding sentence. The creative energy dissipates us and makes us unclean when we are loose, he says, but invigorates and inspires us when we are continent.

Whatever the modern view of this idea, there was a long tradition approving it that he was well aware of. Porphyry had said contemptuously, "[Only] the vulgar . . . think that sensual enjoyments and venery are preservative of health." Opposing the vulgar view, at least with respect to mental and spiritual health, he continued by praising the Jewish sect of Essenes and the philosopher-priests of Egypt for cultivating celibacy, so as to devote themselves to contemplation and divine inspiration. His philosophical justification for chastity follows: "For holy men were of opinion that purity consisted in a thing not being mingled with its contrary, and that mixture is defilement. . . . On this account, venereal connections are attended with defilement. For in these, a conjunction takes place of the female with the male."

So with the other austerities. Similar defilement occurs when the dead flesh of animals is taken into the living body, and the soul is polluted when it is invested with a human form. Thoreau owed a large debt to Porphyry, but he was too much the poet to be concerned with metaphysical arguments. In dealing with chastity—as with vegetarianism and the elevation of spirit over body—he quickly shifts ground from the strict to the liberal meaning of the word. To his own rhetorical question, "What is chastity?" he answers, "If you would be chaste, you must be temperate." (244) This is an accepted definition of chastity in its derived sense: moderation, restraint, avoidance of excess or extravagance.

The whole context of "Higher Laws" prepares for such a broadening of meaning. Throughout, the dual tendencies of man —animal and spiritual; wildness and virtue—have been maneuvered so as to find a temperate way that will combine them both. So, after Thoreau's brief tribute to chastity in its strict sense of sexual abstinence, he brings everything into balance with a modified definition: "All sensuality is one, though it takes many forms; all purity is one. It is the same whether a man eat, or drink, or cohabit, or sleep sensually." Least dramatic of all is the last example, particularly applicable to his own life: "In the student sensuality is a sluggish habit of mind." (243–244)

It was such a liberal view of disciplining the appetites that made the humanism of Oriental ascetics especially appealing to Thoreau. Of all those he read during his apprentice years, according to Sherman Paul, the one that spoke most to his condition was Menu, the "divinely inspired lawgiver" who codified the pattern of behavior for the Brahman, the "superior man" with whom Thoreau identified himself. He first discovered the *Laws of Menu* in 1840, made copious extracts in his Notebook the next year, published the ethical heart of these laws in the *Dial* in

1843, and made a literary essay of them in *A Week* in 1849. From Menu he learned that though celibacy was not required of Hindu priests, it was frequently practiced: "Many thousands of *Brahmans*, having avoided sensuality from their early youth and having left no issue in their families, have ascended . . . to heaven." Similarly, dietary laws and other disciplines were not enjoined on them as strictly as on European ascetics, but the value of moderation was urged: "In lawfully tasting meat, in drinking fermented liquor, in caressing women, there is no turpitude; for to such enjoyments men are naturally prone: but a virtuous abstinence from them produces a signal compensation."

Though not referred to by name in *Walden*, Menu was the Oriental philosopher cited anonymously at the end of "Higher Laws":

> Nothing was too trivial for the Hindoo lawgiver, however offensive it may be to modern taste. He teaches how to eat, drink, cohabit, void excrement and urine, and the like, elevating what is mean, and does not falsely excuse himself by calling these things trifles. (245)

This is the substance of a whole chapter "On Diet, Purification, and Women" in the *Laws of Menu*. Specifically, when Thoreau laments that we today are so impure "we cannot speak simply of the necessary functions of human nature," he is clearly remembering the purity that enabled Menu to speak so frankly of them, as in the following passage:

> All the cavities above the navel are pure, and all below it, unclean; so are all excretions, that fall from the body. . . .
>
> Oily exudations, seminal fluids, blood, dandruff, urine, feces, earwax, nail-parings, phlegm, tears, concretions on the eyes, and sweat, are the twelve impurities of the human frame.

In the succeeding pages detailed rules are given for cleansing these impurities. A more generalized precept concerning purification is included by Thoreau in the *Dial* extracts from Menu: "Bodies are cleansed by water; the mind is purified by truth; the vital spirit, by theology and devotion; the understanding, by clear knowledge." And scattered through the *Laws* there are elaborate regulations for choosing a wife, running a household, and traveling; for births and funerals; for domestic and business relations; for every conceivable human activity.

During the summer of 1840, when Thoreau first discovered this Hindu classic, he recorded in his *Journal* the nature of its appeal to him: "The 'Laws of Menu' are a manual of private devotion. . . . [They] carry us back to a time when purification and sacrifice and self-devotion had a place in the faith of men, and were not as now a superstition." (J, I, 279–280) In the Notebook containing his first gleanings from Menu, he followed them with a comment on the universality of his laws and their applicability to his own needs: "We seem to be dabbling in the very elements of our present conventional or actual and visible life.— Here is a *history* of the *forms* which humanity has in all ages assumed. . . . The book would afford a maxim applicable to any condition in which a man may be found."

Expanding this generalization for his essay in *A Week*, Thoreau added: "Any *moral* philosophy is exceedingly rare. This of Menu addresses our privacy more than most . . . as if it were the primeval conventicle, where how to eat, and to drink, and to sleep, and maintain life with adequate dignity and sincerity, were the questions to be decided." (I, 156) A final passage in this comprehensive acknowledgment of his debt to Menu makes clear the real value he found in all such exotic sources, whether Western or Oriental:

> As for the tenets of the Brahmans, we are not so much concerned to know what doctrines they held, as that they were held by any. We can tolerate all philosophies, Atomists, Pneumatologists, Atheists, Theists,—Plato, Aristotle, Leucippus, Democritus, Pythagoras, Zoroaster, and Confucius. It is the attitude of these men, more than any communication which they make, that attracts us. Between them and their commentators, it is true, there is an endless dispute. But if it comes to this, that you compare notes, then you are all wrong. As it is, each takes us up into the serene heavens . . . and paints earth and sky for us. Any sincere thought is irresistible.

The very austerity of the Brahmans is tempting to the devotional soul, as a more refined and nobler luxury. (I, 159)

They offered "a way," as Sherman Paul has pointed out, that served as a suggestive paradigm for *Walden* rather than a literal model. Thoreau himself says they served as confirmation rather than inspiration: "Like some other preachers, I have added my texts—derived from the Chinese and Hindoo scriptures—long after my discourse was written." (J, II, 192) The manuscript of *Walden* bears this out, showing many such quotations interlined in the second and third versions, written in 1850–1851.

It is only by putting Thoreau's plea for "chastity" (as well as the other austerities) in the context of his reading, and the whole body of his writing, that its full meaning can be explored. It is merely one of the many disciplines by which man aspires toward a higher life. Returning to his central paradox in "Higher Laws" —that to be chaste is simply to be free of all sensuality—one finds still further clarification in two framing sentences, which indicate the essentially religious purpose of all this disciplining of the appetites. The first is a quotation from Mencius, the Chinese philosopher and disciple of Confucius whose work he had read in a French edition during the 1840's, shortly after his first introduction to the Hindu scriptures. He translated numerous passages from it into his Notebook, including the key one that suited his needs in "Higher Laws": "That in which men differ from brute beasts is a thing very inconsiderable; the common herd lose it very soon; superior men preserve it carefully." (242) Then, after elaborating his all-embracing concept of chastity, he phrases his own response to the dictum of Mencius: "He is blessed who is assured that the animal is dying out in him day by day, and the divine being established." (243)

The duality that set the initial tension of this chapter was the two-way pull between "an instinct toward a higher, or, as it is named, spiritual life . . . and another toward a primitive rank and savage one." (232) Now, at the end of "Higher Laws," it is resolved with his unabashed aspiration toward the divine—though in terms of the whole book this resolution is tentative, as will be seen. Man's difficulty in rising above his animal nature, but the absolute necessity of his attempting to do so, is brought to focus in a concluding sentence: "Nature is hard to be overcome, but she *must* be overcome." (244, my italics.) This aphorism, neglected by previous critics, is crucial to an understanding of the quest for perfection that lies at the heart of *Walden*.

A final analogue for the disciplines by which Thoreau sought to purify himself can be found in Christian monasticism. He could have known of it from so many sources there is no need to cite particular works. One so deeply interested in religion would naturally have been concerned with the early history of that church from which he had dramatically "signed off" at maturity in 1837. Whatever his reading, Peter the Venerable's classic formulation of vows for the Carthusian order would have had especial appeal, because it was the only one that also practiced abstinence from animal flesh and because its monks combined the life of hermit and that of cenobite, with solitude predominating. As everyone knows, Western monasticism was founded on the basic vows of poverty, chastity, and obedience. There are striking parallels to these in the austerities Thoreau set up to rule his life, though his version was a transcendental one. Finding in his New England culture no tradition of monastery, or even sanctuary, he created his own. On the shores of Walden Pond he built a one-man cell that served as his retreat for a long poetic year. While his fellow transcendentalists were coming down from their pulpits to devote themselves to good works, Thoreau went to the woods to recover his faith by leading his own kind of holy life.

The first monastic vow, that of poverty, took its sanction from Christ's advice to the rich young man: "Sell all that thou hast, and distribute unto the poor, and thou shalt have treasure in heaven: and come, follow me." The virtues of charity and discipleship emphasized here were certainly foreign to Thoreau's purpose. But his espousal of poverty was close to the broad aims of the early monks: to free aspirants for the holy life from the temptations of materialism. Early in the opening chapter of *Walden* he satirizes luxuries, even what his contemporaries called necessities, as "positive hindrances to the elevation of mankind." Then he takes his vow: "None can be an impartial or wise observer of human life but from the vantage ground of what *we* should call voluntary poverty." (16) The immediate context suggests a secular goal, that of a philosopher rather than of a saint. But it is followed by a long series of metaphors for his true "enterprises," culminating in the elaborate conceit that begins: "If your trade is with the Celestial Empire . . ." (22) Though the practical purpose of Thoreau's withdrawal from the world was to write his books, their tenor is such as to make it clear that he took the vow of voluntary poverty to free himself for his "private business" with heaven—especially as that business concerned the creation of *Walden*.

During the first half of this book the religious note is so subdued by the brassy dialectic of his attack on the impurity and imperfection of the world around him that only attentive ears can hear it. But by the time one reaches "The Ponds," at the center, he begins to hear a deeply religious ground tone, swelling to its first climax two chapters later in "Higher Laws." There, among other disciplines to elevate the spirit, Thoreau pleads the value of chastity. In monasticism this second vow was aimed at enabling holy men to resist the more personal temptations of the flesh. Of many possible books Thoreau may have read on the subject, there was a particularly interesting one in his own library, Hardy's *Eastern Monachism*. It has a long section comparing the practices of Oriental and Western monastic systems. Moreover, a number of passages dealing with the values of the ascetic life are marked in pencil, and there is fairly good evidence that the markings were made by Thoreau. They are concerned with the strict diet of monks, the sparse furnishings of their cells, and other aspects of their asceticism relevant to the Walden regime. "There is in all men a yearning after something that is beyond the limits of the visible world," one generalized commentary begins; it then goes on to designate the kinds of men who are most unworldly—the poet, the hermit, the mystic—concluding, "All these types of mind are united in the recluse of India."

Two other passages deal specifically with chastity. The very earliest one marked in Hardy's volume, an attitude related to both Eastern and Western monasticism, seems to fit Thoreau's life exactly: "Whosoever shall affirm that the conjugal state is to be preferred to a life of virginity or celibacy, and that it is not better and more conducive to happiness to remain in virginity or celibacy, than to be married, let him be accursed." The other, near the end, describes a sect in pre-Christian Judea in terms that apply to several levels of *Walden's* program, in addition to chastity: "The Essenes gave themselves up to a contemplative mode of life, avoided the ordinary pleasures of existence, and repudiated marriage; they despised riches." Chastity clearly owed as much to earlier ascetic cults as to New Testament teaching. In time, Western monasteries (and the clergy as a whole) came to place their emphasis specifically on celibacy, as pre-Christian anchorites had done and as the example of Christ's own life suggested. But the vow of chastity had originally included abstinence from all sensuality, probably a truer imitation of Christ and certainly closer to Thoreau's meaning in "Higher Laws."

The third vow of monasticism came to mean in practice obedience to the rules of the order as formulated by its founder and later as administered by its abbot, a link in the hierarchical obedience to one's spiritual superiors exacted by the Church all the way up to the Pope. Nothing could seem further from all that Thoreau stands for. In *Walden* he begins emphatically, "I do not mean to prescribe rules to strong and valiant natures." (17) And his long introductory chapter ends with a specific disavowal of any desire to found a brotherhood of poor scholars or even to acquire disciples, insisting that each one "pursue *his own* way." (79) Similarly, the body of the book makes clear that he would never submit his own will to that of another, whether individual or organization. In the "Conclusion" (Chapter 18), he makes a memorable figure of his independence by contrasting it with the goose-stepping of the local militia, declaring that he marches to "a different drummer." (358) Thoreau wrote not only an essay on Civil Disobedience but a whole book on Spiritual Disobedience, if one reads *Walden* as a pioneering adventure in holy living independent of all external authority. But St. Benedict, like other founders of Western monasticism, was just such a spiritual pioneer himself at the outset, by-passing established authority and obeying his God alone. His followers in vowing obedience to him and his rules understood them only as surrogates for God and His laws.

Taken in this way the monastic vow of obedience may be seen in a new light, one not quite so alien to Thoreau. All his life—all his thought and his writing—was disciplined by a strict obedience to some "higher power," though as a transcendentalist he was shy of the name God, and as a poet he was not content with finding a new label for what could be evoked only by metaphor or indirection. All his attempts at definition are tentative and shifting, but his search for the right words leads to the heart of his book. The very title of the climactic "Higher Laws" is as near as he ever came to a satisfactory term for the divinity he obeyed, though this is too abstract for any but the initiate reader to find acceptable. So, midway in the chapter he formulates the idea in concrete imagery:

> If one listens to the faintest but constant suggestions of his genius, which are certainly true, he sees not to what extremes, or even insanity, it may lead him; and yet that way, as he grows more resolute and faithful, his road lies. . . . No man ever followed his genius till it misled him. (239)

As a version of the vow of obedience this is indeed heretical, being a proud reliance on the Self-as-god rather than surrender to an external divinity. It is also rendered in deliberately extravagant language: to follow his "genius" to the point of "insanity." He had indulged in the same kind of exaggeration when defining the other austerities by which he disciplined the body for the sake of the spirit: "I can live on board nails"; "I had but ten cents in the world"; "The wonder is how they, how you and I, can live this slimy, beastly life." (72, 91, 241) Even the pledge to "chastity," in order to flower as a poet, is a gesture of extravagance. One comes closer to his true meaning by taking them all as hyperboles. Yet the three vows of poverty, chastity, and obedience do form a ground plan for *Walden,* and however they may differ from the formal vows of monasticism, they are similar in direction and in ultimate purpose.

In terms of the quest for perfection, the entire first half of *Walden* is devoted to a renunciation of the world, though not the world of nature except in a special sense, since the probationer is more pan-theist than Christian theist. Having completed the period of his novitiate, he proceeds in "Higher Laws" to take his vows renouncing the flesh—only symbolically because as a humanist he is still mindful of the classical ideal: a sound mind in a sound body. Almost immediately after undertaking these disciplines to achieve perfection, he has a glimpse of the divinity accessible to those who lead "a life in conformity to higher principles." But he admits his vision is "intangible and indescribable." (239) He aspires toward it not in doctrinal but in poetic terms. First "fragrance," then "star-dust," finally the perfect image: "It is . . . a segment of the rainbow which I have clutched." (239) In his *Journal* for 22 June 1852, he had been more explicit: "Is not the rainbow a faint vision of God's face?" (J, IV, 128) Such "statements" drawn from his *Journal* often make valuable commentaries on the implications of a book like *Walden.* They are themselves evidence of how much less convincing it is to state than to imply, when dealing with the ineffable, at the same time that they support the critic's guess as to the meaning of a particular symbol. Clutching at "a segment of the rainbow" is not quite the same thing as seeing "God's face." But this is the same pathway to heaven he was ascending with winged sandals at the beginning and end of "Baker Farm."

Now in "Higher Laws" he tries on his *talaria* for the boldest flight he has yet attempted:

> Our whole life is startlingly moral. . . . In the music of the harp which trembles round the world it is the insisting on this which thrills us. . . . Listen to every zephyr for some reproof, for it is surely there, and he is unfortunate who does not hear it. . . . [It] is heard

as music, a proud, sweet satire on the meanness of our lives. (241–242)

One of the very first passages Thoreau copied down in his Notebook from the biography by Iamblicus—an account of Pythagoras' use of music to purify his "corporeal nature"—makes a revealing analogue for the *Walden* experience:

> Pythagoras, however, did not procure for himself a thing of this kind through instruments or the voice, but employing a certain ineffable divinity, and which it is difficult to apprehend, he extended his ears, and fixed his intellect in the sublime symphonies of the world, he alone hearing and understanding, as it appears, the universal harmony and consonance of the spheres, and the stars that are moved through them, and which produce a fuller and more intense melody than anything effected by mortal sounds.

The translator, Thomas Taylor, supplied a footnote to this passage that must have caught Thoreau's eye. In answering the question, "Is it true to say, that the sound of divine bodies is not audible by terrestrial ears?" Aristotle declared that if anyone could hear the music of the spheres it would be a man like Pythagoras, who had escaped from his "terrestrial body" into his "celestial vehicle." By purifying the senses, he said, "such a one will perceive things invisible to others, and will hear things inaudible to others." By finding a dolphin in the rainbow and by thrilling to the music of the world harp Thoreau identifies himself, at least temporarily, as "such a one."

Empedocles ascribed these powers to Pythagoras because of "the illustrious nature of the conformation of his mind and body, and its superior accuracy in seeing, hearing, and in intellectual perception." In *A Week*, making a play between sense perceptions and intuition, Thoreau argues that by leading "a *purely* sensuous life" man can attain such transcendence:

> Our present senses are but the rudiments of what they are destined to become. . . . The ears were made, not for such trivial uses as men are wont to suppose, but to hear celestial sounds. The eyes were not made for such groveling uses as they are now put to and worn

out by, but to behold beauty now invisible. May we not *see* God? (I, 408)

In *Walden,* which renders its meanings by suggestion and indirection, he gives up the frontal assault on heaven and reaches for it in two images: " a segment of the rainbow" and "the music of the harp which trembles round the world."

The Middle Way

In similar fashion, the straightforward approach frequently adopted in *A Week* can serve as a gloss on the worldly as well as the other-worldly aspects of *Walden.* A ten-page digression on religion in the "Sunday" chapter of his earlier book argues that the Bible's emphasis on heaven would appall earthbound Christians if they ever really read it. Then, surprisingly enough, he cites this as the very reason for his own unorthodoxy:

> The New Testament treats of man and man's so-called spiritual affairs too exclusively, and is too constantly moral and personal, to alone content me, who am not interested solely in man's religious or moral nature, or in man even. . . . Christ was a sublime actor on the stage of the world. . . . Yet he taught mankind but imperfectly how to live; his thoughts were all directed toward another world. There is another kind of success than his. Even here we have a sort of living to get, and must buffet it somewhat longer. There are various tough problems yet to solve, and we must make shift to live, betwixt spirit and matter, such a human life as we can. (I, 74; 70–80)

This attack on the "Hebrew scriptures"—and his declaration of preference for the "scriptures of the several nations . . . the Hindoos, the Chinese, and the Persians"—brought the charge of irreligion from a reviewer of his first book, which may be one reason there are no such discussions in his second. But a better explanation is that *Walden* is the quest for a middle way between earth and heaven, not a debate on the relative merits of various religions. The Christian Bible, too uncomfortably close to serve as a source for poetry, was frequently used by him for witty attacks on the materialism of the world. The Oriental bibles proved his best source for imagery of the spiritual life.

To return to "Higher Laws," Thoreau's aspirations have now soared dizzily enough, and he must descend to earth if he is to get on with the story of his experiences at Walden Pond. The final paragraph beginning, "John Farmer sat at his door one September evening," may seem an abrupt and irrelevant ending until we realize that it is a resumption of the narrative broken off on the first page of this chapter. This is the same evening on which the narrator returned from his fishing expedition, saw the woodchuck, and began his long meditation on wildness and spirituality that comprises the body of "Higher Laws." The ancedote of John Farmer, somewhat like a seventeenth-century "Character," is one of those masterful one-paragraph vignettes Thoreau uses to bring his pages to life. His very name suggests that he is Emerson's "Man on the farm" instead of the mere planter who "sees his bushel and his cart, and nothing beyond, and sinks into the farmer." In *Walden's* scale-of-being John Farmer comes midway between John Field, mired in the bog, and the poetic woodsman who has gotten *talaria* to his heels. This is borne out by every detail of the anecdote. "Having bathed, he sat down to recreate his intellectual man . . . when he heard some one playing on a flute. . . . But the notes of the flute came home to his ears out of a different sphere from that he worked in, and suggested work for certain faculties which slumbered in him." (245) This brings the narrator into the picture, for the flute-player can be none other than Thoreau. He prided himself on his skill with this instrument, comparing his own magic to that of Orpheus: "In warm evenings I frequently sat in the boat playing the flute, and saw the perch, which I seem to have charmed, hovering around me." (193)

On this climactic evening in *Walden*, having returned from his visit to John Field and having aspired upward into "a different sphere," where he clutched at a rainbow and heard the celestial music of the world harp, he plays on his flute to charm John Farmer out of the dull labors that would make a brute of him.

This is the message the flute notes bring to his ears: "A voice said to him,—Why do you stay here and live this mean moiling life, when a glorious existence is possible for you?" (246) It will be remembered that the music of the spheres Thoreau heard did not transport him out of this world but taught him how to live in it; it was "a proud, sweet satire on the meanness of our lives." (242) And the effect on John Farmer, as recorded in the concluding sentence, was exactly what this whole chapter has tended toward: "All that he could think of was to practise some new austerity, to let his mind descend into his body and redeem it, and treat himself with ever increasing respect." (246) This makes the final distinction between the goal of Pythagoras and that of his Concord disciple. Thoreau did not want to escape from his "terrestrial body" into his "celestial vehicle," but to "let his mind descend *into* his body and redeem it."

Much further along the road to perfection than John Field, Alek Therien, or even John Farmer, Thoreau still has a long pilgrimage ahead of him. But he knows he will not reach his goal by starting from farming, any more than from the other trades and professions of civilization. Surveying some of the occupations that seemed most suited to his talents, he once expressed his need to transcend them all: "I would fain be a fisherman, hunter, farmer, preacher, etc., but fish, hunt, farm, preach other things than usual." (J, VI, 45) In the pre-Walden years, when he was seriously contemplating buying a run-down farm, he cautioned himself in the *Journal:*

> I must not lose any of my freedom by becoming a farmer and landholder. Most who enter on any profession are doomed. . . . My life must undulate still. I will not feel that my wings are clipped when once I have settled on ground which the law calls my own, but find new pinions grown to the old, and talaria to my feet beside. (J, I, 241–242)

When he finally settled at the pond and played the role of farmer on a miniature scale, he did indeed grow talaria to his heels. It soon becomes clear that he sees beyond his bushel and cart and will never "sink into the farmer." In the "Bean-Field" chapter he confesses that he only hoed about half of the two acres he had planted, leaving the rest for the woodchucks. The whole venture is treated either humorously or symbolically, sometimes with a blend of both modes:

> Mine was, as it were, the connecting link between wild and cultivated fields . . . [it] was, though not in a bad sense, a half-cultivated field. They were beans cheerfully returning to their wild and primitive state that I cultivated, and my hoe played the *Ranz des Vaches* for them. (174)

"It was on the whole a rare amusement," he concludes, "which, continued too long, might have become a dissipation." (179) What he learned from the experience was that farming was not the way for him. A passage in the *Week* tells why:

> I am convinced that my genius dates from an older era than the agricultural. I would at least strike my spade into the earth with such careless freedom but accuracy as the woodpecker his bill into a tree. There is in my nature, methinks, a singular yearning toward all wildness. . . . What have I to do with plows? I cut another furrow than you see.

This dedication to wildness, framed by wit and metaphor, points to the other pole of that duality with which "Higher Laws" began. As such it makes a bridge to the next chapter, where the Walden experience comes down from flights of the spirit and is resumed on the level of a life in nature.

6
Wildness

Hermit and Poet

The descent to earth in "Brute Neighbors" from the aspiring flights of "Higher Laws" is cushioned by a dramatic scene, involving a *Hermit* and a *Poet*, that seems a curious digression at first glance. True, the opening sentence makes a narrative link all the way back to "Baker Farm," with its fishing episode: "Sometimes I had a companion in my fishing, who came through the village to my house from the other side of the town, and the catching of the dinner was as much a social exercise as the eating of it." (247) But its basic relevance to the preceding chapters is thematic, rendered both in the roles of the speakers and in the subject of their dialogue. They are discussing the two-way pull between heavenly aspiration and a life lived in nature. It is a departure only in mode, being cast in play form for emphasis. The *Poet* who comes to see the *Hermit* (Thoreau) has usually been identified as Ellery Channing, because he lived in a house on "the other side of town" and because a reference in the third paragraph, "when we were off the coast of Spain," fits with a trip he had recently made to Italy. In the context of the actual Walden residence this identification is convincing, since Channing was Thoreau's best friend, a constant visitor at the pond, and a practicing poet as well. But in the context of this triad of *Walden* chapters both roles fit Thoreau, who was poet as well as hermit. Only when read in this way does the dialogue yield its full meaning. The theme all along has been how he can live simultaneously the life of a philosopher seeking to merge himself in the divine essence and that of a poetic partaker of experience in the sensuous world. Figuratively speaking the whole of *Walden* is such a dialogue.

The passage begins with the *Hermit* in his solitary cabin musing, "I wonder what the world is doing now." Sounds from it come to him faintly through the woods, "a farmer's noon horn" calling the hands to dinner from their labors in the field. He justifies his own idleness by taking the rule laid down by Captain John Smith when planting the first outpost of civilization in Virginia's wilderness and making a witty reversal of it: "He that does not eat need not work." The laboring, reaping, housekeeping of those who are "born too far into life for me" make the *Hermit* resolve: "Better not keep a house. Say, some hollow tree; and then for morning calls and dinner-parties!" (247) The allusion is probably to Saint Bavo, who became famous for living in such an ascetic abode. In the "Conclusion," Chapter 18, this seventh-century saint literally materializes in Walden woods: "There was a man in my neighborhood who lived in a hollow tree. His manners were truly regal. I should have done better had I called on him"—rather than on the inhospitable king who figures in the other half of that miniature fable. (364) This is the kind of companion the *Hermit* obviously prefers. The morning call in "Brute Neighbors" is paid by an equally fabulous character, Thoreau's alter ego. It is prepared for by the theatrical manner of his advent: "Hark! I hear a rustling of the leaves. . . . Eh, Mr. Poet, is it you?" This phrase, a rustling of leaves, reappears in the chapter as a cue for fable.

The familiar stranger immediately interrupts the *Hermit's* "serious meditation" and makes the expected invitation, to go fishing: "That's the true industry for poets. It is the only trade I have learned. Come, let's along." (248) Such a self-dialogue has been prefigured at the end of "Baker Farm" when the narrator, running down the hill to go fishing at Fair Haven, stops to ask himself if this is not a trivial occupation for a man "who had been sent to school and college." (230) And in a later chapter, "Winter Visitors," a similar colloquy between a poet and a philosopher (usually identified as Bronson Alcott)—who are "revising mythology, rounding a fable here and there"—ends with a similar fusion of the two figures, this time in a single image, "the fishes of thought were not scared from the stream." The roles are reversed there and the harmony is achieved by the poet's surrender to the philosopher, which is appropriate to the occasion of that visit, a winter night. (297)

In the present chapter, harmony is reached by the thinker's yielding to the poet-fisher, as befits a summer morning under "a true Mediterranean sky." Also, the thematic movement at this point in the book is from the hermit seeking the divine essence to the poet seeking metaphors in the world's body, from the spiritual level of "Higher Laws" to the primitive one of "Brute Neighbors." The *Hermit* accepts the invitation to go fishing "gladly," only begging a respite to wind up his thoughts. But when he sends the *Poet* off for bait, it is in language more appropriate to fable than fact: "[Dig] down yonder among the ground-nuts, where you see the johnswort waving," or wander farther still "for I have found the increase of fair bait to be very nearly as the squares of the distances." (248)

"*Hermit alone*. Let me see; where was I? . . . I was as near being resolved into the essence of things as ever I was in my life. . . . I will just try these three sentences of Confut-see; they may fetch that state about again." (248, 249) Of the sentences Thoreau had selected for his "Sayings of Confucius," published in the April 1843 issue of the transcendental *Dial*, the most pertinent to the *Hermit's* situation are:

> Silence is absolutely necessary to the wise man. . . . Heaven speaks, but what language does it use to preach to men, that there is a sovereign principle from which all things depend; a sovereign principle which makes them to act and move? Its motion is its language; it reduces the seasons to their time; it agitates nature; it makes it produce. This silence is eloquent.

But the *Hermit* really had lost his train of thought when the *Poet* interrupted his meditations. He was probably not reading Confucius at all but another Oriental, an ascetic of a truly mystical turn. Three sentences transcribed from the *Laws of Menu*, which Thoreau had published in the same series of "Ethnical Scriptures" in the *Dial* (January 1843), could much more easily have induced his present state of near trance. They deal with the final stage of the Brahman's retirement to the forest for a life of solitude "in the haunts of pious hermits":

> Alone, in some solitary place, let him constantly meditate on the divine nature of the soul; for, by such meditation, he will obtain happiness. . . .
>
> Let him reflect also, with exclusive application of mind, on the subtil, indivisible essence of the supreme spirit, and its complete existence in all beings. . . .
>
> Thus, having gradually abandoned all earthly attachments . . . he remains absorbed in the divine essence.

For all its aspiring toward heaven, however, *Walden* is anchored in "earthly attachments." Thoreau, never a mystic, is unwilling to follow the ascetics to the point of being "resolved into the essence of things," as proved by his uncertainty whether the present meditation is "the dumps or a budding ecstasy." Even his role as *Hermit* is just an assumed one, for purposes of the dialogue. When he asks himself the rhetorical question, "Shall I go to heaven or a-fishing?" his answer is a foregone conclusion. To the *Poet,* returning with fish bait, he says without hesitation: "Well, then, let's be off. Shall we to the Concord? There's good sport there." (249) Thus Hermit is dissolved into Poet, and the duality that has provided the tension of these central chapters is resolved, at least temporarily, by the narrator's re-entry into the sensuous world. But his intention is only to fish (or rather to hunt) for poetic meanings there. The fishing expedition is purely symbolic and is abruptly dropped from the text at this juncture. It is replaced by a hunting expedition, equally symbolic, that comprises the rest of the chapter.

Brute Neighbors

In "Higher Laws" Thoreau had said that when the thoughtless youth matures into "a poet or naturalist [he] leaves the gun and fish-pole behind." (235) It is precisely in this role that the narrator now goes forth to hunt in Walden woods, armed with field glasses and a volume of Oriental beast fables. "I suspect that Pilpay & Co. have put animals to their best use," he begins, providing the key to what follows, "for they are all beasts of burden, in a sense, made to carry some portion of our thoughts." (249) Thoreau deliberately uses the popular but erroneous ascription to Pilpay, as author of this famous collection, in order to give a light touch to his erudite reference. For he was well-acquainted with *The Heetopades of Veeshnoo-Sarma*, in the translation by Charles Wilkins, who corrects the error in his preface even as he gives this great work its due praise: "Their [the Hindoos] System of Ethicks is yet preserved, and the fables of *Veeshnoo-Sarma*, whom we ridiculously call *Pilpay*, are the most beautiful, if not the most ancient, collection of Apologues in the world." It is referred to by its correct title in *A Week*, with praise for its "playful wisdom which has eyes behind as well as before, and oversees itself." (I, 153) With this guide to the moral and religious analogies to be drawn from the animal world—and probably an Aesop in his hip pocket—the poetic hunter is now properly equipped. He is ready to see, hear, and make meaningful contact with his "Brute Neighbors," remembering his own profession of faith in *A Week:* "We need pray for no higher heaven than the pure senses can furnish." (I, 408)

Walden teems with animal life. It contains more than seven hundred references in all, an average of two to the page. The vast majority are simple observations of particular fauna, some wild, some domesticated. They are as various as the environment of field, forest, and pond affords—all those encountered in literal hunting and fishing or nature rambles, all those involved with man on the farm or in villages. They are significant in their variety and in the weight of their presence, surrounding the narrator with his private menagerie and serving as a constant pole of his sensibility. But it is the much smaller number of figurative uses, less than a fifth of the total, that reveal the significance of animals in his thought. Some of them compare men with animals. These are usually mere epithets or similes, to sharpen his criticism of society, a few of which have been cited in earlier chapters that deal with Thoreau's satire of the civilized world. Others compare animals with men, or otherwise bring them into a human context. These are images of man's attempt to find kinship with nature, and as such they are relevant to the present inquiry. Thoreau had read Porphyry's long argument that animals are closely related to men—in having similar bodies, skills, societies, speech, reasoning power, possibly souls—and only differ in degree. What is the true human-animal relationship for Thoreau, the final application of all this imagery in *Walden* to man's life? The whole book is a quest for the most important of all animals, not named in the text but being sought there—man in his complete fulfillment. Hence, when the narrator goes out to explore the world of his "Brute Neighbors," he is really hunting for his Self.

The actual number of animals in this chapter is limited to about a dozen, and most of these are only mentioned (phoebe, robin, dove, raccoon, squirrel) or confined to brief vignettes (otter, woodcock, duck). Half the space is taken up with elaborate accounts of two, ants and a loon, that set the limits of the chapter's meaning, as will be seen. Three others are given a full page each; and these offer a good introduction to the symbolic menagerie in Walden woods. Though the specimens chosen are few, the whole swarming life of nature is brought in by invoking the doctrine of plenitude from the Great Chain of Being. "Why has man just these species of animals for his neighbors," Thoreau asks at the outset, "as if nothing but a mouse could have filled this crevice?" (249) For his first quarry, a mouse, the poetic hunter does not have to stray beyond his cabin door, for one is nesting in his cellar. This is not the common kind found in the village, he says, "but a wild native kind [that] probably had never seen a man before." During house-building it gradually grows tame, finally running up his arm to reach his package of lunch and playing "at bopeep" with it. "When at last I held still a piece of cheese between my thumb and finger, it came and nibbled it, sitting in my hand, and afterward cleaned its face and paws, like a fly, and walked away." (250) The scurrying wild mouse is thus domesticated by a simile comparing it to the most familiar of creatures, the housefly. At the end of the chapter this process is enacted in reverse. Though it is not commonly realized, Thoreau says, "the most domestic cat, which has lain on a rug all her days," can on impulse run away and become "quite wild."

This bit of lore introduces his fable about a "winged cat" that had gained notoriety in the neighboring village of Lincoln. His field expedition to investigate is given point by using the courtesy language of formal visiting: "When I called to see her . . . she was gone a-hunting in the woods, as was her wont." (258) Breaking down the barriers between wild and domestic, in himself as well as in animals, is one method of rapprochement between man and the world of nature.

Thoreau had read about the miraculous power of Pythagoras in communicating with animals: how he persuaded a bear not to be carnivorous, "having gently stroked it with his hand"; how he persuaded an ox to give up eating beans and stick to grass, pulling aside the flap of its ear and "whispering in it for a long time." According to his biographer, Pythagoras "possessed the same dominion as Orpheus over savage animals." Thoreau once playfully claimed the same magic when he charmed the perch with his flute, as noted in the preceding chapter. But his more convincing method of rapprochement is by assimilating himself to the conditions of wildness and making himself one with the natural environment. The best-known example is in *A Week*, where he achieves an uncanny intimacy with the sunfish or bream:

> I have thus stood over them half an hour at a time, and stroked them familiarly without frightening them, suffering them to nibble my fingers harmlessly, . . . and have even taken them gently out of the water with my hand; though this cannot be accomplished by a sudden movement, however dexterous, for instant warning is conveyed to them through their denser element, but only by letting the fingers gradually close about them as they are poised over the palm, and with the utmost gentleness raising them slowly to the surface. (I, 25)

So it is in *Walden* when he holds the wild mouse in his hand.

The next anecdote shows him making intimate contact with the chicks of a partridge, in spite of its being "so shy a bird":

> The young suddenly disperse on your approach, at a signal from the mother, as if a whirlwind had swept them away, and they so exactly resemble the dried leaves and twigs that many a traveller

> has placed his foot in the midst of a brood, and heard the whir of the old bird as she flew off, and her anxious calls and mewing, or seen her trail her wings to attract his attention, without suspecting their neighborhood. [But treading with caution Thoreau finds them in their hiding place and lifts them up.] . . . I have held them in my open hand at such a time, and still their only care, obedient to their mother and their instinct, was to squat there without fear or trembling. (250–251)

Having established such a relationship, he can say of the wild partridge and her brood, "These were my hen and chickens," just as the mouse had become his luncheon companion, and the winged cat (if he should meet her on his next visit) would be "the right kind of cat for me to keep, if I had kept any; for why should not a poet's cat be winged as well as his horse?" (252, 250, 258)

One of the few records of a visit to Walden Pond during Thoreau's residence there that is both detailed and relevant to the book is an almost incredible account of his animal taming. It was written by a young friend of the Alcotts, who included him when they went there for a family outing. He was seventeen years old at the time:

> I have a keen recollection of the first time I met Henry David Thoreau. It was upon a beautiful day in July, 1847. . . .
>
> He was talking to Mr. Alcott of the wild flowers in Walden woods when, suddenly stopping, he said: "Keep very still and I will show you my family." Stepping quickly outside the cabin door, he gave a low and curious whistle; immediately a woodchuck came running towards him from a nearby burrow. With varying note, yet still low and strange, a pair of gray squirrels were summoned and approached him fearlessly. With still another note several birds, including two crows, flew towards him, one of the crows nestling upon his shoulder. I remember it was the crow resting close to his head that made the most vivid impression upon me, knowing how fearful of man this bird is. He fed them all from his hand, taking food from his pocket, and petted them gently before our delighted gaze; and then dismissed them by different whistling, always

strange and low and short, each little wild thing departing instantly at hearing its special signal.

One would be tempted to dismiss this as the romantic reminiscence of an old man (his book was published when he was eighty-five), with the now famous *Walden* to color his memory, but the whole fabulous paragraph can be corroborated in Thoreau's own words. "I once had a sparrow alight upon my shoulder for a moment," he recalled of an occasion when he was hoeing in a village garden, "and I felt that I was more distinguished by that circumstance than I should have been by any epaulet I could have worn." (304) In the *Journal* for 1855 he gave a long account of catching a screech owl with his hands and taking it home for a day to study its habits: "I was surprised to find that I could imitate its note as I remember it, by a *guttural* whinnering." (J, VII, 521–525)

Among many such *Journal* notations, the most Pythagorean is his full report of an encounter with a woodchuck that he took by surprise one day in April 1852:

We sat looking at one another about half an hour, till we began to feel mesmeric influences. When I was tired, I moved away, wishing to see him run, but I could not start him. He would not stir as long as I was looking at him or could see him. I walked round him; he turned as fast and fronted me still. I sat down by his side within a foot. I talked to him *quasi* forest lingo, baby-talk, at any rate in a conciliatory tone, and thought that I had some influence on him. He gritted his teeth less. . . . With a little stick I lifted one of his paws to examine it, and held it up at pleasure. I turned him over to see what color he was beneath (darker or more purely brown), though he turned himself back again sooner than I could have wished. . . . I played with him tenderly awhile with the stick. . . . I spoke kindly to him. I reached checkerberry leaves to his mouth. I stretched my hands over him, though he turned his head and still gritted a little. I laid my hand on him, but immediately took it off again, instinct not being wholly overcome. If I had had a few fresh bean leaves, thus in advance of the season, I am sure I could have tamed him completely, . . . stroking him at my leisure.

. . . I respect him as one of the natives. He lies there, by his color and habits so naturalized amid the dry leaves, the withered grass, and the bushes. A sound nap, too, he has enjoyed in his native fields, the past winter. I think I might learn some wisdom of him. His ancestors have lived here longer than mine. He is more thoroughly acclimated and naturalized than I. (J, III, 421–423)

The *Journal* contained a greater wealth of material than such a highly selective book as *Walden* could make use of, though one wonders why such a fine anecdote as this one was omitted. (When he says the woodchuck is "more *thoroughly* naturalized than I" is he punning on his own name, so pronounced during his lifetime?) Perhaps it was because he had already used the woodchuck in "Higher Laws" as a symbol of wildness, arousing the savage instinct to "devour him raw." Perhaps it was because the two examples in the next chapter, "Brute Neighbors," of taming the mouse and the baby partridge, were enough to make his point. Having given them, he generalizes his method into a formula there: "You only need sit still long enough in some attractive spot in the woods that all its inhabitants may exhibit themselves to you by turns." (253)

Another device for penetrating to whatever meaning animals may have for man was to play off the scientific way of knowing nature against the poetic. With the cat, having been given a pair of "wings" she had shed, he describes them in the precise language of a zoologist, then speculates: "Some thought it was part flying squirrel or some other wild animal, which is not impossible, for, according to naturalists, prolific hybrids have been produced by the union of the marten and domestic cat." (258) As for the wild mice he says, "I sent one to a distinguished naturalist, and it interested him much" (the authority in this case being known, Professor Louis Agassiz of Harvard). The same technique is used on a more elaborate scale with the "partridge (*Tetrao umbellus*)." (250) Like a scientific Audubon he describes its appearance, calls, behavior, habitat, protective coloration—all in meticulous detail. Then, having approached with the stealth of an experienced woodsman to bring the chicks into close-range observation, he drops the role of naturalist for that of fabulist: "The remarkably adult yet innocent expression of their open and serene eyes is very memorable. All intelligence seems reflected in them. They suggest not merely the purity of infancy, but a wisdom clarified by experience." (251) The eyes are not windows through which he can see into the real meaning of the partridge. They "suggest" and "reflect"; they mirror qualities in the observer or at least qualities he is seeking, "purity" and "wisdom." Whether scientist or poet he can never know the reality "out there," only his perception of it, what he himself "creates." But he can draw on external nature as a reservoir of imagery. A *Journal* entry in 1853, as his great book was going through its final revision, points to the two chief functions of animals in "Brute Neighbors." If the writer is in close harmony with the natural world, fully alive and rich in experiences that demand expression, Thoreau declares, "all nature will *fable*, and every natural phenomenon be a myth." (J, V, 135)

The Battle of the Ants is the most celebrated fable in *Walden*. It is drawn out in great detail, and it has a lesson applicable to man such as one finds in Aesop and Veeshnoo-Sarma, though the moral is not hammered home as in the works of the classic fabulists. Here his basic technique for turning a commonplace incident in nature into an allegory of man is an ingenious pretense of using the laboratory method of science. It begins quite casually one day at his chopping block when he "observes" two ants locked in mortal combat on a wood chip, one red, one black and twice its size, and another red ant coming to the rescue. Taking the chip into his house, he puts it under a microscope for closer observation. In life he might well have used this instrument to study the ants' anatomy like an entomologist. But in his book it is used to magnify the combatants to human size. The gory details of their battle—"assiduously gnawing at the near fore leg of his enemy," his own breast "all torn away, exposing what vitals he had"—are merely grotesque in their violence until they take on Swiftian overtones. The eye witness continues:

They struggled half an hour longer . . . , and when I looked again the black soldier had severed the heads of his foes from their bodies, and the still living heads were hanging on either side of him like ghastly trophies at his saddle-bow, still apparently as firmly fastened as ever, and he was endeavoring with feeble struggles, being without feelers and with only the remnant of a leg, and I know not how many other wounds, to divest himself of them. (255, 256)

When the victor finally frees himself of his "spoils" and crawls away in crippled state, the fabulist comments: "I thought that his industry would not be worth much thereafter." (256) This gives a new twist to the biblical proverb, "Go to the ant, thou sluggard," industriousness being the last lesson Thoreau cared to draw from these tiny insects. The moral implication in *Walden* is the other way round. Man also is an animal, and the meaningless brutality of his own endless warfare is "fabled" in the battle of the ants.

The satire is heightened when the combatants are blown up into epic heroes by an allusion to Homer—one of the two notable additions Thoreau made to his *Journal* account of this anecdote when translating it into his book. At the chivalric crux of the battle, when the second red ant comes to the aid of the first, the commentator speculates whether he has already despatched his own foe "Or perchance he was some Achilles, who had nourished his wrath apart, and had now come to avenge or rescue his Patroclus." As attentive readers will remember, it was a passage from the *Iliad* about these same two heroes that the narrator in an earlier chapter had read aloud for the diversion of the Canadian woodchopper, himself described as "a true Homeric or Paphlagonian man." (159, 160) This brings into conjunction the animallike man and the menlike animals, and together they make the witty suggestion that the "heroic" archetype is man most closely assimilated to his "Brute Neighbors." Thus the mock epic dimension is added.

Having now firmly established the human allegory by magnifying glass and Homeric allusion, Thoreau can return to the larger battle raging outside at the chopping block. For the ants are not merely engaged in "a *duellum*, but a *bellum*." The small surrounding area, littered with chips, is expanded into a field where full-scale armies clash. "The legions of these Myrmidons covered all the hills and vales in my wood-yard, and the ground was already strewn with the dead and dying . . . the red republicans on the one hand, and the black imperialists on the other." (253) The allusive language here swings the comparison from Achilles' tribe in the Trojan War to the split American loyalties in the Mexican War, which was favored by the slave-holding South and opposed by liberals in the North. Other scattered references to Austerlitz and the Hôtel des Invalides extend the comparison to the Napoleonic Wars. A more detailed allusion brings it home to the Battle of Concord Bridge and the Revolutionary War: "And certainly there is not the fight recorded in Concord history, at least, if in the history of America, that will bear a moment's comparison with this, whether for the numbers engaged in it, or for the patriotism and heroism displayed." The front line reporter is sure the armies of these embattled ants "had their respective musical bands stationed on some eminent chip," could he only hear their stirring strains; and "I have no doubt that it was a principle they fought for, as much as our ancestors," were there only a way to find it out. (255)

If human battles were stripped of their martial fanfare and the rhetoric of war propaganda, the moral implies, they would be no different in violence from the battles of ants. This is what the modern fabulist makes us read between the lines: Go to the ant, thou brute; consider this neighbor's ways in warfare, and be wise to thy own. Aesop and Veeshnoo-Sarma took no chances when they had a lesson for man. They spelled it out. Thoreau made only one slip from implication to statement: "I was myself excited somewhat even as if they had been men. The more you think of it, the less the difference." (255) But his moral, confined to two sentences out of four pages, is much less insisted on than in the classic fables where it often occupies half the space.

The Battle of the Ants in "Brute Neighbors" is a satiric fable, fusing two kinds of "heroic" brutality to remind men of their animal heritage. But it concludes with a pretended appeal to science for validation. Kirby and Spence, the authorities cited, were authors of a four-volume compendium published in 1815 that served as a standard text on insects during the first half of the nineteenth century. But their scholarly tomes are passed over in favor of a more popular work which they issued during the period of the Walden residence. This single volume was limited to the "manners and economy" of insects, as having more interest for the general reader than the earlier technical volumes by these authors dealing with "the anatomy, physiology, orismology, &c. of the science." It was even written in "the epistolary form," because that admitted of disgressions and allusions, of a concern with style and imagination. In their accounts of battles among ants there are many parallels to the one in *Walden*, such as: "They will sooner be torn limb from limb than let go their hold; and after their battles, the head of a conquered enemy may often be seen suspended to the antennae or legs of the victor, a trophy of his valor." There is even one passage that may have given Thoreau the clue for turning his own battle of ants into a mock epic: "As the exploits of frogs and mice were the theme of Homer's muse, so, were I gifted like him, might I celebrate on this occasion the exhibition of Myrmidonian valor." Thoreau may also have been attracted by the authors' prefatory avowal of their prime object, "to direct the attention of their readers 'from nature up to nature's God,'" merely redefining their terms to suit himself.

The only actual reference to Kirby and Spence in "Brute Neighbors," however, is of a very different order. Its purpose is not to validate Thoreau's anecdote scientifically nor to give away his literary source. Instead, it cites a supporting anecdote to enhance his fable by proving that ants have served as human analogy since ancient times:

"Æneas Sylvius," say they, "after giving a very circumstantial account of [a battle of ants] contested with great obstinacy by a great and small species on the trunk of a pear tree," adds that " 'This action was fought in the pontificate of Eugenius the Fourth.' "

The medieval anecdote provides the model for Thoreau's own eloquent conclusion, four hundred years later: "The battle which I witnessed took place in the Presidency of Polk, five years before the passage of Webster's Fugitive-Slave Bill" (1850). None of this, neither the scientific flourish nor the historical one, is included in Thoreau's *Journal* account of a battle of the ants, for an obvious reason. Recorded as taking place on January 21, 1852, long after he had left the pond and returned to his family's house in Concord, it is only a partial source for the *Walden* anecdote.

The fictive dating as the fall of 1845 serves several important functions. It places the ant warfare in the first year of his residence at the pond and also at the outbreak of the Mexican War, which was involving contemporary Americans in meaningless violence according to Thoreau. He had made clear his own stand on that issue: by refusing to pay taxes to support a war that would extend the "slave empire," going to jail for it, and writing his most famous essay, "Civil Disobedience." In *Walden* this incident is touched on only in casual asides—here by the tags "black imperialists" and "red republicans." Also by using the Fugitive-Slave Bill of 1850 as the point of reference in dating his Battle of the Ants in "Brute Neighbors," he may be taking a side glance at another kind of brutality, slavery itself, that was to lead a decade later to the worst carnage in American history, the impending Civil War. Such extensions and revisions from *Journal* to book, the very techniques that make *Walden* what it is, are generalized into a theory of the creative process in an entry just a month later, 18 February 1852. If his facts can be "transmuted into the substance of the human mind," they can be turned into poetry. (J, III, 311) This is what he means by saying that "all nature will *fable*" for him.

Thus the longest episode in "Brute Neighbors," located at its center, reveals its chief mode as one suited to a modern bestiary, closer kin to the classic Oriental collection of Veeshnoo-Sarma than to the medieval Christian ones. The second longest, at the chapter's end, adds the dimension of myth. "In the fall the loon (*Colymbus glacialis*) came, as usual, to moult and bathe in the pond," it begins, "making the woods ring with his wild laughter." (258) ("Our moulting season, like that of the fowls," Thoreau says elsewhere, "must be a crisis in our lives.") (26) The arrival of sportsmen from town in pursuit of this rare quarry is announced in the same fabling language that had brought the Poet to the Hermit's cabin at the beginning of the chapter: "They come rustling through the woods like autumn leaves." That they are not exactly orthodox hunters is proved by their coming to see as well as to shoot the wild loon, bringing both spyglasses and guns. The hunt itself is only a mock one, carried off in the spirit of high comedy. For "no loon can be heard or seen," and the foiled sportsmen soon "beat a retreat to town and shop and unfinished jobs." The *Journal* passage recording such an actual foray into his woods, dated conjecturally 1845–1847, explains that the loon had already vanished "in that morning rain, with one loud, long, hearty laugh." (J, I, 422) In *Walden* this is translated into myth-making language: the October wind rises and the waves on the pond dash angrily, "taking sides with all waterfowl"; that is, nature helps her fabulous wild bird escape his pursuers. At this point the only *Journal* account of a loon's visit during the Walden residence breaks off.

The core of the anecdote in "Brute Neighbors," the loon chase by Thoreau alone, was not recorded in his *Journal* until 1852, years after he had left the pond. (J, IV, 379–81) This account is almost identical with the one in the book. The reason seems clear: it was a trial draft for *Walden*, which was undergoing revisions and extensions at this time. Hence the mythical tone is present in both versions, and it is quite possible that both are literary creations, whether or not based on an actual experience. As a poetic huntsman, who has sold his gun before coming to the woods, he goes in pursuit of the loon with boat and paddle "one very calm October afternoon." When this *Journal* extension (the private loon chase) was transcribed into the book, only one addition was needed. It is a brief passage to enhance the elusive nature of the pursued, as the pursuer seeks vainly to drive this wildlife into a corner for closer observation: "It was a pretty game, played on the smooth surface of the pond, a man against a loon. Suddenly your adversary's checker disappears beneath the board, and the problem is to place yours nearest to where his will appear again." (260) For the rest, *Journal* and book are almost identical.

The game is played out at considerable length and comprises the amusing part of the anecdote—but not its meaning, for the overall intent is far from comic. Throughout, the reader gradually becomes aware, this chase on the pond has the artless inconsequence and unfinished quality frequently found in myth. It does not really come to a conclusion. It simply drifts off at the end, with the loon "disappearing far away on the tumultuous surface." (262) On each of his escapes the elusive bird has mocked the hunter with "his wild laugh." Finally, "when he had balked me most successfully . . . he uttered a long-drawn unearthly howl." The narrator's comment seems merely a fitting end to a fruitless hunt: "I concluded that he laughed in derision of my efforts, confident of his own resources." (261) But an appended sentence gives the indisputable clue to a mythical interpretation:

> This was his looning,—perhaps the wildest sound that is ever heard here . . . as if calling on the god of loons to aid him, and immediately there came a wind from the east and rippled the surface, and filled the whole air with misty rain, and I was impressed as if it were the prayer of the loon answered, and his god was angry with me. (261, 262)

The sudden rising of "a wind from the east," a prayer to "the god of loons," and its answer in the coming of "a misty rain"—these phrases turn the narrative toward legend and send the critic from ornithology to birdlore in his search for meanings. The loon or great northern diver, even when divested of older mythical trappings, is even today considered an augur of rain among simple folk. In the centuries before *Walden* he was the center of a whole cluster of myths. To the Algonquin Indians (who inhabited the part of Canada Thoreau knew and who are cited by him in "Higher Laws") the loon was the messenger of their culture-hero Kuloscap, "The Master"; it was he who gave them their human-sounding cry so they could pray to him when they needed help. A modern authority, after recounting the sequel to this legend, whereby they became men, and yet another legend, in which a fisherman became a loon, remarks: "Once again folklore reveals the primitive mentality which makes no clear distinction between man and animals, and regards shape-changing as normal." In the widely diffused loon mythology, he adds, they are sometimes thought to escort the dead to the spirit world, conceived as lying beneath the waters:

> There are indications that this idea may have been overlaid by later notions concerning a heavenly world. In the Algonquin myth already mentioned the loons fly around and act as messengers for The Master. The Buriats believe that spirits often appear in the shape of divers [loons]. . . . Neither Buriats nor Yakuts will kill divers nor disturb their nests for fear of disaster befalling them. Among the Tungus the diver [is] sacred.

The relevance of all this to *Walden,* particularly to its central triad of chapters, is obvious—the kinship between men and animals, nature as a source of symbolic significance for human lives, even the loon as a possible heavenly messenger. It seems clear that Thoreau at this point made use of the myths and legends of American Indians as his final guide to fabled meanings in "Brute Neighbors." His life-long interest in this subject is common knowledge. Not so well known is his avid reading of all available records during the 1850's and his voluminous note-taking for an ambitious Indian book he did not live to write. In just what volume he may have found the Algonquin loon myth has not yet been discovered, but its pertinence to the anecdote under consideration is undeniable.

As always in his use of sources, Thoreau gives a new meaning to the loon's mythical character by putting the emphasis on his wildness, something entirely missing from the Indian legends. His "looning," it will be remembered, was "perhaps the wildest sound that is ever heard here." A sentence in the first version of this chapter (which was not included in the published book) reinforces this: "There is always a wild and yet a wilder life somewhere sustaining itself at any moment than we allow for—which corresponds to the rareness of some of our thoughts." This was probably dropped because it came too close to statement, but it makes an interesting gloss on "wildness," a theme that runs all through Thoreau's writing. The word in its several forms—wild, wilderness, wildness, and so on—recurs some seventy times in *Walden*, a luminous thread in its fabric. The concept itself functions significantly at three places in the book, most elaborately in this triad of chapters, but also near the beginning and near the end, as will be pointed out later on.

In the opening paragraph of "Higher Laws," after resisting the temptation to seize a woodchuck and devour him raw, Thoreau continues: "Once or twice, however, while I lived at the pond, I found myself ranging the woods, like a half-starved hound, with a strange abandonment, seeking some kind of venison which I might devour, and no morsel could have been too savage for me." (232) This passage was not added until the fifth version of *Walden*, in 1853. But an even more extravagant expression of the same pose can be found in a letter a dozen years earlier, written to Emerson's sister-in-law:

> I grow savager and savager every day, as if fed on raw meat, and my tameness is only the repose of untamableness. I dream of looking abroad summer and winter, with free gaze, from some mountain-side, while my eyes revolve in an Egyptian slime of health,—I to be nature looking into nature with such easy sympathy as the blue-eyed grass in the meadow looks in the face of the sky. From some such recess I would put forth sublime thoughts daily, as the plant puts forth leaves.

Such passages taken literally would seem to be sheer nonsense. Yet Thoreau's woodland life seemed wild enough to his more staid fellow townsmen. About 1845, Emerson commented in his journal: "Henry Thoreau is like the wood-god who solicits the wandering poet and draws him into antres vast and desarts wild, and bereaves him of his memory, and leaves him naked, plaiting vines and with twigs in his hand." And Alcott, after a visit to

Walden cabin in the winter of 1847, recorded of his young friend: "The ruddiest and nimblest genius that has trodden our woods, he comes amidst mists and exhalations, his locks dripping with moisture." But the quality of wildness in Thoreau's life is of less interest than its use as a symbol in his writings. Since it is a clue to meaning, possibly of great import, it must be followed out by an exploration of the *Journal*, the essays, and the lesser books.

The Tonic of Wildness

In "Winter Animals" (Chapter 15), to begin with the actual state of wildness around Concord, Thoreau speaks with nostalgia of former times when bear, moose, deer, wildcats abounded in the township. Of the animals that still thrive there, he adds: "It is hardly as if you had seen a wild creature when a rabbit or a partridge bursts away, only a natural one." (308–309, 310) This lament is elaborated in a *Journal* passage two years after *Walden* was completed:

> I spend a considerable portion of my time observing the habits of the wild animals, my brute neighbors. By their various movements and migrations they fetch the year about to me. . . . But when I consider that the nobler animals have been exterminated here,—the cougar, panther, lynx, wolverene, wolf, bear, moose, deer, the beaver, the turkey, etc., etc.,—I cannot but feel as if I lived in a tamed and, as it were, emasculated country. Would not the motions of those larger and wilder animals have been more significant still? . . . I am reminded that this my life in nature, this particular round of natural phenomena which I call a year, is lamentably incomplete. (J, VIII, 220–221)

So it is not surprising when news comes that a lynx has been killed in nearby Carlisle, in 1860, to find Thoreau one of the first on the scene. He scrutinizes and measures, then describes it in his *Journal* in great detail, citing scientific authorities for the purpose of classification. Most interesting of all is his quickness to claim it as local, not a straggler from the far north:

It is remarkable how slow people are to believe that there are *any* wild animals in their neighborhood. . . .

While the man that killed my lynx (and many others) thinks it came out of a menagerie, and the naturalists call it the Canada lynx, and at the White Mountains they call it the Siberian lynx, —in each case forgetting, or ignoring, that it belongs here,—I call it the Concord Lynx. (J, XIV, 85, 142)

But he admits that it is "very rare hereabouts."

Foxes, on the other hand, were still fairly common around Concord. Raiders on the periphery of civilization, they were the most accessible form of wildlife in Massachusetts and had become a favorite quarry for huntsmen. On one occasion Thoreau gave chase alone, without benefit of hounds, and recorded it in his *Journal*, 30 January 1851. The anecdote is remarkable enough to deserve quotation in full:

Suddenly, looking down the river, I saw a fox some sixty rods off, making across to the hills on my left. As the snow lay five inches deep, he made but slow progress, but it was no impediment to me. So, yielding to the instinct of the chase, I tossed my head aloft and bounded away, snuffing the air like a fox-hound, and spurning the world and the Humane Society at each bound. It seemed the woods rang with the hunter's horn, and Diana and all the satyrs joined in the chase and cheered me on. Olympian and Elean youths were waving palms on the hills. In the meanwhile I gained rapidly on the fox; but he showed a remarkable presence of mind, for, instead of keeping up the face of the hill, which was steep and unwooded in that part, he kept along the slope in the direction of the forest, though he lost ground by it. Notwithstanding his fright, he took no step which was not beautiful. The course on his part was a series of most graceful curves. It was a sort of leopard canter, I should say, as if he were nowise impeded by the snow, but were husbanding his strength all the while. When he doubled I wheeled and cut him off, bounding with fresh vigor, and Antaeus-like recovering my strength each time I touched the snow. Having got near enough for a fair view, just as he was slipping into the wood, I gracefully yielded him the palm. He ran as though there were not a bone in his back, occasionally dropping his muzzle to the snow for a rod or two, and then tossing his head aloft when satisfied of his course. When he came to a declivity he put his fore feet together and slid down it like a cat. He trod so softly that you could not have heard it from any nearness, and yet with such expression that it would not have been quite inaudible at any distance. So, hoping this experience would prove a useful lesson to him, I returned to the village by the highway of the river. (J, I, 186–187)

By identifying himself with the fox instead of with the hunter, Thoreau links himself with the wild. This is just a means to an end. For the spiritual is present also in the "Elean youths waving palms." Elea was the seat of a Greek school of philosophy that taught the universal unity of being, that the All is One.

Knowing that only a "maimed and imperfect nature" was available to him in the civilized world of Concord, he was constantly yearning for something more primitive. "I would like to go into perfectly new and wild country," he writes in the *Journal* for 1852: "I wish to lose myself amid reeds and sedges and wild grasses that have not been touched." (J, IV, 329) This was a chief motive for two of his longest journeys from home, one taken during the Walden residence, the other while the book was being finished. In *Cape Cod* he records the wildness and brutal violence of the ocean:

The seashore is a sort of neutral ground, a most advantageous point from which to contemplate this world. . . .

It is a wild, rank place, and there is no flattery in it. Strewn with . . . whatever the sea casts up,—a vast *morgue,* where famished dogs may range in packs, and crows come daily to glean the pittance which the tide leaves them. The carcasses of men and beasts together lie stately up upon its shelf, rotting and bleaching in the sun and waves, and each tide turns them in their beds, and tucks fresh sand under them. There is naked Nature,—inhumanly sincere, wasting no thought on man, nibbling at the cliffy shore where gulls wheel amid the spray. (IV, 186–187)

If this effectively separates Thoreau from the Victorian tendency to sentimentalize nature, how much more so his descriptions of the *Maine Woods*. Finding himself buried in a wholly uninhabited wilderness, stretching off to Canada on either hand, he says that here one "must front the true source of evil," since there is no society nor institutions to blame it on.

On top of Mount Katahdin, Thoreau being probably the fifth man ever to have reached it, he finds the epitome of wildness:

> It is difficult to conceive of a region uninhabited by man. We habitually presume his presence and influence everywhere. And yet we have not seen pure Nature, unless we have seen her thus vast and drear and inhuman. . . . *Nature* was here something savage and awful, though beautiful. . . . This was that Earth of which we have heard, made out of Chaos and Old Night. Here was no man's garden, but the unhandseled globe. It was not lawn, nor pasture, nor mead, nor woodland, nor lea, nor arable, nor waste land. It was the fresh and natural surface of the planet Earth, as it was made forever and ever,—to be the dwelling of man, we say,—so Nature made it, and man may use it if he can. Man was not to be associated with it. It was Matter, vast, terrific,—not his Mother Earth that we have heard of. . . . It was a place for heathenism and superstitious rites,—to be inhabited by men nearer of kin to the rocks and to wild animals than we.

The sheer materiality of the natural world in this remote place fills him with awe and, for the moment, makes his own physical body seem strange to him. "Talk of mysteries!" he exclaims: "Think of our life in nature,—daily to be shown matter, to come in contact with it,—rocks, trees, wind on our cheeks! the *solid* earth! the *actual* world! the *common sense! Contact! Contact! Who* are we? *where* are we?" (III, 79) This is not melodramatic if read symbolically: the astonished Self confronting the unconscious Wild. A terror inspired by wild beasts would have been far less effective.

Such was his response to the Maine wilderness during a trip in 1846, leaving Walden cabin on August 31 and returning several weeks later. On that occasion the emphasis was on mountain climbing, boating on lakes and rivers, tasting the "quality" of wildness. On his second trip, seven years later, the emphasis is on hunting and the life of loggers and pioneers. His reaction to this experience is ambivalent:

I think that I could spend a year in the woods, fishing and hunting just enough to sustain myself, with satisfaction. This would be next to living like a philosopher on the fruits of the earth which you had raised, which also attracts me. But this hunting of the moose merely for the satisfaction of killing him,—not even for the sake of his hide,—without making any extraordinary exertion or running any risk yourself, is too much like going out by night to some wood-side pasture and shooting your neighbor's horses. . . . What a coarse and imperfect use Indians and hunters make of nature! (III, 132–33)

Frontiersmen are just as bad, he adds, exploiting and laying waste the wilderness for profit. It is the poet who makes the truest use of nature, preserving its life rather than destroying it.

This second journey into the *Maine Woods* led Thoreau to revise his attitude toward wildness as an actual state of being. Returning to Concord, he writes an epilogue to his essay:

Nevertheless, it was a relief to get back to our smooth but still varied landscape. For a permanent residence, it seemed to me that there could be no comparison between this and the wilderness, necessary as the latter is for a resource and a background, the raw material of all our civilization. The wilderness is simple, almost to barrenness. The partially cultivated country it is which chiefly has inspired, and will continue to inspire, the strains of poets, such as compose the mass of any literature. Our woods are sylvan, and their inhabitants woodmen and rustics; that is *selvaggia*, and the inhabitants are *salvages*. . . . The poet's, commonly, is not a logger's path, but a woodman's. The logger and pioneer have preceded him, like John the Baptist; eaten the wild honey, it may be, but the locusts also; banished decaying wood and the spongy mosses which feed on it, and built hearths and humanized Nature for him. . . .

But for beauty, the poet must, from time to time, travel the logger's path and the Indian's trail, to drink at some new and more bracing fountain of the Muses, far in the recesses of the wilderness. (III, 171–173)

It is this modified concept of the wild, symbolic instead of literal, that found its way into *Walden*. "We need the *tonic* of wildness"—a typical expression of the new attitude—was added in this very year of 1853 as the conclusion to his chapter on the rank new life of "Spring."

For the poet there is little need of far journeys to take him to what is essentially an interior world. From an early date the *Journal* is filled with reminders that "to see wild life" one simply fares forth "at a wild season," and that the student by wandering only a few steps from his study will find himself in a place "unaccountably strange and wild." (J, II, 375; III, 444) After several excursions with Ellery Channing, he plots out four great uninhabited tracts near Concord, one being Walden woods, that make "a paradise for walkers." (J, V, 239–240) After one such walk, just a few miles from home, his *Journal* commentary is so pertinent to the present inquiry as to demand full quotation:

I seemed to have reached a new world, so wild a place that the very huckleberries grew hairy and were inedible. . . . What's the need of visiting far-off mountains and bogs, if a half-hour's walk will carry me into such wildness and novelty? . . .

I see that all is not garden and cultivated field and crops, that there are square rods in Middlesex County as purely primitive and wild as they were a thousand years ago, which have escaped the plow and the axe and the scythe and the cranberry-rake, little oases of wildness in the desert of our civilization, wild as a square rod on the moon, supposing it to be uninhabited. I believe almost in the personality of such planetary matter, feel something akin to reverence for it, can even worship it as terrene, titanic matter extant in my day. . . . I would fain improve every opportunity to wonder and worship, as a sunflower welcomes the light. The more thrilling, wonderful, divine objects I behold in a day, the more expanded and immortal I become. (J, IX, 42, 44–46)

The relation of this to the description of Mount Katahdin in Maine is clear, even to the parallel phrasing. The chief difference is that what inspired a terrified awe in that distant wilderness creates a feeling of reverence and kinship near at home. Or, rather, the difference is that the former was actual wildness, the latter imagined. The interior quality of what he is seeking is made explicit in this same *Journal* passage: "It is in vain to dream of a wildness distant from ourselves. There is none such. It is the bog in our brain and bowels, the primitive vigor of Nature in us, that inspires that dream. I shall never find in the wilds of Labrador any greater wildness than in some recess in Concord, *i.e.* than I import into it." (J, IX, 43)

Much of Thoreau's exploration of the idea of wildness was brought to focus in a composition which he gave as a lecture now and again throughout the 1850's, then shortly before his death prepared for publication as one of his longest and best essays. Its title is "Walking," but the subject is wildness. By the extravagance of his language he makes the idea dramatic. By putting it in a traditional context he makes it poetically credible. "I wish to speak a word for Nature, for absolute freedom and wildness, as contrasted with a freedom and culture merely civil," he begins in the bold introductory paragraph: "I wish to make an extreme statement, if so I may make an emphatic one, for there are enough champions of civilization." (V, 205) Wildness is to serve as a counterweight to tameness, he says, a yearning for the fresh and untried so as to escape from the stale and conventional. The poet is drawn toward it but by the very definition of what he is—a cultivated rather than a natural man—he can never become one with it:

Here is this vast, savage, howling mother of ours, Nature, lying all around, with such beauty, and such affection for her children, as the leopard; and yet we are so early weaned from her breast to society. . . .

For my part, I feel that with regard to Nature I live a sort of border life, on the confines of a world into which I make occasional and transient forays only, and my patriotism and allegiance to the state into whose territories I seem to retreat are those of a moss-trooper. (V, 237, 242)

He uses another metaphor to make the same point in another late essay, "Wild Apples," saying they are "wild only like myself," having "strayed into the woods from the cultivated stock." (V, 301)

Besides the traditional context of primitive versus civilized, Thoreau puts the yearning for wildness in another and more provocative perspective in "Walking." It symbolizes the search for a native American "way" in preference to the old European one:

When I go out of the house for a walk, uncertain as yet whither I will bend my steps, and submit myself to my instinct to decide for me, I find, strange and whimsical as it may seem, that I finally and inevitably settle southwest. . . . It is hard for me to believe that I shall find fair landscapes or sufficient wildness and freedom behind the eastern horizon. . . . I must walk toward Oregon, and not toward Europe. . . .

The West of which I speak is but another name for the Wild; and what I have been preparing to say is, that in Wildness is the preservation of the World. . . . From the forest and wilderness come the tonics and barks which brace mankind. . . . Give me a wildness whose glance no civilization can endure,—as if we lived on the marrow of koodoos devoured raw. (V, 217–18, 224–25)

The call for an original American literature, free from European imitation, had been repeated tiresomely throughout the nineteenth century. Thoreau avoided the patriotic motif and found a new meaning by rendering this appeal for originality in the imagery of wildness. "In literature it is only the wild that attracts us," he says five pages further on, translating his metaphor: "Dullness is but another name for tameness." The trouble with English literature is that it "breathes no quite fresh and, in this sense, wild strain." The qualities set forth above were the very ones that Europe first deplored, then came to admire, in one of the mainstreams of American literature, from Melville to Faulkner. Wildness in this sense is what gives distinction to *Walden* also: a style as tangy as the wild huckleberry, a subject matter that could have sprung only from American soil.

Wildness, then, must be reckoned as a poetic aspect of Thoreau's writing rather than a literal aspect of his world. If we bear in mind his boast that he could find no greater wildness in Labrador than in some "recess" in Concord, "*i.e.* than I *import into it*," it will be instructive to point out some images of the wild he "created" from what he saw in the environs of his village, then gave them a local habitation there. Of a walk along the Mill Brook just beyond Emerson's place one January day, he records:

> I hear faintly the cawing of a crow far, far away. . . . It mingles with the slight murmur of the village, the sound of children at play, as one stream empties gently into another, and the wild and tame are one. What a delicious sound! It is not merely crow calling to crow, for it speaks to me too. I am part of one great creature with him; if he has voice, I have ears. . . . Ah, bless the Lord, O my soul! bless him for wildness, for crows that will not alight within gunshot! and bless him for hens, too, that croak and cackle in the yard! (J, VII, 112-13)

The crow serves well enough as a representative of the "border life" between the wild and the tame, shunning man yet a plague to the farmer. But it has long been customary to treat this bird humorously, so here the incident is given a light rather than a serious turn.

To Thoreau the hawk, of all the creatures inhabiting his world, was the perfect symbol of wildness and freedom. This soaring bird appears again and again in his writings, always with the same signification and frequently as an image of the poet, with which he identifies. One of the most interesting accounts is a long *Journal* passage in June 1853. It begins with his stealthy approach:

> Visited my nighthawk on her nest. Could hardly believe my eyes when I stood within seven feet and beheld her sitting on her eggs,

her head to me. She looked so Saturnian, so one with the earth, so sphinx-like, a relic of the reign of Saturn which Jupiter did not destroy, a riddle that might well cause a man to go dash his head against a stone. It was not an actual living creature, far less a winged creature of the air, but a figure in stone or bronze, a fanciful production of art, like the gryphon or phoenix. . . . It was enough to fill one with awe. (J, V, 230–31)

When he reports his discovery in the village, the immediate reaction of his neighbors is to take a rifle and go after it. They would not hesitate to kill a hen-hawk, now "so rare in the landscape," just to save a few of their hens, he mocks. But this is a "narrow and grovelling" economy, sacrificing the greater value to the less. "I would rather never taste chickens' meat nor hens' eggs than never to see a hawk sailing through the upper air again," he winds up: "This sight is worth incomparably more than a chicken soup or a boiled egg." (J, V, 246)

When he returns to the hawk six years later, he drops both the anecdotal and the satirical modes and gives us a poem in prose, highly pertinent to the present inquiry:

The hen-hawk and the pine are friends. The same thing which keeps the hen-hawk in the woods, away from the cities, keeps me here. That bird settles with confidence on a white pine top and not upon your weathercock. That bird will not be poultry of yours, lays no eggs for you, forever hides its nest. Though willed, or *wild*, it is not willful in its wildness. The unsympathizing man regards the wildness of some animals, their strangeness to him, as a sin; as if all their virtue consisted in their tamableness. He has always a charge in his gun ready for their extermination. What we call wildness is a civilization other than our own. The hen-hawk shuns the farmer, but it seeks the friendly shelter and support of the pine. It will not consent to walk in the barn-yard, but it loves to soar above the clouds. It has its own way and is beautiful, when we would fain subject it to our will. So any surpassing work of art is strange and wild to the mass of men, as is genius itself. No hawk that soars and steals our poultry is wilder than genius, and none is more persecuted or above persecution. It can never be poet laureate, to say "Pretty Poll" and "Polly want a cracker." (J, XI, 450–51)

This passage is as intricate a structure of wit and metaphor as the best in *Walden,* where it might well have been used if created in time. For readers of Thoreau, at any rate, it adds a new dimension to their understanding of wildness and of the kind of book he intended: free and soaring, strange in its difference from the tame and the known. The punning etymology of wild as willed, tucked in as an added surprise, he extends elsewhere by citing Richard Chenevix Trench, a poetically-minded linguist of the day:

> Trench says a wild man is a *willed* man. Well, then, a man of will who does what he wills or wishes, a man of hope and of the future tense. . . . The perseverance of the saints is positive willedness, not a mere passive willingness. The fates are wild, for they *will*; and the Almighty is wild above all, as fate is. (J, IV, 482)

Here he begins with a new self-portrait and ends with a new definition of God, linking the two in wildness.

If the hawk is a symbol for the poet so is the thrush, in a complementary sense. In one, wildness stands for the freedom of genius, in the other for untamed lyric beauty. Among nearly three-score references to the thrush in his *Journal,* several are particularly relevant:

> All that was ripest and fairest in the wilderness and the wild man is preserved and transmitted to us in the strain of the wood thrush. It is the mediator between barbarism and civilization. . . . This is the only bird whose note affects me like music, affects the flow and tenor of my thought, my fancy and imagination. . . . The thrush alone declares the immortal wealth and vigor that is in the forest. Here is a bird in whose strain the story is told, though Nature waited for the science of aesthetics to discover it to man. Whenever a man hears it, he is young, and Nature is in her spring. Whenever he hears it, it is a new world and a free country, and the gates of heaven are not shut against him. (J, V, 292–93; IV, 190)

Here is the generalized idea of the wild beauty of the singer, to fit any poet.

There are other aspects of the thrush that make it specifically suitable to Thoreau. He is convinced that there is no such "unexplored wildness" in the nightingale, a bird which he had never heard but which he knew as emblematic of the Romantic poet, as in Keats' great ode. His preference for the thrush implies something far beyond mere bird song. "I doubt if they have anything so richly wild in Europe," he declares: "It will only be heard in America, perchance, while our star is in the ascendant. ... Why, then, was I born in America? I might ask." (J, IV, 263) He answers his own question, in a later *Journal* entry, that he also is to sing just such a new native song. The American thrush is not only remote from Europe but remote from its own cities, whose culture is still too derivative of the Old World. There can be little doubt that Thoreau has himself in mind when he writes: "The true poet will ever live aloof from society, wild to it, as the finest singer is the wood thrush, a forest bird." (J, VI, 257)

The thrush makes its appearance several times in *Walden*, once significantly in connection with the tanager. Listing the advantages of where he had chosen to live, an airy cabin in the woods above the pond, he says he has caged himself nearer to the birds, especially "those wilder and more thrilling songsters of the forest which never, or rarely, serenade a villager,—the wood thrush, ... the scarlet tanager." (95) This links the wilderness beauty of color to that of sound. The two in combination make a memorable passage in the *Journal* on a May evening in 1853:

At Loring's Wood heard and saw a tanager. That contrast of a *red* bird with the green pines and the blue sky! Even when I have heard his note and look for him and find the bloody fellow, sitting on a dead twig of a pine, I am always startled. ... That incredible red, with the green and blue, as if these were the trinity we wanted. ... I am transported; these are not the woods I ordinarily walk in. He sunk Concord in his thought. How he enhances the wildness and wealth of the woods! ... I have passed the Rubicon of staying out. I have said to myself, that way is not homeward; I will wander further from what I have called my home—to the home which is forever inviting me. In such an hour the freedom of the woods is offered me, and the birds sing my dispensation. (J, V, 187)

This is indeed an artist's paradise: his gods a trinity of colors, bird songs his dispensation. It is a new religion, a re-ordering of the world under the divine authority of the poet.

Two more *Journal* passages complete Thoreau's symbolic heightening of wildness. One takes off from the tanager:

> We soon get through with Nature. She excites an expectation which she cannot satisfy. The merest child which has rambled into a copeswood dreams of a wilderness so wild and strange and inexhaustible as Nature can never show him. The red-bird which I saw on my companion's string . . . I thought but the outmost sentinel of the wild, immortal camp,—of the wild and dazzling infantry of the wilderness,—that the deeper woods abounded with redder birds still; but, now that I have threaded all our woods and waded the swamps, I have never yet met with his compeer, still less his wilder kindred. The red-bird which is the last of Nature is but the first of God. . . . I expected a fauna more infinite and various, birds of more dazzling colors and more celestial song. (J, VI, 293–94)

There is a similar passage in the *Week*, about a red-bird on his companion's string exciting hopes that he might find one in the solitude of the forest "stranger and more dazzling" yet. It is followed by a sentence that translates one meaning of his symbol: "Still less have I seen such strong and wilderness tints on any poet's string." (I, 56–57)

The second *Journal* passage begins with Thoreau's actual discovery of wildness in the form of a new species of bream in Walden Pond, previously unknown in spite of two centuries of fishermen there. At first he attempts to find its proper classification, saying tentatively, "Where the *Pomotis obesus* swims must be a new country, unexplored by science." (J, XI, 350) But as he commented elsewhere, the scientific term never gives us the thing itself, being only a confession of our larger ignorance: "Natural objects and phenomena are in this sense forever wild and unnamed by us." (J, XIII, 141) His interest now is far from that of the scientist:

> I cannot but see still in my mind's eye those little striped breams poised in Walden's glaucous water. They balance all the rest of the world in my estimation at present, for this is the bream that I have just found. . . . How wild it makes the pond and the township to find a new fish in it! America renews her youth here. But in my account of this bream I cannot go to a hair's breadth beyond the mere statement that it exists,—the miracle of its existence, my contemporary and neighbor, yet so different from me! I can only poise my thought there by its side and try to think like a bream for a moment. . . . I only see the bream in its orbit, as I see a star, but I care not to measure its distance or weight. The bream, appreciated, floats in the pond as the centre of the system, another image of God. (J, XI, 358–59)

In his *Journal* and in his lesser writings, on occasions, Thoreau could be as transcendental as Emerson. Extravagances of this particular sort are kept in strict control by the creator of *Walden*, and that is one of the reasons it does not seem dated today. There too nature "must be overcome," but not by treating it as something one can "put his foot through"—as a veil he can penetrate and see God.

To return now to the myth at the end of "Brute Neighbors," where the wildest of all birds disappears over the horizon, eluding the grasp of the poetic hunter. Was the loon's god angry with him for trying to go beyond mortal bounds, and so answered its prayer? It is only in this faint way that Thoreau's masterpiece echoes the transcendentalism of the *Journal:* the bream floating in the pond "as the centre of the system, another image of God"; the red-bird "which is the last of nature [and] the first of God." These glosses extend the possible implications of the loon chase and the meaning of wildness. But in the strict terms of *Walden* this episode merely dramatizes nature at its most elusive. The reason the loon's god is angry is that the hunter was trying to bring it to quarry, by outwitting its elusiveness. If man tries to make game of nature, whether as hunter or fisher, he will come back empty-handed or at best with a biological specimen. Thoreau, however, was not hunting the substance of the loon, either as a stuffed bird for his collection or as a dish for his dinner, but was seeking its essence—its wildness. This was even more elusive. But in establishing communion with his brute neighbors the poetic hunter has made great strides. He has observed tame animals running wild, like the cat; he has succeeded in domesticating some of the shyest, like the partridge; ants have been metamorphosed into Homeric heroes. Yet the loon, ultimate symbol of the wild, mocks and escapes him. He can have only "a yearning toward all wildness" to balance his unattainable yearning for holiness and heaven, then find his human way in between.

To recapitulate, this is the real quest of the central triad of chapters. Thoreau was too skillful an architect to construct his pyramid out of three discrete and repellant blocks of material. Instead, they were subtly articulated. The boggy field of "Baker Farm" was framed by images of soaring. The ascent to "Higher Laws" took its long start from the primitive level of fishing and hunting. The descent to "Brute Neighbors" began with a dialogue that gently mocked his recent attempt to rise to spiritual heights. And the rainbow threw its aspiring arch over all three chapters, just as wildness ran along the earth throughout—from the self-exhortation, "Grow wild according to thy nature," to its celebration in hunter and fisher, and its final proper embodiment in the animals of his bestiary. So the separate elements of his structure were not only interrelated but meshed into a unit. And the dialectical pattern implicit in each chapter became explicit in the whole triad. Thoreau's fluctuations between two poles was not a meaningless wavering. He knew that the reality he sought lay in a proper balance between each of the pairs of dualities that make up the tensions of *Walden*. In these chapters it has been shown to be a balance between the savage world and the spiritual, between earth and heaven, wildness and virtue. The same quest is continued through the rest of the book.

7

Circles

The open sesame to *Walden* is a single magical word, "circle." For Thoreau it is a major symbol and one of great complexity. It stands first and most obviously for the daily and annual cycles, which will be discussed in great detail shortly. One quotation from the *Journal* that links the largest image with the greatest speed seems appropriate now: "As the planet in its orbit and around its axis, so do the seasons, so does time, revolve, with a rapidity inconceivable." (J, IV, 350) More unusual is the literary use to which he puts the illusion of roundness with which the world is pictured to the human eye, the circular horizon with its dome above and man as the ever-moving center of the spectacle. In one of his earliest notebooks Thoreau transcribed from Lavater, the German poet and physiognomist, an extension of this idea that was especially attractive to transcendentalists: "As in looking upward each beholder thinks himself the centre of the sky; so Nature formed her individuals, that each must see himself the centre of being." He used it in *A Week* with something of this suggested meaning. "The universe is a sphere whose centre is wherever there is intelligence," he says: "The sun is not so central as man." (I, 373)

Thoreau always tied the transcendent idea to the observed reality, however. In his constant concern in the *Journal* with problems of perception, he returns again and again to this particular phenomenon, stressing its illusory quality. "I am always struck by the centrality of the observer's position," he records in 1851, for example: "He always stands fronting the middle of the arch, and does not suspect at first that a thousand observers on a thousand hills behold the sunset sky from equally favorable positions." (J, II, 296) It is in this sense that it is put to use in *Walden*, with a touch of wit. Speaking of the farms he considered buying, so that he might have "a *sedes*, a seat" in the country, he says: "Wherever I sat, there I might live, and the landscape radiated from me accordingly." (90)

On one occasion his comment indicates his awareness of the psychological illusion that explains this: the horizon appears round because the eye sees to the same maximum distance in all directions; then the mind transforms the shapeless sky into a dome to fit this "circular" horizon. As he puts it in *A Week:*

Let us wander where we will, the universe is built round about us, and we are central still. If we look into the heavens they are concave, and if we were to look into a gulf as bottomless, it would be concave also. The sky is curved downward to the earth in the horizon, because we stand on the plain. *I draw down its skirts.* (I, 353; my italics)

The only problem for the poet was how to turn these phenomena into images that would carry his meaning. One way was to emulate the processes and patterns of nature. A *Journal* passage in 1842, possibly inspired by Walden Pond, is pertinent at this point:

Pond.—Nature is constantly original and inventing new patterns, like a mechanic in his shop. . . . All things, indeed, are subjected to a rotary motion, either gradual and partial or rapid and complete, from the planet and system to the simplest shellfish and pebbles on the beach; as if all beauty resulted from an object turning on its own axis, or others turning about it. It establishes a new centre in the universe. As all curves have reference to their centres or foci, so all beauty of character has reference to the soul, and is a graceful gesture of recognition or waving of the body toward it. (J, I, 332)

Orbs, spheres, circular paths and flights, daily and seasonal cycles, orbiting stars and ripples on water—all these form an important part of Thoreau's subject matter and provide him with another way of looking at the world. The imagery ranges from insects to the cosmos and is applied to a great variety of things: animals, plants, ponds, sights, sounds, people. The very structure of his book is circular, almost a Ptolemaic system of cycles and epicycles, and this complicates the critic's task. Books that are linear in structure, like history and biography, have a beginning-middle-end so that their forms do not complicate the problem of understanding their meanings. Of course, in one sense the casual reader will also go straight through *Walden* from beginning to end, getting what understanding he can out of its sequence of chapters. But the close reader, aware of its intricate patterning, will want to go beyond subject matter and follow out some of the interrelations of its themes, which are often suggested by the chapter titles themselves. He will set "The Pond in Winter" (chapter 16) against the central "Ponds" (chapter 9); tie in the later "Winter Visitors" and "Winter Animals" (chapters 14 and 15) with the summer "Visitors" and "Brute Neighbors" (chapters 6 and 12); and look for more than mere sequence in the progress from house-building in spring (chapter 1) to "House-Warming" in autumn (chapter 13). Finally, the critic, if convinced that *Walden* is a poem, will find himself seeking its meanings through the same circuitous routes used by Thoreau for rendering his quest—through the interweaving of key symbols, such as "wildness" and "circles."

Circle Images

The first elaborate use of a circle as symbol, in the early chapter "Sounds," relates it significantly to the theme of wildness. At the very beginning of his story, speaking of the "clearing" he made in Walden woods for the site of his cabin, Thoreau comments on the "deficiency of domestic sounds" there—like those of the churn, the spinning wheel, and the singing kettle. More to the point there was no cat nor dog, no cow nor pig, in his woodland world; not even rats in the wall of his house: "No cockerels to crow nor hens to cackle in the yard. No yard! but unfenced nature reaching up to your very sills . . . and no path to the civilized world." (141–142) Such is the symbolic wilderness he has withdrawn to—a mile and a half from town.

In Concord men live on small square lots "fenced . . . and reclaimed from Nature," with a path leading from house to street and thence to the town center. At Walden, Thoreau's circular clearing touches at all points a "vast range and circuit . . . of unfrequented forest," and he is drawn not to any center of civilization but to an exploration of his private wilderness on the circumference. (144) His companions are only wild creatures, he says: shy woodland birds, the fox and woodchuck, the otter and skunk, "a flock of wild geese or a laughing loon on the pond." (142) There, during the early weeks of adjustment to his solitary life in the woods, he tells what made him feel that the near neighborhood of man was not essential: "I was so distinctly made aware of the presence of something kindred to me, even in scenes which we are accustomed to call wild and dreary, and also that the nearest of blood to me and humanest was not a person or a villager." (146) He who is learning to grow wild according to his own nature finds his proper society in such a solitude.

In addition to the double circle described above—the hermit's clearing surrounded by the unspoiled woods—his association with its inhabitants leads to other circles of much subtler significance. In a *Journal* passage about observing the habits of wild animals (quoted in the long section on wildness in the preceding chapter) Thoreau gave as its reason for his careful study: "By their various movements and migrations they fetch the year about to me." In another *Journal* entry, referring to the migration and hibernation of animals, their seasons of mating and moulting,he declares:

> God did not make this world in jest; no, nor in indifference. . . . I love the birds and beasts because they are mythologically in earnest. I see that the sparrow cheeps and flits and sings adequately to the great design of the universe; that man does not communicate with it, understand its language, because he is not at one with nature. (J, III, 368)

Perhaps, instead of pursuing nature by the direct approach, he could become at one with it and communicate with its wild creatures better by putting himself in harmony with their motions. This is the directive in two other *Journal* passages written during the same year in which the loon chase was recorded, 1852. Instead of catching the loon, he urges himself: "Catch the pace of the seasons. . . . Let your life be a leisurely progress through the realms of nature." (J, III, 182) Again, a few months later, he asks himself: "What are threescore years and ten hurriedly and coarsely lived to moments of divine leisure in which your life is coincident with the life of the universe?" (J, IV, 433)

A life coincident with that of the universe would be circular. But man's life seems inescapably a straight line from beginning to end, a pilgrimage from cradle to grave as the proverb has it, and thought of in these terms he is trapped in his own mortality. Thoreau seems to be asking: How can he shape his life into a circular pattern? The way most obviously available in *Walden* is the one that encompasses its whole narrative, the annual cycle of the seasons. But first a glance at some small circular patterns on the earth itself. The most charming but least seriously intended are the movements of animals and birds in numerous passages scattered throughout the book, always with the same significance. When they are in motion about a center that Thoreau occupies, literally or figuratively, they are "communicating." In straight flight they are silent. In his first mention of birds he says explicitly, they "sang around or flitted noiseless." (124) The question of scientific accuracy is irrelevant here, and in the examples given in the ensuing pages, since all are for metaphorical or humorous purposes.

For those who think of Thoreau as a transcendentalist of high seriousness, it is salutary to recall that two of his "communions" with the animal world, achieved by slipping into their orbits, are presented in the vein of farce and ribald satire. On one occasion he likens the dismal screams of owls to Ben Jonson's midnight hags, to fallen souls, to "suicide lovers remembering the pangs and delights of supernal love in the infernal groves." When other birds are silent, their wailing serenades him from the dark forest around his clearing: "*Oh-o-o-o-o that I had never been bor-r-r-n!* sighs one on this side of the pond, and circles with the restlessness of despair to some new perch on the gray oaks . . . and—*bor-*

r-r-r-n! comes faintly from far in the Lincoln woods." They express one of the meanings of nature, however, and are admirably suited to swamps and twilight woods. "I rejoice that there are owls," he concludes with a mock moral: "Let them do the idiotic and maniacal hooting for men." (138–139)

Again, with a deft reworking of Aristophanes, he presents a great ring of bibulous frogs passing cup and song around the shore of Walden Pond. They are described as "the sturdy spirits of ancient wine-bibbers and wassailers, still unrepentant, trying to sing a catch in their Stygian lake." There is probably no drinking contest of wider circumference in all literature, and certainly no wittier demonstration that nature has something more to communicate to man than sermons in stones. This wine has lost its flavor and become "only liquor to distend their paunches, [to the point of] mere saturation and waterloggedness." Yet the wassail continues all night, the password of "*tr-r-r-oonk, tr-r-r-oonk, tr-r-r-oonk!*" being repeated from cove to cove until it has made "the circuit of the shores." The flabbiest paunched frogs are the "leakiest" and hence first to drink themselves "under the pond." Finally, the patriarch in seniority and girth, "his chin upon a heart-leaf, which serves for a napkin to his drooling chaps," bellows his accusation that everybody is "*tr-r-r-oonk!*" and the sun comes up to disperse the morning mists. (139–140) The spectator-reader is left to draw his own moral from this satiric skit.

Thoreau's normal use of the circle as symbol in these bird and animal movements is not comic, as in the samples just given from the early chapter "Sounds"; on the other hand, he does not attempt to make it a profound way of probing for meanings. For the most part such circles are simply poetic images for his achievement of rapport with nature. They recur throughout the book, increasingly in the last half. For example, there is his comment on the wild ducks as he watches them "circle round and round and over the pond" before coming in to light: "what beside safety they got by sailing in the middle of Walden I do not know, unless they love its water for the same reason that I do." (262) Similarly, near the end of the book, one of the sure signs that spring has come at last is the arrival from Southern bayous of a flock of wild geese that, with a honk from their leader as signal, "wheeled and settled in the pond." (345) Again, in the earlier "Brute Neighbors," he tells how when he stumbled on a woodcock and her brood "she would leave her young and circle round and round me," making a noise to distract attention from her chicks. (252–253)

In "Winter Animals" there is a long passage about former times when hunters were "a numerous and merry crew here," (308) constantly out with their hounds in pursuit of the fox. "Sometimes a pack hunting by themselves would pass my door, and circle round my house, and yelp and hound without regarding me," he recalls: "Thus they circle until they fall upon the recent trail of a fox, for a wise hound will forsake everything else for this." Then he concludes by drawing on hunting lore to authenticate the meaning he wants to give to his circle image: "They tell me that if the fox . . . would run in a straight line away no fox-hound could overtake him; but, having left his pursuers far behind, he stops to rest and listen till they come up, and when he runs he circles round to his old haunts, where the hunters await him." (305–306) Falling into the right circle, Thoreau implies, is literally a way to overtake the wild.

The hawk, with its particular pattern of soaring, makes an especially attractive circular image by extending the symbolism of freedom and wildness it also stands for (as pointed out in the preceding chapter). Two *Journal* entries during the period of *Walden's* final revisions show him shaping the materials of actual observation for literary use. In 1853 Thoreau went out with a spyglass to watch a family of hawks, posting himself about a half mile from their nest, where he could see the young hawk sitting and could study the wild anger in its eye. The mother, he reports, "is incessantly circling about and above its charge" to defend it against intruders. But what he brings away from that afternoon's observation is not a lesson in domestic sentiment. It is a purely esthetic image: "Meanwhile the male is soaring, apparently quite undisturbed, at a great height above, evidently not hunting, but amusing or recreating himself in the thinner and cooler air, as if pleased with his own circles, like a geometer, and enjoying the sublime scene." (J, V, 235–236) Nor is this entirely poet's fancy. Thoreau was a keen enough bird watcher to know that even the hawk's eye could not fix its prey at such a height. The conclusion is flat and convincing: "He probably descends to hunt."

The second *Journal* passage, a year and a half earlier, goes further still but quickly discounts the literalness of the observation reported. This time Thoreau is on top of Fair Haven Hill, looking down on a large hawk that is soaring above a pine wood on the edge of the pond:

> Travelling ever by wider circles. What a symbol of the thoughts, now soaring, now descending, taking larger and larger circles, or smaller and smaller! It flies not directly whither it is bound, but advances by circles, like a courtier of the skies. . . . But the majesty is in the imagination of the beholder, for the bird is intent on its prey. Circling and ever circling. . . . The poetry of motion. Not as preferring one place to another, but enjoying each as long as possible. Most gracefully so surveys new scenes and revisits the old. As if that hawk were made to be the symbol of my thought, how bravely he came round over those parts of the wood which he had not surveyed, taking in a new segment, annexing new territories! (J, III, 143)

"Flights of imagination, Coleridgean thoughts," he concludes, spelling out the analogy with a quotation from "Lycidas"—"ever to fresh woods and pastures new."

These observations and images coalesce in a *Walden* vignette that lifts his "Bean-Field" labors from utility to beauty. He has just turned up some Indian arrowheads with his hoe and as he leans on it, thinking of that primitive age long past, he glances up at the sky and gives a sample of the kind of experiences that made him prolong his work beyond the morning stint on such occasions:

> The nighthawk circled overhead in the sunny afternoons—for I sometimes made a day of it—like a mote in the eye, or in heaven's eye, falling from time to time with a swoop and a sound as if the heavens were rent, torn at last to very rags and tatters, and yet a seamless cope remained. . . . Or sometimes I watched a pair of

hen-hawks circling high in the sky, alternately soaring and descending, approaching and leaving one another, as if they were the embodiment of my own thoughts. (175–176)

Thus the *Journal* is of value in making explicit what is only implicit in *Walden.* There he leaves his simile to speak for itself (*as if* an embodiment of his thoughts); and he sidesteps the moral analogy by adding that such sights and sounds are merely "a part of the inexhaustible entertainment which the country offers."

Two of Thoreau's finest circle images have religious overtones. One is that of the whippoorwills in "Sounds," chanting "their vespers" as he sits at his door. They begin every evening almost with the precision of a clock ("within five minutes of a particular time"), and continue for half an hour. "Sometimes I heard four or five at once in different parts of the wood, by accident one a bar behind another"—that is, singing a *round,* as well as "around." "Sometimes one would circle round and round me in the woods a few feet distant as if tethered by a string"—the perfect compass image. So they keep up their song through the night "at intervals," the technical term suggesting the harmony of nature's music to his ears. (137)

If birds can worship nature's god in an evensong, so can flowers in a ritual dance. A "hymn" celebrating this was copied down in one of Thoreau's literary notebooks, immediately following his extracts from the *Life of Pythagoras.* Among the attractions of that pre-Socratic philosopher, one may recall, were his magical powers of communicating with animals and his use of nature as a way to the truth. After transcribing numerous passages from the *Life,* Thoreau concluded with one from Proclus, quoted in the notes. Though it remained unused, this complementary circle image would have fitted perfectly in the *Walden* sequence given above:

Hence the sun-flower, as far as it is able, moves in a circular dance towards the sun; so that if any one could hear the pulsation made by its circuit in the air, he would perceive something composed by a sound of this kind, in honor of its king, such as a plant is capable of framing.

This would be as miraculous as the music of the spheres heard by Pythagoras, the Neoplatonist implies, "if any one could hear"! In *Walden* Thoreau says less effectively: "The birds with their plumage and their notes are in harmony with the flowers" and all nature is at one, lamenting that man alone finds it difficult to become part of this whole. (222) But there are approaches other than the passive ones of listening and looking which have just been described.

When the circle is radial rather than orbital, man at the center is generator of the sound waves. As the bells of Concord ring out to the horizon, they are modulated by nature until they reach Walden "partly the voice of the wood." For an echo, he says, is to some extent "an original sound, and therein is the magic and charm of it." (136–137) A passage in "The Ponds" (Chapter 9) clearly establishes the echo as a circular medium of communication:

> When, as was commonly the case, I had none to commune with, I used to raise the echoes by striking with a paddle on the side of my boat, filling the surrounding woods with circling and dilating sound, stirring them up as the keeper of a menagerie his wild beasts, until I elicited a growl from every wooded vale and hillside. (193)

Thus nature transforms the sounds made by man in returning them to him, as in the preceding circles man altered natural voices, turning the trumping of frogs into a drinking song and the cry of whippoorwills into chanted vespers. The closer he draws into the orbit of nature the more man participates in its harmony, until the communion becomes reciprocal.

At the very heart of the book lies Walden Pond, the central circle image. All paths lead into this chapter, "The Ponds"; all lines of meaning radiate from it. Here Thoreau found his ideal Self in that symbol of perfection which was the exact opposite of all those imperfections he had inveighed against in the life of society. The other ponds form a ring around Concord—

Goose Pond, Flint's, White, Fair Haven—the circle of his endless saunterings. At their center lies Walden, and at its center Thoreau glimpses the end of his quest. "This is my lake country," he says laconically. (219) Then to heighten the fabulous quality of his chosen pond, he makes it the subject of a special creation. After recounting an Indian fable of its origin, he contributes an original one more pertinent to his text:

It is very certain, at any rate, that once there was no pond here, and now there is one . . . that ancient settler whom I have mentioned, who remembers so well when he first came here with his divining-rod, saw a thin vapor rising from the sward, and the hazel pointed steadily downward, and he concluded to dig a well here. (202–203)

Is this verbal play, the Divine One suggested by "his divining-rod"? A few pages later in the chapter the creator of Walden Pond is specifically called the "Maker," who "rounded this water with his hand, deepened and clarified it in his thought, and in his will bequeathed it to Concord." (214–215)

Walden is actually oblong rather than circular, but since ponds are generally thought of as being round, Thoreau takes a poet's license and throws up a shower of circle imagery in its praise. "It is a clear and deep green well," he says in one place, "a perennial spring." (195) There is much about the matchless transparency of its waters and its all but indescribable color, "a vitreous greenish blue . . . such as watered or changeable silks and sword blades suggest." (196–197) This is followed by extended comparisons with other ponds and a discussion of the causes for color in water, as if he were interested solely in the science of optics, only to conclude with the real image he had in mind: "Lying between the earth and the heavens, it partakes of the color of both. . . . Such is the color of its *iris*." (196, my italics)

Then come several jewel images. "It is a gem of the first water which Concord wears in her coronet," he puns adroitly (199); next, "a perfect forest mirror, set round with stones as precious to my eye as if fewer or rarer." The latter image is elaborated into a conceit: "It is a mirror which no stone can crack, whose quicksilver will never wear off, whose gilding Nature continually repairs . . . a mirror in which all impurity presented to it sinks, swept and dusted by the sun's hazy brush." (209) Perhaps for the sake of bringing these fanciful images back to earth, he then indulges in a flat-footed pun: "one might suppose that it was called originally *Walled-in* Pond," referring to its actual stony shore. (203) The imagery closes with a series of concentric and overlapping circles. When the leaves are off the trees, he says: "I have been surprised to detect encircling the pond . . . a narrow shelf-like path in the steep hillside . . . as old probably as the race of man here, worn by the feet of aboriginal hunters." (199–200) When its mirror surface is momentarily broken, this is caused only by the "dimpling circles" where waterbugs are skating, or by the "circling undulations" made when pickerel dart after them. (208) Otherwise it is a reflecting glass that brings within man's reach "a lower heaven," the grandest circle of all. (96)

This imagery, varied and diffuse as it may seem, all tends in one direction. In his search for the perfect phrase to describe Walden Pond he even borrows from Emerson, but without naming his source: "One proposes that it be called 'God's Drop.'" Emphasizing his divergence from the other transcendentalists, Thoreau's own phrase is complementary. "It is earth's eye," he says, and the rest of his sentence makes the image fit his quest exactly: "looking into which the beholder measures the depth of his own nature." (206–207) Lying between earth and heaven, Walden partakes of both in more than color. "This pond," he concludes, "was made deep and pure for a symbol" (316)—not so much a symbol of the immanent God or Oversoul as of Thoreau's own soul or transcendent self.

All the remaining pages of *Walden*, like all the pages that went before, are aimed at making himself worthy of this perfection. The pond has achieved purity "by living thus reserved and austere, like a hermit in the woods" (215), and he resolves to match his own life to it as best he can. His dream of doing this is the subject of some halting verses inserted in the middle of the chapter:

> I cannot come nearer to God and Heaven
> Than I live to Walden even.

But if the pond is a symbol of his transcendent self, Thoreau is the first to admit that his actual self is something far different: "I am its stony shore." (215) An early manuscript version of this poem, celebrating the heavenly beauty of Walden Pond, contains two omitted lines that refer indirectly to a transcendental belief frequently appearing in his writings:

> It is a part of me which I have not prophaned
> I live by the shore of me detained.

The underlying doctrine received its classic statement in Wordsworth's "Intimations of Immortality": heaven lies about us in our infancy, and though shades of the prison house begin to close about the youth he is still "Nature's Priest," still attended by the splendid vision.

Thoreau not only knew this famous ode but adopted it as a kind of spiritual autobiography, with recurrent allusions to it in his *Journal*. In 1851, he writes that none of his mature experiences are comparable with those of his boyhood, and further that even then, as far back as he could remember, he always unconsciously referred to the experiences of a previous state of existence: "For life is a forgetting," etc. The inaccuracy of the quotation is merely evidence that the poem has been assimilated, for what follows is a highly original embodiment of Wordsworth's essential meaning:

> My life was ecstasy. In youth, before I lost any of my senses, I can remember that I was all alive, and inhabited my body with inexpressible satisfaction; both its weariness and its refreshment were sweet to me. This earth was the most glorious musical instrument, and I was audience to its strains. . . . I said to myself,—I said to others,—"There comes into my mind such an indescribable, infinite, all-absorbing, divine, heavenly pleasure, a sense of elevation and expansion, and [I] have had nought to do with it. I perceive that I am dealt with by superior powers. . . ." The morning and the evening were sweet to me, and I led a life aloof from the society

of men. I wondered if a mortal had ever known what I knew. . . . For years I marched as to a music in comparison with which the military music of the streets is noise and discord. I was daily intoxicated, and yet no man could call me intemperate. (J, II, 306–307)

Several years later he returns to the same music metaphor, in the context of remembering childhood rambles into the wilderness as compared with the more prosaic walks of the mature naturalist:

I go about to look at flowers and listen to the birds. There was a time when the beauty and the music were all within, and I sat and listened to my thoughts, and there was a song in them. I sat for hours on rocks and wrestled with the melody which possessed me. I sat and listened by the hour to a positive though faint and distant music, not sung by any bird, nor vibrating any earthly harp. When you walked with a joy which knew not its own origin. When you were an organ of which the world was but one poor broken pipe. I lay long on the rocks, foundered like a harp on the seashore, that knows not how it is dealt with. You sat on the earth as on a raft, listening to music that was not of the earth, but which ruled and arranged it. Man *should be* the harp articulate. When your cords were tense. (J, VI, 294)

The fractured syntax and the impressionistic style suggest the act of remembering as well as the wonder and glory of lost childhood.

Near the end of Thoreau's life, when he was over forty, the comparison in his *Journal* between youth and age is more dramatic, the former idealized and the latter satirized, with faint Wordsworthian gleams still discernible in the imagery:

The young man is a demigod; the grown man, alas! is commonly a mere mortal. He [the youth] is but half here, he knows not the men of this world, the powers that be. They know him not. Prompted by the reminiscence of that other sphere from which he so lately arrived, his actions are unintelligible to his seniors. He bathes in light. He is interesting as a stranger from another sphere. He really thinks and talks about a larger sphere of existence than this world. It takes him forty years to accommodate himself to the carapax of this world. This is the age of poetry. Afterward he may be the president of a bank, and go the way of all flesh. But a man of settled views, whose thoughts are few and hardened like his bones, is truly mortal, and his only resource is to say his prayers. (J, XIII, 35)

But Thoreau remained young longer than most men, that being one of the chief goals of his life. The Walden experiment was specifically aimed at recovering his youth, and the dynamic book he made out of it testifies to his success. A month after *Walden* was published, he summed up his life down to 1854:

I thought with what more than princely, with what poetical, leisure I had spent my years hitherto, without care or engagement, fancy-free. I have given myself up to nature; I have lived so many springs and summers and autumns and winters as if I had nothing else to do but *live* them. . . . It has been my vacation, my season of growth and expansion, a prolonged youth. (J, VII, 46)

The boast is made good in the vigorous and elastic spirit of his masterpiece, without need of being spelled out there. Nor did he allow echoes from Wordsworth's ode, the source of his inspiration, to find their way into his book. But the theme of youth pervades it. In the central chapter, "The Ponds," he says of Walden: "It is perenially young . . . it is itself unchanged, the same water which my youthful eyes fell on; all the change is in me." (214) Unlike the pond, Thoreau must earn the right to be young again. The austere discipline of his year in the woods prepares him to take part in the renewal he sees in nature. In the grass that "flames up on the hillsides like a spring fire" he finds a "symbol of perpetual youth." (343) When the ice finally melts he sees "the face of the pond full of glee and youth" and identifies with it, so as to share in the miracle of rebirth that follows immediately. (344) So in *Walden*, with novel images that free him from imitating Wordsworth and with the realistic framework provided by his prose narrative, Thoreau's search to discover his ideal self becomes a quest to recover his lost youth in a second spring. In this way the annual cycle becomes the encompassing image of his book.

Cycle of the Seasons

How can man "catch the pace of the seasons"? Plants and animals already move with the universal rhythm, but man with his too-conscious mind has somehow lost touch with this charmed circle. Such was the Romantic belief during the early nineteenth century. Thoreau's solution for the dilemma, it has been urged recently with much cogency, was to try, through learning, to understand nature so thoroughly that he could recover the equivalent of his lost instinct. "Anticipation," by knowing perfectly well what is coming next, says Professor Baym, was the goal of his program of nature study, which was identical with his quest for personal salvation. One of the "enterprises" to which Thoreau says he has devoted his life, as set forth in Chapter 1, is described in such terms: "To anticipate, not the sunrise and the dawn merely, but, if possible, Nature herself!" (19) Thus early in *Walden* he plants a clue to his final revelation in "Spring" (Chapter 17).

Ellery Channing, his friend and first biographer, tells how Thoreau formed an ambition, by limiting himself to a small territory like Concord township, to "construct a chart or calendar which should chronicle the phenomena of the seasons in their order." He seems to have begun this in earnest during the years between the Walden residence and the completion of his book. A *Journal* entry in 1856 tells how he had worked out his method, some six years before, though he never attempted to be a systematic botanist:

I wanted to know my neighbors, if possible,—to get a little nearer to them. I soon found myself observing when plants first blossomed and leafed, and I followed it up early and late, far and near, several years in succession, running to different sides of the town and into the neighboring towns, often between twenty and thirty miles in a day. I often visited a particular plant four or five miles distant, half a dozen times within a fortnight, that I might know exactly when it opened, beside attending to a great many others in different directions and some of them equally distant, at the same time. At the same time I had an eye for birds and whatever else might offer. (J, IX, 157–158)

This activity was continued with considerable enthusiasm for eight or ten years, and recorded in as many volumes of the *Journal.* According to an entry in 1853, if he makes a correct observation of nature this year and is able to repeat it with illustrations the next, "the season and life itself is prolonged." (J, V, 100) But his tables are constantly being upset by erratic and baffling factors, like the weather. By 1859 he is trying to convince himself that he simply has not lived long enough to learn the phases of nature and to know that one year is like another: "A man must attend to Nature closely for many years to know when, as well as where, to look for his objects, since he must always anticipate her a little." (J, XII, 347) By 1860 he has come to recognize that the sense organs are inadequate instruments and that one lifetime is too short to discover the vast pattern of "regularity" that must lie behind and include these seeming irregularities. "It takes us many years to find out that Nature repeats herself annually," he admits in his *Journal*: "But how perfectly regular and calculable all her phenomena must appear to a mind that has observed her for a thousand years!" (J, XIII, 279) The task he had set himself was impossible, and this is what accounts for the tedious bird and flower lists and for the increasing sense of frustration and defeat in the last volumes of the *Journal.* That the task might be accomplished some day by impersonal science was irrelevant to a poet for whom the only purpose of "anticipation" was its use by man, as a way for becoming one with nature.

Thoreau's failure may have wrecked the late *Journal* but it did not touch his great book. According to Professor Baym:

> The problem of the irregular universe does not arise in *Walden* because the correspondence of the protagonist's life to the seasons is on the largest and most general levels only. The hero must anticipate the limit of winter, believe in the return of spring, know when to plant beans and when to sound the pond.

Since Walden is a poem, it is not structured by argument and demonstration, whether scientific or philosophical. "Anticipation" as a method of studying nature would have been confined to the *Journal* in any case, even if it had proved successful. But Thoreau's exploration of it as a concept is relevant for readers of the book, because there also it functions significantly, once at the beginning and again at the end, as will be seen. "Anticipation" for the author of *Walden* is not a method but a metaphor, representing his desire for genuine participation in the circle of nature.

One way he could make poetry out of his endless observations of the annual cycle was to use these data for breaking down the customary assumption about the seasons: that the year is divided into four distinct parts, each lasting three months. Most men are so indifferent to the natural world that it takes something spectacular—a snowstorm, heat wave, the first chorusing of birds, maples flaming on a hillside—to make them take note of a change of season. Then they come to for a moment and salute winter, summer, spring, or fall—but only as separate and equal segments of a linear year, unaware of the continuous changes that mark the progress of the annual cycle from day to day. Thoreau could on occasion adopt the conventional belief, to be sure, as when making a generalized comment about the fine contrasts offered by the New England climate: "We really have four seasons, each incredible to the other." (J, III, 233) But the saunterer in all weathers, the keen observer and obsessed reporter of nature knew better.

On a Sunday in May 1852, for example, he took a long walk to Trillium Wood in the morning and another to the hill north of Walden Pond in the afternoon. The *Journal* account of this day is filled with the profusion of what he saw and heard, not bare lists but ecstatic notations of more than fifty birds, animals, flowers, trees, and other aspects of the natural scene. After three pages about such signs of the season's progress, he comments: "These are the warm-west-wind, dream-frog, leafing-out, willowy, haze days. Is not this summer, whenever it occurs?"—the date being only the ninth of May. (J, IV, 43; 40–43) On about the same date during the previous year, he not only announced the start of summer a month ahead of his townsmen but emphasized the suddenness with which it followed spring. "It seems to take but one summer day to fetch the summer in," he records in the *Journal* for May 18: "The turning-point between winter and summer is reached." (J, II, 196–197) Just two months later, on July 19, he follows this up with: "Yesterday it was spring, and to-morrow it will be autumn. Where is the summer then?" (J, II, 318) On 30 July 1852 he summarizes:

> The fore part of this month was the warmest weather we have had; the last part, sloping toward autumn, has reflected some of its coolness, for we are very forward to anticipate the fall. Perhaps I may say the spring culminated with the commencement of haying [first week in July], and the summer side of the year in mid-July. (J, IV, 267)

Anyone inclined to brand this time scheme as perverse, or even whimsical, might keep such a nature calendar for a few months; then he would see how little his own life has kept pace with the seasons.

Thoreau turned to literary advantage his special knowledge of calendar time. He was well-versed in the effects produced by the intricate patterns in nature's seasonal cycle, and he imitated them for poetic effects in his books. "Friday," the final chapter of *A Week on the Concord and Merrimack Rivers*, begins with a reference to the last night spent ashore before embarking on the return trip. "That night was the turning-point in the season," he says: "We had gone to bed in summer, and we awoke in autumn; for summer passes into autumn in some unimaginable point of time, like the turning of a leaf." The symbolism is pertinent to his conclusion. The voyage outward-bound took place in summer, the proper time for action. Now he is sailing home in autumn, the season for thought, for transforming the trip into a book.

These "unimaginable points of time" that mark the turnings from one season to another are followed around the calendar by Thoreau. On 18 March 1853, for example, he comments in his *Journal*: "Yesterday at this hour it was more raw and blustering than the past winter; to-day it seems more mild and balmy than summer." He might well have added, Where then is spring? Instead, he says quite simply, "I have rarely known a greater contrast." (J, V, 25). In the next-to-last chapter of *Walden,* just before the final coming of spring, this point is rendered dramatically. Describing the contrast between winter and spring, just as the ice suddenly begins to break up on the pond, he says of the transition: "It is seemingly instantaneous at last." (344) What follows is the climax of the book. The whole passage, discussed in full later, was added only in Version VII, at a date later than the *Journal* entry above, which is similar enough to be called a first draft. Having been prepared by this and the many other confirming observations in the *Journal,* readers will not be likely to write off the "instantaneous" appearance of spring in *Walden* as an impossible miracle.

Closely related to these sudden transitions from one season to another is the fact that no single season really fits the supposed three-months' duration. Different kinds of observations tend to expand or contract them. A *Journal* entry in August 1851 combines the two ideas:

> The seasons do not cease a moment to revolve, and therefore Nature rests no longer at her culminating point than at any other. If you are not out at the right instant, the summer may go by and you not see it. How much of the year is spring and fall! how little can be called summer! (J, II, 405)

In November of the following year he takes an opposite view: "Four months of the green leaf make all our summer . . . and there are about four months when the ground is white with snow. That would leave two months for spring and two for autumn." (J, IV, 403–404) Then he continues his time game by asking in February 1854: "Is not January alone pure winter? December belongs to the fall . . . February, to the spring." This is why January is the hardest month to get through: "When you have weathered that, you get into the gulf-stream of winter, nearer the shores of spring." (J, VI, 112, 91)

A final *Journal* entry completes this playing around the seasons with the most significant expansion of all, caught in a graphic image. "There is really but one season in our hearts," he declares; "For we are hunters pursuing the summer on snow-shoes and skates, all winter long." (J, IX, 164) A similar maneuvering resulted in the special temporal patterning of *Walden*. Readers who think of it as an even-paced sauntering around the calendar will be surprised at the results of a simple check. To the extent that the actual seasons are a structural principle in the body of the book (the fifteen chapters framed by introduction and conclusion), one may say that the first ten chapters hover around an endlessly prolonged summer, the "one season in our hearts," while the last five carry the story rapidly through autumn and winter to the second spring. This emphasis on summer is most appropriate, since *Walden* is largely an unroofed book. Yet it is necessary for the narrator to go into winter quarters so that he will be prepared to emerge again in the spring and complete his symbolic circle.

The inner time scheme of *Walden* is more complex still. There are anticipations of winter needs in the summer chapters, promises of spring in the autumn, and once an explicit statement that all four seasons are mirrored by the pond in a single day. These interlacings of the calendar, so important to the book's meaning, were first explored in the *Journal*. It will be interesting to trace a few of them from original draft to final expression. For example, on 8 November 1850 he records:

> It is warm somewhere any day in the year. You will find some nook in the woods generally, at mid-forenoon of the most blustering day, where you may forget the cold. I used to resort to the northeast side of Walden, where the sun, reflected from the pine woods on the stony shore, made it the fireside of the pond. It is so much pleasanter and wholesomer to be warmed by the sun when you can, than by a fire. (J, II, 87)

When this is transcribed into *Walden*—set in November just before he "went into winter quarters . . . like the wasps"—the first two sentences are dropped and the last two kept, so as to fix the vignette on the pond. Then he adds a final touch: "I thus warmed myself by the still glowing embers which the summer, like a departed hunter, had left." (265–266) This symbolic figure, the hunter who "shoots at beauty," recurs only for a moment before going indoors for the barren months.

Similarly, Thoreau interweaves the diurnal and the annual cycles. "I am struck by the perfect correspondence of a day—say an August day—and the year," he writes in the *Journal* in 1853; "I think that a perfect parallel may be drawn between the seasons of the day and of the year." Then in another entry: "The day is an epitome of the year." (J, V, 385, 393) These two records come together in the book, transferred to spring and set on the pond to enrich its symbolism:

> The phenomena of the year take place every day in a pond on a small scale. Every morning, generally speaking, the shallow water is being warmed more rapidly than the deep . . . and every evening it is being cooled more rapidly until the morning. The day is an epitome of the year. The night is the winter, the morning and evening are the spring and fall, and the noon is the summer. (332)

The inherent triteness of the comparison here is avoided by equating morning and spring only as a preparation for his symbolic rebirth, the recovery of his lost youth. The subtle evocation of this in the ensuing pages, as will be seen, is a vast improvement over the flat statement that concludes the *Journal* original: "Perhaps after middle age man ceases to be interested in the morning and in the spring." (J, V, 393)

Before Thoreau can "anticipate" spring he must learn to measure the limit of winter and have faith that he can outlast it. "Brute Neighbors" (Chapter 12), with its charming fables of friendship with the animals, is the last of *Walden's* summer chapters. It concludes with the loon chase on the pond "one calm October afternoon" and this fair weather continues into the next chapter, the only one devoted to autumn, as he goes out to gather wild apples, grapes, and a supply of chestnuts for winter. But its title, "House-Warming" (Chapter 13), is verbal play for building his chimney and plastering the cabin walls against the coming cold. It was well into November before he finished, and freezing winter had set in. It was too late for any housewarming in the ordinary sense. But as usual he found a companion in his solitude. "I withdrew yet farther into my shell, and endeavored to keep a bright fire both within my house and within my breast," he says: "It was I and Fire that lived there." (275, 279)

The theme of winter as the season for thinking, summer for action, runs all through the *Journal* and some of Thoreau's other writings before it culminates in this striking *Walden* image. A few samples will suffice. A passage in 1851 says of the superior man:

In summer the animal and vegetable in him are perfected as in a torrid zone; he lives in his senses mainly. In winter cold reason and not warm passion has her sway; he lives in thought and reflection; he lives a more spiritual, a less sensual, life. . . . He migrates into his mind, to perpetual summer. (J, III, 70)

Later in the same year: "Winter, with its *inwardness*, is upon us. A man is constrained to sit down and to think." (J, III, 83) In 1854 there is an extended metaphor of winter as the greatest harvest season of the year, "the harvest of thought":

The winter was not given to us for no purpose. We must thaw its cold with our genialness. We are tasked to find out and appropriate all the nutriment it yields. If it is a cold and hard season, its fruit, no doubt, is the more concentrated and nutty. It took the cold and bleakness of November to ripen the walnut, but the human brain is the kernel which the winter itself matures. Not till then does its shell come off. The seasons were not made in vain. (J, VI, 85)

Perhaps the most suggestive expression of all, and one that looks forward to *Walden*, comes at the end of *A Week*. It is both a summing up and a prophecy:

In summer we live out of doors, and have only impulses and feelings, which are all for action, and must wait commonly for the stillness and longer nights of autumn and winter before any thought will subside; we are sensible that behind the rustling leaves, and the stacks of grain, and the bare clusters of the grape, there is the field of a wholly new life, which no man has lived. (I, 403)

His first book ends too soon in the year (early September) to realize this possibility, but it sets the design for his masterpiece. In *Walden* the long summer activity is all a preparation for surviving the winter into "a wholly new life" in the spring.

The struggle to survive is an annual theme in the *Journal*, too. It recurs throughout the whole period of Thoreau's maturity. One year, as brilliant October gives way to leafless November, he writes: "Nature now, like an athlete, begins to strip herself in earnest for her contest with her great antagonist Winter. In the bare trees and twigs what a display of muscle!" (J, XI, 260) Again, in November 1853 referring to the now silent frogs, hylodes, crickets: "Nature is desert and iron-bound; she has shut her door. How different from the muggy nights of summer, teeming with life! That resounding life is now buried in the mud, returned into Nature's womb." (J, V, 499) The year before, even this dedicated worshipper of nature confessed: "In November, a man will eat his heart, if in any month." (J, IV, 405) This refrain is repeated from year to year in varying form, as for example on 13 November 1851: "Such a day as will almost oblige a man to eat his own heart. A day in which you must hold on to life by your teeth." (J, III, 110) Again, several years later: "November Eat-heart,—is that the name of it?" (J, X, 203) Then when January comes, the other hardest month to get through, the figure is even grimmer: "The winter, cold and bound out as it is, is thrown to us like a bone to a famishing dog, and we are expected to get the marrow out of it." (J, VI, 84–85) This entry is in January 1854, when he was putting the finishing touches on the winter chapters of *Walden*.

Two other *Journal* passages of the same period, with even more effective animal imagery, were among the very last additions to his book (in Version VII), made just before it went to the printer in March. The first is in December 1853: "In winter even man is to a slight extent dormant . . . the weather oftener shuts him up in his burrow; he begins to feel the access of dormancy and to assume the spherical form of the marmot." (J, VI, 38) When used in "The Ponds" the simile is attached to Walden itself, rather than to its hermit: "Like the marmots in the surrounding hills, it closes its eyelids and becomes dormant for three months or more." (313) The second is a long *Journal* passage for 5 February 1854 that is transcribed bodily into "House-Warming," with only some sharpening of style:

The animal merely makes a bed, which he warms with his body, in a sheltered place; but man, having discovered fire, boxes up some air in a spacious apartment, and warms that, instead of robbing himself, makes that his bed, in which he can move about divested of more cumbrous clothing, maintain a kind of summer in the midst of winter, and by means of windows even admit the light, and with a lamp lengthen out the day. Thus he goes a step or two beyond instinct, and saves a little time for the fine arts. (280; J, VI, 96)

The artistic use to which he put this extra time during his hibernation at Walden Pond was in writing the first draft of *A Week*, parts of which he read to Alcott during the winter months of 1847, it will be recalled. But to give the *Journal* passage a context especially relevant to his new book, he adds several sentences that specify this box nest as his own cabin and relate his survival of the winter to one of the major themes of *Walden*. The occasion is his return from a wintry walk, during which he was so exposed to the rudest blasts that his whole body has grown torpid; but "when I reached the genial atmosphere of my house I soon recovered my faculties and prolonged my life." This leads him to speculate how the human race may be destroyed at last: "It would be easy to cut their threads any time with a little sharper blast from the north." (280) If man can survive the winter he can, hopefully, revive in the spring.

Another way to "anticipate" spring is to find the promise of it in autumn and winter, signs that the life cycle is continuous. Once again it is interesting to trace this idea from *Journal* to book. In November 1850 he writes:

There seems to be in the fall a sort of attempt at a spring, a rejuvenescence, as if the winter were not expected by a part of nature. . . . If you penetrate to some warm recess under a cliff in the woods, you will be astonished at the amount of summer life that still flourishes there. No doubt more of the summer's life than we are aware thus slips by and outmaneuvers the winter, gliding from fence to fence. (J, II, 99, 104)

Again, when he finds several kinds of ferns "still green and much in fruit" on the last day of October, he comments: "Even in them I feel an argument for immortality. Death is so far from being universal. The same destroyer does not destroy all." (J, X, 149, 150) Of all the hoped-for correspondences between man and nature none is more hackneyed, or less convincing, than this supposed evidence of immortality.

Thoreau redeems the passage by wit, choosing for his second witness a plant whose coarse leaves and offensive smell have kept previous poets from singing its praise:

If you are afflicted with melancholy at this season, go to the swamp and see the brave spears of skunk cabbage buds already advanced toward a new year. . . . Is it the winter of their discontent? Do they seem to have lain down to die, despairing of skunk-cabbagedom? . . . Mortal human creatures must take a little respite in this fall of the year; their spirits do flag a little. There is a little questioning of destiny. . . . But not so with the skunk-cabbage. Its withered leaves fall and are transfixed by a rising bud. Winter and death are ignored; the circle of life is complete. Are these false prophets? Is it a lie or a vain boast underneath the skunk-cabbage bud, pushing it upward and lifting the dead leaves with it? . . . There is no can't nor cant to them. They see over the brow of winter's hill. They see another summer ahead. (J, X, 150–151)

If this had not been written too late, 1857, it would have deserved inclusion in *Walden*. It is certainly better than the feeble punning there when he tries to give a humorous twist to the pre-spring evidences of continuity in the life cycle:

When the ground was partially bare of snow, and a few warm days had dried its surface somewhat, it was pleasant to compare the first tender signs of the infant year just peeping forth with the stately beauty of the withered vegetation which had withstood the winter . . . decent weeds, at least, which widowed Nature wears. (341–342)

The trouble here clearly is that the grandeur of Thoreau's theme in "Spring" calls for a different mode, not wit but the highest reaches of metaphor.

Turning to the *Journal* once more, one finds an interesting analogy to "human beings in the November of their days" in connection with another observation of spring-life linked with autumn-death in nature: "I notice that many plants about this season of the year or earlier [November 17], after they have died down at the top . . . put forth fresh radical leaves which sustain the life in their root still, against a new spring." (J, V, 508–509) This idea is embodied in one of the most memorable images in *Walden's* penultimate chapter:

> The grass flames up on the hillsides like a spring fire,—"et primitus oritur herba imbribus primoribus evocata,"—as if the earth sent forth an inward heat to greet the returning sun . . . the grass blade, like a long green ribbon, streams from the sod into the summer, checked indeed by the frost, but anon pushing on again, lifting its spear of last year's hay with the fresh life below. (343)

Modern taste might prefer the metaphor alone, without the Latin tag from Varro's *Rerum Rusticarum* ("And now arises the grass, called forth by the first rains"), which adds nothing to the passage but a classical flourish. Even *Walden* did not always escape the literary conventions of the day.

Thoreau's treatment of the annual cycle has been moving steadily from objective reporting to metaphor. A late *Journal* entry takes him all the way into the poet's inner climate: "These regular phenomena of the seasons get at last to be—they were *at first*, of course—simply and plainly phenomena or phases of my life. The seasons and all their changes are in me." (J, X, 127) If nature is Maya, simultaneously Illusion and Reality, the poet can control it, as in the following dizzy spin around the calendar in three *Journal* passages. On 15 May 1853 he writes:

> The first cricket's chirrup which I have chanced to hear now falls on my ear and makes me forget all else; all else is a thin and movable crust down to that depth where he resides eternally. He already foretells autumn. . . . His voice has set me thinking, philosophizing,

moralizing at once. . . . At one leap I go from the just opened buttercup to the life-everlasting. This singer has antedated autumn. His strain is superior (inferior?)[1] to seasons. It annihilates time and space.

[1] Exaltedly inferior. (J, V, 158) [Thoreau's note]

Next, in an extraordinary *Journal* passage four years after *Walden* was published, he inverts all the customary meanings of time and space by making an elaborate metaphor out of the then popular form of entertainment called a cyclorama or "panorama"—a series of pictures of a landscape presented on a continuous surface moving around the audience. Here the seasons become just such a set of unchanging stage scenery circling timelessly about Thoreau, one of the spectators, who is unmoving but constantly changing because he is growing older with each annual revolution:

The November twilights just begun! It appeared like a part of a panorama at which I sat spectator, a part with which I was perfectly familiar just coming into view, and I foresaw how it would look and roll along, and prepared to be pleased. Just such a piece of art merely, though infinitely sweet and grand, did it appear to me. . . . Yet I sat the bench with perfect contentment, unwilling to exchange the familiar vision that was to be unrolled for any treasure or heaven that could be imagined. . . . It was as if I was promised the greatest novelty the world has ever seen or shall see, though the utmost possible novelty would be the difference between me and myself a year ago. This alone encouraged me, and was my fuel for the approaching winter. That we may behold the panorama with this slight improvement or change, this is what we sustain life for with so much effort from year to year. . . . Give me the old familiar walk . . . with this ever new self, with this infinite expectation and faith, which does not know when it is beaten. We'll go nutting once more. We'll pluck the nut of the world, and crack it in the winter evenings. (J, XI, 273–274)

This fine conceit was coined too late for inclusion in his book. Yet the same idea—of the intricate relation between the perceiving mind and some aspect of nature it is trying to grasp —appears briefly but significantly in "The Ponds." After more than two decades of intimate association with his chosen pond, he declares: "Walden wears best, and best preserves its purity. . . . It is itself unchanged, the same water which my youthful eyes fell on; all the change is in me. . . . It is perennially young." This is the spring from which he must drink if he is to recover his lost youth. "Many men have been likened to it," he concludes, "but few deserve that honor." (214) A third and final *Journal* passage completes his symbolic whirl around the seasonal cycle. After a walk to Conantum in the autumn of 1851 he writes:

> The witch-hazel here is in full blossom on this magical hillside, while its broad yellow leaves are falling. . . . It is an extremely interesting plant,—October and November's child, and yet it reminds me of the very earliest spring . . . suggesting amid all these signs of autumn, falling leaves and frost, that the life of Nature, by which she eternally flourishes, is untouched. . . . While its leaves fall, its blossoms spring. The autumn, then, is indeed a spring. All the year is a spring. . . . It [the hillside covered with witch-hazel] is a faery place. This is a part of the immortality of the soul. (J, III, 59–60)

By the poet's transforming power, out-maneuvering time and turning objects into thoughts, Thoreau has achieved "The perfect correspondence of Nature to man, so that he is at home in her!" (J, X, 127) This is made explicit in a late *Journal* entry:

> Each season is but an infinitesimal point. It no sooner comes than it is gone. It has no duration. It simply gives a tone and hue to my thought. Each annual phenomenon is a reminiscence and prompting. Our thoughts and sentiments answer to the revolutions of the seasons, as two cog-wheels fit into each other. We are conversant with only one point of contact at a time, from which we receive a prompting and impulse and instantly pass to a new season or point of contact. A year is made up of a certain series and number of sensations and thoughts which have their language in nature. Now I am ice, now I am sorrel. Each experience reduces itself to a mood of the mind. (J, IX, 406–407)

Having now turned the calendar from an outer fact to an inner one, Thoreau knows he can survive winter and find renewal in spring, since both are metaphors. So he can await the coming of actual spring with serene confidence.

Second Spring

"One attraction in coming to the woods to live was that I should have leisure and opportunity to see the Spring come in." (333) The very location of his cabin favored this purpose because Walden Pond, for a complex of reasons (which he sets forth with the expertise of a scientist), "indicates better than any water hereabouts the *absolute* progress of the season." (333, 330, my italics) So Thoreau begins his penultimate chapter "Spring." Then, taking the melting and breaking up of ice as the sign of the new season, he records the exact day when the pond was "first completely open" in every year from 1845 (when he built his cabin) through 1854 (when *Walden* went to press). "It commonly opens about the first of April," he sums up, and this average date will have to serve since he does not pinpoint the day of the advent of spring in his climactic chapter, for very good reasons. The statistical data at the beginning of this chapter, though accurate enough, are not there for scientific purposes. Like the other factual matter in *Walden*, they provide a foundation to support the myth he is creating—here the miracle of rebirth.

Long before the "absolute" arrival of spring he has a vision of the pond breaking up, as he watches the ice-cutters at Walden in the dead of winter. For several weeks on its frozen surface "I saw from my window a hundred men at work," he says; "and now they are all gone, and in thirty days more, probably, I shall look from the same window on the pure sea-green Walden water there." Then he adds, "Perhaps I shall hear a solitary loon laugh as he dives and plumes himself." (328) With the final advent of spring, some twenty pages later, this prophecy is fulfilled: "I saw a loon in the pond." (351) Once again this wild bird serves as a symbolic figure, heralding the rebirth of the year. The vision occurred, presumably, about the end of February. There comes a period at the end of winter, he says in the *Journal* for March 1853, when "we are daily expecting spring." (J, V, 13) His most extravagant example of "anticipating" spring, in the phenomenon of thawing sand and clay, takes place at just such a period, in the early part of March. The episode is not dated in the book, but the original drafts were made in the *Journal* on 12 March 1852 and 2 March 1954.

The deep "cut" on the railroad, through which Thoreau often passed on his way to the village, was composed of fine sand mixed with a little clay "of various rich colors." This begins to flow down the slope in fantastic shapes, he says, whenever the frost comes out of the ground—a phenomenon "not very common on so large a scale." His delight in it is so great that he indulges in five pages of ecstatic imagery, tinged with wit, that must be quoted at some length:

> As it flows it takes the forms of sappy leaves or vines, making heaps of pulpy sprays a foot or more in depth, and resembling as you look down on them, the laciniated, lobed, and imbricated thalluses of some lichens; or you are reminded of coral, or leopards' paws or birds' feet, of brains or lungs or bowels, and excrements of all kinds. It is a truly *grotesque* vegetation, whose forms and color we see imitated in bronze, a sort of architectural foliage more ancient and typical than acanthus, chiccory, ivy, vine. . . . You find thus in the very sands an anticipation of the vegetable leaf. No wonder that the earth expresses itself outwardly in leaves, it so labors with the idea inwardly. The atoms have already learned this law, and are pregnant by it. The overhanging leaf sees here its prototype. (336–337, 338)

The source of this leaf metaphor, as the universal type of life, was undoubtedly Goethe's *Metamorphosis of Plants* (1790). There is no specific proof that Thoreau read this little book, though the likelihood is strong. He did read *Italienische Reise* with great care, in German, and it was on the Italian journey, in Sicily, that Goethe first got the notion that all flowering plants are comparable and can be brought together in a single concept.

The full development of this theory in Goethe's monograph

has all the verve and freshness of an enthusiastic amateur, and there are several passages that would have appealed to the poet-scientist of *Walden*. "When now the plant vegetates, blooms, or fructifies, so it is still *the same organs* which, with different destinies, and under protean shapes, fulfil the part prescribed by Nature," he could have read in the *Metamorphosis*, for example. The value of this little book lay in the unifying quality of Goethe's mind, his search for a fundamental law. Its influence has been on thinkers and poets rather than on scientists. As might be expected, he preferred to call himself a *Naturschauer*, not a *Naturforscher*, and it is as a gazer into nature rather than as an investigator that he would have influenced Thoreau.

The leaf as prototype may have come from Goethe, but the metaphoric embodiment of it in sand foliage is entirely original. So are the punning etymologies by which Thoreau extends the universal leaf form to include liver and lungs, the feathers of birds, the lumpish grub and airy butterfly; finally by grotesque analogy he extends it to human fingers and toes, lips and ear lobes. These exaggerations give him a new circle image and a new version of man's original creation from the earth. "The very globe continually transcends and translates itself, and becomes winged in its orbit," he declares. Then asks, "What is man but a mass of thawing clay?" (338, 339) In conclusion he turns the whole phenomenon into a grand conceit for the creativity of the Artist:

> Thus it seemed that this one hillside illustrated the principle of all the operations of Nature. The Maker of this earth but patented a leaf. What Champollion will decipher this hieroglyphic for us? . . . I am affected as if in a peculiar sense I stood in the laboratory of the Artist who made the world and me,—had come to where he was still at work, sporting on this bank, and with excess of energy strewing his fresh designs about. . . . This is the frost coming out of the ground; this is Spring. It precedes the green and flowery spring, as mythology precedes regular poetry. (337–338, 340)

This metaphysical leap of the imagination makes Emerson's "Snow-Storm" seem merely fanciful, with its analogy of the Over Soul manifesting itself in the "frolic architecture" of the snow.

The sand foliage makes an image of retiring winter, however, not of the spring's resurgence. But it means that the hero, like nature, has survived the contest with his most formidable antagonist. Having witnessed this "anticipation of the vegetable leaf" in the pre-spring thaw, he is now on the alert for the true spring, the "green and flowery" one. In the *Journal* for 7 March 1853, Thoreau asks himself:

What is the earliest sign of spring? The motion of worms and insects? The flow of sap in trees and the swelling of buds? Do not the insects awake with the flow of sap? Bluebirds, etc., probably do not come till insects come out. Or are there earlier signs in the water?—the tortoises, frogs, etc. (J, V, 8)

Four years later he is beginning to despair: "No mortal is alert enough to be present at the first dawn of the spring." (J, IX, 295) By March 1860 he is reduced to listing some of the myriad signs of spring, over one hundred of them, without comment; his hope of establishing a chart whereby he could really anticipate nature had failed. (J, XIII, 208–210)

In the "Spring" of *Walden*, however, he has entire confidence since this is a book of poetry—not the quasi-scientific observations of the *Journal*:

I am on the alert for the first signs of spring, to hear the chance note of some arriving bird, or the striped squirrel's chirp, for his stores must be now nearly exhausted, or see the woodchuck venture out of his winter quarters. On the 13th of March, after I had heard the bluebird, song sparrow, and red-wing, the ice was still nearly a foot thick. (333–334)

This is the last date given before the actual advent of spring—left dateless, presumably to enhance its mythical quality. The next ten pages, covering presumably a full two weeks more, consist of a succession of expectations and postponements that enhance the drama of anticipation. They culminate in a paragraph that begins:

The first sparrow of spring! The year beginning with younger hope than ever! . . . What at such a time are histories, chronologies, traditions, and all written revelations? The brooks sing carols and glees to the spring. The marsh hawk, sailing low over the meadow, is already seeking the first slimy life that awakes. (342–343)

Then comes the bright image of the new grass, flaming up on the hillsides "like a spring fire," previously quoted. Then follows the climax, a double one. "Walden is melting apace," he says: "It is glorious to behold this ribbon of water sparkling in the sun, the bare face of the pond full of glee and youth." The rebirth of nature takes place in a single startling sentence: "Walden was dead and is alive again." (343–344) This does not appear in the original *Journal* draft, 20 March 1853, which uses, instead, the trite phrase "resurrection of the year." (J, V, 29) How much more effective to transfer to the pond those famous words in the parable of the prodigal's return, for like that son, Walden had been only figuratively dead because of its journey into the "far country" of winter.

The rebirth of the hero fills the next paragraph. The original draft of this remarkable experience is written down in the *Journal* under a date that records it as coming with spring in the first year of his residence at Walden. Because of the climactic importance of this passage the *Journal* and book versions will now be placed side by side (my italics in both quotations). This will make clear the greatly enhanced meaning achieved by subtle reworking:

March 26, 1846. The change from foul weather to fair, from dark, sluggish hours to serene, elastic ones, is a memorable crisis which all things proclaim. The change from foulness to serenity is instantaneous. *Suddenly an influx of light, though it was late, filled my room.* I looked out and saw that the pond was already calm and full of hope as on a summer evening, though the ice was dissolved but yesterday. *There seemed to be some intelligence in the pond which responded to the unseen serenity in a distant horizon.* (J, I, 400)

The improvement in diction when this was transcribed into the book will be obvious enough. But the real significance of the revisions consisted in emphasizing the quality of miracle (here indicated by italics). In *Walden* the advent of spring is undated:

> The change from storm and winter to serene and mild weather, from dark and sluggish hours to bright and elastic ones, is a memorable crisis which all things proclaim. It is seemingly instantaneous at last. *Suddenly an influx of light filled my house, though the evening was at hand, and the clouds of winter still overhung it, and the eves were dripping with sleety rain.* I looked out the window, *and lo!* where yesterday was cold gray ice there lay the transparent pond already calm and full of hope as in a summer evening, *reflecting a summer evening sky in its bosom, though none was visible overhead, as if it had intelligence with some remote horizon.* (344)

In the book not only is winter darkness literally turned into spring light but the invisible is made visible—a kind of epiphany.

Light is one of the principal symbols of deity in all three of the religions that interested Thoreau—Christian, Hindu, Greek. The idea of God as light, the sun as a symbol of the risen Christ, is present in Thoreau's "Spring" only as a kind of vague background he could expect his readers to bring with them. Hence the merest suggestion was enough, as with the other allusions to Christianity in Walden. The relevance of Hindu religious ideas and images throughout the book, not so readily apparent to Western eyes, has been pointed out frequently before in the present study. Another one of them, the highest state aimed at by yoga, the *pabhassara* or attainment of the unstainable purity of light, may have been in the back of Thoreau's mind when he wrote of his epiphany on the pond. It is definitely so in a semimystical passage in *A Week*:

> Every man casts a shadow; not his body only, but his imperfectly mingled spirit. . . . The divine light is diffused almost entirely around us, and by means of the refraction of light, or else by a certain self-luminousness, or, as some will have it, transparency, if we preserve ourselves untarnished, we are able to enlighten our shaded side. (I, 375–376)

The oriental origin of this is suggested in a passage immediately following, describing "the whole race of yellow flowers," on every hill and in every valley, "like Brahminical devotees, turning steadily with their luminary from morning till night." A reflection of this divine light may be found near the end of *Walden's* "Spring":

Ah! I have penetrated to those meadows on the morning of many a first spring day . . . when the wild river valley and the woods were bathed in so pure and bright a light as would have waked the dead, if they had been slumbering in their graves, as some suppose. There needs no stronger proof of immortality. All things must live in such a light. (349)

Most pertinent to the advent of spring in *Walden* is another series of images, obvious in their reference to the sun but submerged with reference to the cult of Apollo. It will be remembered, however, that this god of light and also of poetry was, appropriately, the one out of all the Greek pantheon with whom Thoreau identified himself. Images of the sun appear and reappear throughout the book. Early in the first chapter, telling of his desire to "anticipate . . . the sunrise" and of his going about this enterprise "many mornings, summer and winter," he comments with such lightness as to obscure the suggestion of worship: "It is true, I never assisted the sun materially in his rising, but, doubt not it was of the last importance only to be present at it." (19) This surely alludes to the tradition that Apollo's son, Orpheus, whose life and poetry Thoreau was familiar with, climbed a hill every morning to salute the sun. At the other end of the book, the concluding sentences read: "Only that day dawns to which we are awake. There is more day to dawn. The sun is but a morning star." (367) In between he declares himself "a worshipper of Aurora" (sister of Helios) and one of those poets who, like her son Memnon, "emit their music at sunrise." (98, 99)

The sun is also central to all the aspects of rebirth and renewal in "Spring." It causes the thawing of sand, with which Thoreau identifies his body. It causes the re-awakening to life of Walden, with which he identifies his spirit—the influx of light flooding the pond and his room simultaneously. It is the cause of regeneration in nature on the literal level every year, and on the symbolic level now, for this spring is clearly to be the fulfillment of his promise, at the beginning of the book, of "the spring of springs" when he would "rise to a higher and more ethereal life." (46)

One further extension of sun imagery may be suggested at this point. Thoreau was acquainted with Orphism, a religious reformation in Greece that tried to mediate between the cults of Apollo and Dionysus, both of whom were worshipped at the same Oracle of Delphi, though at different seasons of the year. Feeling that the heavenly aspiration of the former was too austere, and that the orgiastic ecstasies of the latter should be modified, priests of the new religion attempted a synthesis that would symbolize the dualism of man's nature. It seems reasonable to suggest that this might serve as another analogue to Thoreau's duality of wildness and spirituality in "Higher Laws," a theme discussed at length in the preceding chapter. At any rate Thoreau knew the *Hymns* attributed to Orpheus and during the 1840's copied down a dozen pages of "Fragments" in his *Literary Notebook*, including part of a hymn to the sun. He probably also knew the one quoted by Thomas Taylor (a favorite translator of the classics among transcendentalists) as an example of the final stage of Orphic initiation, when the deity is revealed as resplendent light:

> *He comes! The god of light! the god's at hand!*
> . . . Apollo's eyes endure
> None but the good, the perfect, and the pure.

These symbols of divine light in the religions Thoreau was familiar with, as well as the pervasive images of the sun throughout *Walden*, are valid aids for those who would read in depth the meaning of the sudden "influx of light" on the pond. It remains to be seen what effect the sense of rebirth and renewal had on him. This was possibly the most difficult task he faced in completing his book, since he was trying to write a poetically acceptable myth of himself and not a saint's life. An extravagant *Journal* passage in the spring of 1852 seems a trial flight:

A mild spring day. . . . I lean over a rail to hear what is in the air, liquid with the bluebird's warble. My life partakes of infinity. . . . I go forth to make new demands on life. I wish to begin this summer well; to do something in it worthy of it and of me; to transcend my daily routine and that of my townsmen; to have my immortality now, that it be in the *quality* of my daily life; to pay the greatest price, the greatest tax, of any man in Concord, and enjoy the most! ! I will give all I am for *my* nobility. I will pay all my days for *my* success. I pray that the life of this spring and summer may ever lie fair in my memory. May I dare as I have never done! May I persevere as I have never done! May I purify myself anew as with fire and water, soul and body! May my melody not be wanting to the season! May I gird myself to be a hunter of the beautiful, that naught escape me! May I attain to a youth never attained! I am eager to report the glory of the universe; may I be worthy to do it; to have got through with regarding human values, so as not to be distracted from regarding divine values. . . . (J, III, 350–351)

Pertinent as these clamorous resolutions for the new year may be to the themes of *Walden,* the mode is all wrong and he was wise to exclude it.

To return to the epiphany in "Spring," instead of using any such rhetoric Thoreau finishes his climactic paragraph with the simple but transcendent image of a robin, traditional symbol of happiness and of hope:

I heard a robin in the distance, the first I had heard for many a thousand years, methought, whose note I shall not forget for many a thousand more,—the same sweet and powerful song as of yore. O the evening robin, at the end of a New England summer day! If I could ever find the twig he sits upon! I mean *he*; I mean *the twig*. This at least is not the *Turdus migratorious*. (344)

On one level the sudden influx of light that appears on the pond and illuminates the Hermit-Poet of Walden is simply the sun of a new year, and it brings the promise of another New England summer, if not a vision of heaven. If it is also the divine light of an eternal spring, offering escape from the mortal cycle, this will have to appear from a further examination of the imagery of *Walden* rather than from its argument. "As it grew darker," the passage ends quietly, "I came in, and shut the door, and passed my first spring night in the woods." (345) This sentence brings the Walden year around to its second spring (the previous one having been devoted to house-building). It is preceded and followed by circling images of wild geese and wild ducks arriving at the pond.

There is a lacuna in the *Walden* sequence at this point that is filled so perfectly by a *Journal* passage one marvels it was not included. It is recorded on 18 April 1852, in the very period when Thoreau was undertaking those rewritings that were to transform his narrative of life in the woods into a poem. "For the first time I perceive this spring that the year is a circle," he begins: "I see distinctly the spring arc thus far. It is drawn with a firm line. Every incident is a parable of the Great Teacher." To this major image he then links a major idea, in the paragraph immediately following:

> Why should just these sights and sounds accompany our life? Why should I hear the chattering of blackbirds, why smell the skunk each year? I would fain explore the mysterious relation between myself and these things. I would at least know what these things unavoidably are, make a chart of our life, know how its shores trend, that butterflies reappear and when, know why just this circle of creatures completes the world. Can I not by expectation affect the revolutions of nature, make a day to bring forth something new? (J, III, 438)

The overall design of *Walden* is contained in this image of the year coming full circle in spring, though it is never explicitly so stated in the book. And the great chapter entitled "Spring" concludes with a resounding hymn of praise to this idea of plenitude. Thoreau knows he must merge himself ever more harmoniously with the cycle of time and the circle of nature before he can transcend either.

The *Journal* for a quarter-century is filled with evidence that he was aware of the traditional concept of the Great Chain of Being and all its component ideas: the plenitude, gradation, and continuity of life from the simplest forms all the way up through man to the throne of God. The reference is specific when on 10 December 1840, he discovers a strange track on the snow in his back yard and decides it is that of a migrating otter, quite rare in Concord. "I cannot but smile at my own wealth, when I am thus reminded that every chink and cranny of nature is full to overflowing," he records: "Such an incident as this startles me with the assurance that the primeval nature is still working." (LJ, 187) That Thoreau took the naturalistic rather than the Christian view of this doctrine is proved by the twist he gives it in *Walden*. When in "The Pond in Winter" he tells of the "wild men" who come to drop their fishing lines through holes cut in the ice, he muses: "The perch swallows the grub-worm, the pickerel swallows the perch, and the fisherman swallows the pickerel; and so all the chinks in the scale of being are filled." (314)

Though his attitude was unorthodox, Thoreau did take a kind of religious joy in the profusion of nature's life. "How much richer we feel for this unused abundance and superfluity!" he says, commenting on the annual harvest of inedible chokeberries: "Nature would not appear so rich . . . if we knew a use for everything." (J, V, 368) A more detailed account of the same response may be found in a very early *Journal* entry:

> Surely joy is the condition of life. Think of the young fry that leap in ponds—the myriad of insects ushered into being of a summer's evening—the incessant note of the hyla with which the woods ring in the spring, the *nonchalance* of the butterfly carrying accident and change painted in a thousand hues upon its wings—or the brook-minnow stemming stoutly the current, the lustre of whose scales worn bright by the attrition is reflected upon the bank! (LJ, 144)

But he steered clear of all the contemporary sentimentalizing of nature, especially the tendency to prettify it. He wanted to know all sides, to see nature steady and see it whole. Once, noticing carrion flowers and wild roses growing near each other in a small swamp, he comments: "All things, both beautiful and ugly, agreeable and offensive, are expressed in flowers,—all kinds and degrees of beauty and all kinds of foulness." Then queries, "For what purpose has nature made a flower to fill the lowlands with the odor of carrion?" (J, IV, 149)

He may begin by sounding like a Victorian moralist when he writes of the beauty and fragrance of the white lotus: "How significant that the rich black mud of our dead stream produces the water-lily,—out of that fertile slime springs this spotless purity!" (J, V, 283) But he is quick to point out the impossibility of finding a perfect bloom, since they are attacked by bugs and begin to disintegrate as soon as fully open. Just two days before, 17 June 1853, he fills five pages of the *Journal* with an account of a grotesque giant fungus, almost obscene in its shape and in its tendency to fall into decay as suddenly as it had shot up into life. "It suggests a vegetative force which may almost make man tremble for his dominion," he says: "It carries me back to . . . the age of the saurus and pleiosaurus and when bullfrogs were as big as bulls." Then he asks, of this toadstool, eighteen inches high: "What part does it play in the economy of the world?" He answers himself with another question, "Is it not a giant mildew or mould?" then goes on to turn it into an allegory of evil, "the flower of humid darkness and ignorance." (J, V, 270–275) So of the great mud turtles, which he follows from the egg buried in sand to full growth at sixty or seventy pounds:

If Iliads are not composed in our day, snapping turtles are hatched and arrive at maturity. It already thrusts forth its tremendous head, —for the first time in this sphere,—and slowly moves from side to side,—opening its small glistening eyes for the first time to the light,—expressive of dull rage, as if it had endured the trials of this world for a century. When I behold this monster thus steadily advancing toward maturity, all nature abetting, I am convinced that there must be an irresistible necessity for mud turtles. With what tenacity Nature sticks to her idea! (J, VI, 474)

Not just the plenitude of creatures in all their range and diversity fascinates him but the endless chain of eater and eaten. During one January thaw he comments on the insects that swarm up out of the grass roots only to be devoured by crows, the musquashes betrayed to the hunter by the piles of clam shells outside their burrows, the caterpillars and crickets and other bugs washed up out of their winter quarters, some to drown and the rest to become food for birds. (J, XI, 419–422) Such observations could lead him to say: "Nature by her bounteousness thus disgusts us with a sense of repletion—and uncleanness even." (J, VII, 504) More characteristic is his determination to see both sides of the picture: "Shall the earth be regarded as a graveyard, a necropolis, merely, and not also as a granary filled with the seeds of life? Is not its fertility increased by this decay?" (J, VI, 162)

Life and death, growth and decay, waste and replenishing out of the fullness of creative power—he must accept it all if he is to be at home in nature. Once, seeing life delivered from the jaws of death by sheer accident, he records the incident with a balance of tragic and comic that matches nature's acceptance of it as part of the scheme of things:

> I saw a snake by the roadside and touched him with my foot to see if he were alive. He had a toad in his jaws, which he was preparing to swallow with his jaws distended to three times his width, but he relinquished his prey in haste and fled; and I thought, as the toad jumped leisurely away with his slime-covered hind-quarters glistening in the sun, as if I, his deliverer, wished to interrupt his meditations,—without a shriek or fainting,—I thought what a healthy indifference he manifested. Is not this the broad earth still? he said. (J, II, 423)

Again, watching the dead carp that float to the surface annually, as the Concord River floods the great meadows, he can finally say:

> When I realize that the mortality of suckers in the spring is as old a phenomenon, perchance, as the race of suckers itself, I contemplate it with serenity and joy even, as one of the signs of spring.

. . . [This] proves its necessity and that it is part of the *order,* not disorder, of the universe. (J, IX, 310)

The superb paean to plenitude at the end of "Spring" is based on such close observation and sympathetic understanding over a long period of years. It is the most concentrated dose of nature in all of *Walden,* and the squeamish will probably prefer to skim over it. But for those who would follow the whole way Thoreau's merging with nature, it must be quoted in full:

Our village life would stagnate if it were not for the unexplored forests and meadows which surround it. We need the tonic of wildness,—to wade sometimes in marshes where the bittern and the meadow-hen lurk, and hear the booming of the snipe; to smell the whispering sedge where only some wilder and more solitary fowl builds her nest, and the mink crawls with its belly close to the ground. At the same time that we are earnest to explore and learn all things, we require that all things be mysterious and unexplorable, that land and sea be infinitely wild, unsurveyed and unfathomed by us because unfathomable. We can never have enough of nature. We must be refreshed by the sight of inexhaustible vigor, vast and titanic features, the sea-coast with its wrecks, the wilderness with its living and decaying trees, the thunder-cloud, and the rain which lasts three weeks and produces freshets. We need to witness our own limits transgressed, and some life pasturing freely where we never wander. We are cheered when we observe the vulture feeding on the carrion which disgusts and disheartens us, and deriving health and strength from the repast. There was a dead horse in the hollow by the path to my house, which compelled me sometimes to go out of my way, especially in the night when the air was heavy, but the assurance it gave me of the strong appetite and inviolable health of Nature was compensation for this. I love to see that Nature is so rife with life that myriads can be afforded to be sacrificed and suffered to prey on one another; that tender organizations can be so serenely squashed out of existence like pulp,—tadpoles which herons gobble up, and tortoises and toads run over in the road; and that sometimes it has rained flesh and blood! With the liability to accident, we must see how little account is to be made of it. The impression made on a wise man is that of universal innocence. Poison is not poisonous after all, nor are any wounds fatal. Compassion is a very untenable ground. (349–351)

This passage achieves distinction not by its substance but by its expression. The idea of the internecine warfare in nature was widespread in the decade that ended with the publication of Darwin's *Origin of Species*. It found its way into much of the literature of the day, but characteristically in a kind of fastidious flirting with "Nature red in tooth and claw," as in Tennyson's *In Memoriam*. Thoreau accepts the struggle for survival without qualms, then employs the skills of the writer's art to realize his special effects: precise diction, fresh imagery, modulation of tone, understatement, surprise, and paradox.

The structure of the paragraph is a sequence of nature miniatures that are cumulative and climactic. Their full meaning is developed only gradually, but the direction is set in the opening sentence: Our life needs renewal by contact with the primitive, "the tonic of wildness." The series of images that follow suggest the diversity of nature, but are unified by the fact that all have wild settings. They culminate at mid-point in a succinct summary: "We can never have enough of nature." The second half of the paragraph consists of a series of vignettes that are increasingly violent and revolting, building up to a climactic paradox. "I love to see that Nature is so rife with life," he declares, but this is immediately followed by demonstrations of the universality of death in nature. When he concludes that "sometimes it has rained flesh and blood!"—in parody of a nonsensical folk saying (it rained cats and dogs)—the horrific becomes comic. It is now clear that he has adopted a mode of mock horror only in order to express as startlingly as possible his yearning for wildness.

The entertainment is over. But several terse statements are appended for probing its true meaning, by relating his theme of wild nature to basic ideas in the Old and New Testaments. When he defines the wholesale carnage he has been describing as "universal innocence," he is correcting the popular misconception of what Eden was like before the Fall. Then man also lived like an animal in nature, it is implied, without the moral conscience and self-awareness that made possible the development from innocence to the human condition. The concluding sentence, "Compassion is a very untenable ground," puts a sharp limitation on what has always been taken as the most appealing attribute of Christ. His was compassion for the suffering of mankind. Thoreau warns that to carry this over to nature, to be distressed by pain and violence there, is to take a sentimental and hence a partial view. Destruction is a necessary aspect of the abundant health and vitality of nature. It is not a world of two conflicting forces, life and death, but of a single triumphant vital force. Thus he justifies the ways of nature to man, who must find empathy with its wildness if he is to be at home there.

The passage just interpreted must now be fitted into the larger design of *Walden*. It shows the capacity of the narrator to accept the natural world on the Dionysian level. The passage previously subjected to close reading, the miraculous influx of light at the advent of spring, showed him capable of rising above nature to an Apollonian vision. Does he now go on to achieve a synthesis such as that offered by Orphism? Initiates of this ancient cult believed that if they could sufficiently transcend the Dionysian world, they could escape from the perpetual process of change, revolving in a cycle, by finding an inner mystical spring which is eternal. There are echoes of this at the end of *Walden's* "Spring." At one point he says, "the coming in of spring is like the creation of Cosmos out of Chaos and the realization of the Golden Age." (346) Two pages later he quotes ten lines from Ovid's *Metamorphoses* to show that the Golden Age was a time of "eternal spring." These are not applied directly to the narrator, it is true, but there are also hints of a transformation going on inside himself. He speaks of "our own recovered innocence," and again he says: "our prospects brighten on the influx of better thoughts." (346) Most suggestive of all is a reference to the soaring of a hawk, frequently a symbol of his higher self: "It was the most ethereal flight I had ever witnessed." But despite all these veiled prophecies, after a reference to seeing a loon on the pond early in May, the chapter ends: "And so the seasons went rolling on into summer." (351) He is still revolving in the circle of nature and time. This is why one more chapter is necessary, to make his "Conclusion."

8
The Leap

"Thus was my first year's life in the woods completed; and the second year was similar to it. I finally left Walden September 6th, 1847." (351) These are the last two sentences of "Spring," but they have no real relation to that ecstatic and expectant chapter. Instead they are a postscript to the whole volume. By this abrupt change of key to the flat and factual, the reader is put right back where he was when he read the opening paragraph of *Walden:*

When I wrote the following pages, or rather the bulk of them, I lived alone, in the woods, a mile from any neighbor, in a house which I had built myself, on the shore of Walden Pond, in Concord, Massachusetts, and earned my living by the labor of my hands only. I lived there two years and two months. At present I am a sojourner in civilized life again. (3)

These two laconic bits of autobiographical summary frame the transcendent experience that lies between. Each is a linear image, a walk out from Concord and a return journey, the entrance and exit to the magic circle of Walden. But the natural world has turned out to be a place of ambiguous value for the poet, if lived in too long and too deeply. "I seem to be more constantly merged in nature," Thoreau warned himself once, "but perchance less obedient to spirit." (J, III, 66) If he felt the need to escape from entrapment in the cycle of nature the simplest way to do it was to take the straight path back to the civilized world he had left, a mile and a half by the Lincoln Road or less by the railroad cut.

"I left the woods for as good a reason as I went there," the author of the "Conclusion" to *Walden* says: "Perhaps it seemed to me that I had several more lives to live, and could not spare any more time for that one." (355) Why Thoreau, the man, terminated his residence at Walden Pond has always baffled readers even more than why he went there in the first place. He himself is forced into paradox and metaphor when trying to explain it on the literal level. The *Journal* passage of 22 January 1852 that was condensed into the sentences quoted above from the book offers a more elaborate but hardly more clarifying set of reasons:

> But why I changed? why I left the woods? I do not think that I can tell. I have often wished myself back. I do not know any better how I ever came to go there. Perhaps it is none of my business, even if it is yours. Perhaps I wanted a change. There was a little stagnation, it may be. About 2 o'clock in the afternoon the world's axle creaked as if it needed greasing, as if the oxen labored with the wain and could hardly get their load over the ridge of the day. Perhaps if I lived there much longer, I might live there forever. One would think twice before he accepted heaven on such terms. A ticket to Heaven must include tickets to Limbo, Purgatory, and Hell. (J, III, 214–215)

On the next page of the *Journal*, Thoreau makes a final try at explaining: "I must say that I do not know what made me leave the pond. I left it as unaccountably as I went to it. To speak sincerely, I went there because I had got ready to go; I left it for the same reason." The answer was, quite plainly, that he was as baffled as any one. Explaining one's motives to conduct in actual life is hard enough, if one really seeks the truth. The explanation of actions in mythology is harder still, if not impossible, and so they are invariably left ambiguous. The residence at Walden Pond took place on both levels, in real life and in the book he wrote about it. In the latter, Thoreau was both the contriver and the exemplar of his own myth. There could be no better proof of this than the fact that he falls ineluctably into myth-making language when trying to account for the literal act of going to the pond and leaving it, so fused were his life and his art at this point. A power beyond his knowing or coping with seems to have led him there and brought him back.

The skeleton plot of *Walden* is the archetypal monomyth of the hero's retreat from society, his initiation, and final return—as epitomized by Joseph Campbell: "A hero ventures forth from the world of common day into a region of supernatural wonder: fabulous forces are there encountered and a decisive victory is won: the hero comes back from this mysterious adventure with the power to bestow boons on his fellow men." This heroic subject matter is greatly simplified and its expression muted by Thoreau, of course, since he was writing for a modern audience that had rejected traditional mythology and embraced realism. But the special mythical character of his book has already been sufficiently manifested, and now it is echoed in the hyperbole of his reason for leaving the pond, "I had several more lives to live," even though he qualifies it with "perhaps." The new life he begins on his return to Concord is not the subject of his last chapter; it is, instead, the boon he brings back from the Walden experience to give his fellow men. This is not a practical gift, like the fire Prometheus brought, unless *Walden* itself can be so considered. It is a bundle of gifts, summed up by him in the first chapter of his book as "a simple and irrepressible satisfaction with the gift of life," (87) which he has received and is now eager to share with others.

The temptation to preach is almost irresistible for a poet who is convinced he has had a vision of a better life. Thoreau usually kept this tendency in control, but the very title of his final chapter, "Conclusion," doubled the temptation. He was, it must be admitted, a kind of Jeremiah in reverse, not calling his people back to the altar of their fathers but advising them instead to break away from the old and pioneer a new way of praising God. In drawing his conclusions, he sometimes demeans the poetic mode of *Walden* by pointing the finger of a moralist at his audience:

> However mean your life is, meet it and live it; do not shun it and call it hard names. It is not so bad as you are. It looks poorest when you are richest. . . . Cultivate poverty like a garden herb, like sage. Do not trouble yourself much to get new things, whether clothes or friends. Turn the old; return to them. Things do not change; we change. Sell your clothes and keep your thoughts. God will see that you do not want society. (361)

This kind of writing, here partly redeemed by the verbal play, could easily become tedious.

Since he felt the urge, quite understandably, to make some sort of statement before letting his readers go, it was much more acceptable to rejoice at his own gains than to task them for their shortcomings, as above:

> I learned this, at least, by my experiment; that if one advances confidently in the direction of his dreams, and endeavors to live the life which he has imagined, he will meet with a success unexpected in common hours. He will put some things behind, will pass an invisible boundary . . . and he will live with the license of a higher order of beings. In proportion as he simplifies his life, the laws of the universe will appear less complex, and solitude will not be solitude, nor poverty poverty, nor weakness weakness. (356)

This is consonant with the Vedantic teaching that informs so much of his great book, but it violates the mode and so would spoil the effect if continued too long. Sometimes his sententiousness rises into effective aphorism: "It is life near the bone where it is sweetest." (362) Or better still into a parable: "If you have built castles in the air, your work need not be lost; that is where they should be. Now put the foundations under them." (356) Best of all is his substitution of metaphor for the mode of didacticism in his last chapter, as he had replaced it by wit in his first. The finest thing about his "Conclusion" is a series of memorable images, linear instead of circular, that complete the meaning of *Walden*.

Another circle from which Thoreau felt the constant need to escape was that of convention, even when it was only conformity to his own round of habits. This is given as an additional reason for leaving Walden Pond. "I had not lived there a week before my feet wore a path," he confesses: "It is remarkable how easily and insensibly we fall into a particular route, and make a beaten track for ourselves." (355) But he did not return to Concord village to fall into any of its routines. Out of the goose-stepping of the local militia, one of the most hackneyed symbols for conformity, he created a new metaphor of the marching hero that has become famous through repeated quotation: "If a man does not keep pace with his companions, perhaps it is because he hears a different drummer. Let him step to the music which he hears, however measured or far away." (358–359) This image of the self-reliant man has a long and interesting history in Thoreau's writings. It first appears in a brief *Journal* passage in 1840, which was transcribed the same year into "The Service," his earliest completed essay: "A man's life should be a stately march to an unheard music, and when to his fellows it may seem irregular and inharmonious, he will be stepping to a livelier measure, which only his nicer ear can detect." When submitted to the transcendental *Dial* the essay was rejected, much to Thoreau's chagrin, and it remained unpublished until forty years after his death.

The image was salvaged, however, and reappears greatly extended in *A Week*. It is attached to the incident of hearing an actual drummer in the night, though described as a "stray sound from a far-off sphere," that comes to his ear as he is falling asleep on the bank of the Merrimack. It sets him musing:

> A strain of music reminds me of a passage of the Vedas, and I associate with it the idea of infinite remoteness, as well as of beauty and serenity, for to the senses that is farthest from us which addresses the greatest depth within us. It teaches us again and again to trust the remotest and finest as the divinest instinct, and makes a dream our only real experience. . . . That harmony which exists naturally between the hero's moods and the universe, the soldier would fain imitate with drum and trumpet. When we are in health, all sounds fife and drum for us. . . . Marching is when the pulse of the hero beats in unison with the pulse of Nature, and he steps to the measure of the universe. (I, 181, 183)

With such ease the hero of *A Week*, replacing the militia's fife and drum with sphere music, walks straight out of his mundane life into a life that is in harmony with the universe. One may rightly prefer to all this strident rhetoric the quietly controlled image in *Walden*, where all depends on the suggestiveness of a "different drummer" and music that comes from "far away." But readers seem to have missed what is clearly the follow up of Thoreau's martial metaphor in this book four pages later: "I delight to come to my bearings,—not walk in procession with pomp and parade, in a conspicuous place, but to walk even with the Builder of the universe, if I may,—not to live in this restless, nervous, bustling, trivial Nineteenth Century, but stand or sit thoughtfully while it goes by." (363) *Walden* has its own images of transcendence, all the more acceptable to modern readers for not being too insisted on.

In "Spring," it has been shown, Thoreau escaped from the limitations of Time by maneuvering it into an intricate pattern of life, death, and rebirth. Having collapsed the two years and more of his actual residence into one, he then extended that year to include two springs so he could bend linear time into a circle —a movement from the given spring of youth to the earned one of a remade spirit. Finally, to escape entrapment in this annual cycle, he reworked his design into a spiral by making the second spring rise to a much higher level than the first. In "Conclusion" he makes another kind of escape, this one from the limitations of Space, by means of an extraordinary cluster of travel images.

The journey motif permeates Thoreau's writings. *A Week on the Concord and Merrimack Rivers*, *Cape Cod*, *The Maine Woods* and *A Yankee in Canada* are all records of actual trips or voyages. Many of his best essays are likewise the fruit of excursions, sometimes stated in their titles ("Walking" and "A Winter Walk"), sometimes clearly implied ("Wild Apples" and "Autumnal Tints"). Even the fourteen-volume *Journal* is a kind of journey, through the days and the years. All of this, as related to his unusually wide reading in travel literature, has been made the subject of a recent book, *Thoreau as World Traveller*, a fine ironic label for the most-rooted author in American literary history. *Walden* is the final and unique expression of this theme. It contains a fair amount of travel on the literal level: trips to and from the village, rambles in the woods and visits to neighboring people and places, walks around Walden Pond and around the circle of ponds. But the symbolic journey is what really counts, as Professor Christie phrases it so astutely:

To explore oneself through an exploration of the natural world—that total world of the geographer, its natural features and its human environmental phenomena together—this was a route so characteristically Thoreau's that its definition in the analogy [of travel] which unified *Walden* already seemed familiar and unobtrusive by 1854. To write a travel book about a traveler who explores one place thoroughly, that he may thereby discover the resources of his own nature and spirit, is only the logical extension of the metaphor toward which all Thoreau's travel experience pointed. . . . Seen in this light, the book is Thoreau's characteristic presentation of truth through paradox, an account of a traveler's stay in one place.

Thoreau's attachment to his locale is well known, but two of his most important statements about it have been overlooked, curiously enough. In the *Journal* for 11 November 1853 he gives his reasons for preferring rootedness to travel:

I cannot but regard it as a kindness in those who have the steering of me that, by the want of pecuniary wealth, I have been nailed down to this my native region so long and steadily, and made to study and love this spot of earth more and more. What would signify in comparison a thin and diffused love of the whole earth instead, got by wandering? The traveller's is but a barren and comfortless condition. (J, V, 496–497)

The second comment, several years later, adds time to place and makes an aphorism out of his contentment: "I have never got over my surprise that I should have been born into the most estimable place in all the world, and in the very nick of time, too." (J, IX, 160) It remains now to bring into focus the special travel imagery in *Walden,* and in the *Journal,* that will illuminate the theme of the present study.

Once, in a characteristic etymological game, Thoreau elevates the secular walker into the religious pilgrim. It occurs in the context of his laments about the rarity of the person with "a genius

. . . for sauntering," one who does not walk for exercise or to get somewhere but "to succeed to the highest and worthiest ends by the abandonment of all specific ends." Then comes the verbal play:

And this word "saunter," by the way, is happily derived "from idle people who roved about the country [in the Middle Ages] and asked charity under pretense of going *à la Sainte Terre*," to the Holy Land, till, perchance, the children exclaimed, "There goes a *Sainte-Terrer*," a Holy-Lander. They who never go to the Holy Land in their walks, as they pretend, are indeed mere idlers and vagabonds.

This *Journal* passage from 1851 was incorporated in "Walking," a posthumously published essay celebrating his forays into "wildness"—another example of his familiar dichotomy of savage and spiritual. As such it is highly relevant to *Walden* and would undoubtedly have been used there had it not been put to another purpose, as the opening gambit in his lecture on "Wild and Walking," his chief offering when responding to lecture invitations during the 1850's. Though this fabling etymology is not included in his book, the idea is. The word appears there only twice, but the same doubleness of meaning is encompassed. In "Visitors" it is applied to the Canadian woodchopper, that wild "Paphlagonian" man, who is seen "sauntering through the village" like "a prince in disguse." (164) In "Winter Visitors" it is applied to Alcott, the "blue-robed" saint: "Of yore we had sauntered and talked, and effectually put the world behind us." (296–297) But it is the narrator himself, with all his symbolic journeyings, who is the true "saunterer" in *Walden*, though not explicitly so named.

"I have travelled a good deal in Concord," (4) Thoreau announces at the very beginning of his book, an extravagance that has won a kind of indulgent renown. Even when one points out that "Concord" refers not to the town but to the township of about fifteen square miles, it still seems only the amusing exaggeration of a parochial boaster. But understood in the full context of its *double entendre*, it is one of the best pieces of wit in *Walden*. Even in terms of local geography his meaning goes beyond the literal. "It takes a man of genius to travel in his own country, in his native village; to make any progress between his door and his gate," he comments in the *Journal* of August 1851. (J, II, 376) A few months later he adds: "The question is not where did the traveller go? . . . but *who* was the traveller?" (J, III, 183)

Thoreau is constantly expressing his preference for solitary walks, once justifying his refusal to take a companion by saying: "the woodpath [is] my studio, where I maintain a sacred solitude and cannot admit promiscuous company." (J, XII, 333) An interesting variant, when he broke his rule in order to respond to the call of civic duty, is recorded in the *Journal* of the same period, September 1851:

> On Monday, the 15th instant, I am going to perambulate the bounds of the town. As I am partial to across-lot routes, this appears to be a very proper duty for me to perform. . . . It is a sort of reconnoissance of its frontiers authorized by the central government of the town, which will bring the surveyor in contact with whatever wild inhabitant or wilderness its territory embraces. (J, II, 498–499)

His reaction to this experience is a combination of wit and vituperation. The men he had been forced to live with during the week of perambulating he found to be "narrow-minded . . . grovelling, coarse, and low-lived." No amount of scenery could redeem such a walk:

> I feel as if I had committed suicide in a sense. . . . Though I have been associating even with the *select* men of this and the surrounding towns, I feel inexpressibly begrimed. My Pegasus has lost his wings; he has turned a reptile and gone on his belly. . . . It is a charmed circle which I have drawn around my abode, having walked not with God but with the devil. (J, III, 23, 5, 24)

This explosion is saved from being merely perverse and antisocial by the conclusion, so pertinent to the travel imagery in *Walden:*

> The poet must keep himself unstained and aloof. Let him perambulate the bounds of Imagination's provinces, the realms of faery, and not the insignificant boundaries of towns. The excur-

sions of the imagination are so boundless, the limits of towns are so petty. (J, III, 5)

"To travel and 'descry new lands' is to think new thoughts, and have new imaginings," he had written in his *Journal* a decade before: "The deepest and most original thinker is the farthest travelled." (LJ, 153) This is what is meant, on the second and more significant level, by his whimsical remark: "I have travelled a good deal in Concord." Throughout *Walden*, local images are extended to global ones by imaginary travel. As he looks across the pond from his cabin door, "the opposite shore . . . stretched away toward the prairies of the West and the steppes of Tartary." (97) When the ice is cut in winter to be shipped to Asia by Yankee clipper, as has been pointed out, the pure Walden water is mingled with the sacred water of the Ganges. This is not cartographic window dressing. Instead, these are gleanings from his great storehouse of reading in Western and Oriental travel books; more importantly, they are allusions to the culture of American Indians and East Indians that he studied so intensively. Concord township is linked, by thought and imagination, to the lands and literatures of the world.

The final chapter of *Walden* contains the greatest concentration of travels, travelers, and foreign parts to be found in any one place in all Thoreau's writings. But the facts here, as always, are only starting points for figures of speech. There are two kinds of travel images, linear and circular. The latter carry only negative meanings. Brief mention is made of the migrations of the goose and bison, each of whom "keeps pace with the seasons," only to remind us of the annual cycle he is still trying to escape from. Globe-trotting is lightly disparaged as an exercise in futility, actually going in circles. Who wants to rush off to South Africa "to chase the giraffe," to go on expeditions to the North Pole or the sources of the Nile, to search out "a Northwest Passage around this continent"? He dismisses the whole business by saying, "It is not worth the while to go round the world to count the cats in Zanzibar," pointing his satire by reference to an actual triviality he had picked up from a recent travel book. A final circular image of travel is especially interesting because of its ambiguity. In the context of globe-trotting, and so presumably with disparagement, he says: "Our voyaging is only great-circle sailing." (352) This is the navigator's term for sailing along any of the "great circles" like the equator, such a course being the shortest between any two points on the earth's surface. That is, it fits the definition of a straight line, the illusion experienced by the voyager, but it is actually an arc of the earth's sphere, and following it, he eventually comes back to where he started from.

It is only by linear images of travel that Thoreau could annihilate space. The most soaring one in *Walden* over-leaps all boundaries and leaves the planet. But first a *Journal* entry for 1851 that offers a substantial launching pad for his space flight: "We experience pleasure when an elevated field or even road in which we may be walking holds its level toward the horizon at a tangent to the earth, is not convex with the earth's surface, but an absolute level." (J, II, 422) Although Thoreau was well aware of the optical illusion involved in the actual phenomenon, he did not hesitate to use it metaphorically in his book. There, in "Conclusion," it becomes his greatest leap of the spirit:

> Start now on that farthest western way, which does not pause at the Mississippi or the Pacific, nor conduct toward a wornout China or Japan, but leads on direct, a tangent to this sphere, summer and winter, day and night, sun down, moon down, and at last earth down too. (354–355)

There is an even more extravagant flight in an early *Journal* passage, too fanciful to have been included in *Walden* but deserving quotation here because it links a linear travel image of migrating birds with the rebirth imagery in "Spring":

> To-day I feel the migratory instinct strong in me, and all my members and humors anticipate the breaking up of winter. If I yielded to this impulse, it would surely guide me to summer haunts. This indefinite restlessness and fluttering on the perch do, no doubt, prophesy the final migration of souls out of nature to a serene summer, in long harrows and waving lines in the spring weather, over

what fair uplands and fertile Elysian meadows winging their way at evening and seeking a resting-place with loud cackling and uproar! (J, I, 176)

This is indeed an unusable flight of fancy, whether for bird or man, here merged into one as a symbol of the soul in its final transmigration to eternal summer.

Thoreau's other linear travel image is entirely valid, not an escape into outer space but a journey downward into the Self. The original *Journal* draft for the opening page of "Conclusion," rich in its references to external travel, ends with an alternative recommendation: "Let us migrate interiorly without intermission." (J, I, 131) In *Walden* this is expanded into a two-page conceit for internal travel. It is "validated," appropriately, by citation of two metaphysical authors, a minor poet and a master of prose. Thoreau launches his journey with a quotation from William Habington's poetic epistle to a friend, though without naming author or title:

> Direct your eye right inward, and you'll find
> A thousand regions in your mind
> Yet undiscovered. Travel them, and be
> Expert in home-cosmography.

This is followed by several questions posing the alternatives of external and internal travel: "What does Africa,—what does the West stand for? Is not our own interior white on the chart? [That is, unexplored.] . . . Is it the source of the Nile, or the Niger, or the Mississippi, or a Northwest Passage around this continent, that we would find?" (353) At this point the second and most important allusion comes into play. It is much more subtle, being merely the ingestion of an idea from Sir Thomas Browne's *Religio Medici*, without quotation or any direct clue to the source. About the year 1840, Thoreau had copied down in his commonplace book a passage in which Browne says he can match all that the Nile and the North Pole have to offer, "in the cosmography of myself," without the bother of travel: "We carry with us the wonders we seek without us. There is all Africa and her prodigies in us."

Just how completely Thoreau assimilated this idea is shown by the answer he gives in *Walden* to his own rhetorical questions, quoted above: "Be rather the Mungo Park, the Lewis and Clark and Frobisher, of your own streams and oceans; explore your own higher latitudes. . . . Nay, be a Columbus to whole new continents and worlds within you, opening new channels, not of trade, but of thought." (353) Again, this is not name-dropping but a pertinent reference to the authors of travel books he was intimately acquainted with—accounts of exploring expeditions to the heart of Africa, the American West, and a possible route around America to Cathay—topped with a salute to the symbolic explorer of new worlds. "If you would travel farther than all travellers," he concludes—"Explore thyself." (354) So he gives new life to an old cliché.

His final linear image of travel annihilates all space by drawing it into himself, making it an idea in the mind and a metaphor on the page. "As travellers go round the world and report natural objects and phenomena," he suggests in a *Journal* entry of 1851, "so faithfully let another stay at home and report the phenomena of his own life,—catalogue stars, those thoughts whose orbits are as rarely calculated as comets. . . . A meteorological journal of the mind." (J, II, 403) This is a perfect description of his own book, being completed at the time, with its program of the most intensive kind of living symbolized by the most extensive kind of travel. When reading Gibbon's memoirs he once commented: "To my mind he travels as far when he takes a book from the shelf, as if he went to the barrows of Asia." (LJ, 182) One might say the same thing after reading *Walden,* the unique memoir of Henry Thoreau.

The poet draws all things into himself—Space and Time, Nature and God—only so that he can give them out again recreated as metaphors. Just as Thoreau merged himself with all these by learning to orbit in their circles, so he learned to escape from all entrapments by vertical leaps into a newly identified life. There could be no happier way to conclude this reading of his "one book of poetry" than by examining several of those purely linear images that will point to some of the final meanings in *Walden*, the two most memorable ones coming in its "Conclusion."

One of the earliest in the book occurs in that often cited list of "enterprises" to which he has dedicated himself: "In any weather, at any hour of the day or night, I have been anxious to improve the nick of time, and notch it on my stick too; to stand on the meeting of two eternities, the past and future, which is precisely the present moment; to toe that line." (18) This is his witty version of the transcendental formula for escaping from the wheel of time by living in the Eternal Now. Again, in the same introductory chapter, "Economy," noting that the seed sends its radicle downward so that it can send its shoot upward with equal confidence, he invokes another transcendental doctrine: "Why has man rooted himself thus firmly in the earth, but that he may rise in the same proportion into the heavens above." (17) The same moral analogy is made in the next to last chapter, drawn from the new grass that shoots up in "Spring": "So our human life but dies down to its root, and still puts forth its green blade to eternity." (343) Thoreau is not often so solemnly didactic, but he found it hard to dodge the idea of Correspondence when looking for intimations of immortality.

Much more in keeping with the style of *Walden* at its best is a vignette in his central chapter "The Ponds." He begins by telling how sometimes, returning late from the village, "partly with a view to the next day's dinner, [I] spent the hours of midnight fishing from a boat by moonlight." What follows is one of those miniature anecdotes, moving by surprise from factual to figurative language, that adorn his narrative and point up his meanings. In a timeless mood he drifts about the pond until he feels a slight vibration along the line:

At length you slowly raise, pulling hand over hand, some horned pout squeaking and squirming to the upper air. It was very queer, especially in dark nights, when your thoughts had wandered to vast and cosmogonal themes in other spheres, to feel this faint jerk, which came to interrupt your dreams and link you to Nature again.

It seemed as if I might next cast my line upward into the air, as well as downward into this element, which was scarcely more dense. Thus I caught two fishes as it were with one hook. (194–195)

In a much earlier chapter a similar image occurs in brief: "I would . . . fish in the sky, whose bottom is pebbly with stars." (109) And far along in the book, in "The Pond in Winter," when he cuts a hole in the ice and peers down into the "quiet parlor" of the fishes looking as serene as in summer, he creates an answering image: "Heaven is under our feet as well as over our heads." (313) Walden Pond, with its transparent waters and its calm reflecting surface, was a perfect source of metaphors for the heavenward leap that transcends the limitations of earth.

The complementary aspects of pond and sky lead to a series of images by which he tries to probe for himself. In an early *Journal* entry he says: "I cannot see the bottom of the sky, because I cannot see to the bottom of myself. It is the symbol of my own infinity." (J, I, 150) Turning to Walden Pond, a more accessible point for measurement, he makes it into a lens of magical powers: "It is earth's eye; looking into which the beholder measures the depth of his own nature." (206–207) This image-and-idea from "The Ponds" is picked up seven chapters later in "The Pond in Winter." Many people have tried to sound the bottom of Walden without success, he says, "paying out the rope in the vain attempt to fathom their truly immeasurable capacity for marvellousness." Then he adds, with feigned condescension, "While men believe in the infinite some ponds will be thought to be bottomless." (316) Having pretended to ally himself with science, he then spreads out his survey of the pond over some five or six pages, with the precise detail of a limnologist.

His conclusion sounds like that of a scientific researcher: "I . . . found, to my surprise, that the line of greatest length intersected the line of greatest breadth *exactly* at the point of greatest depth." (319, 315–320) But the use to which he puts this new fact gives the game away. "What I have observed of the pond is no less true in ethics," he says, and then proceeds to apply the "rule of the two diameters" to man for the purpose of measuring the "height or depth of his character." (321–322) The page-long *jeu d'esprit* that follows has been called by one critic "a kind of superb topographical phrenology." It is actually a compounding of the device of arguing by analogy: the shape of the pond added to the shape of the human head to find correspondences in the character of the man within. Phrenology by mid-century had been recognized as only a pseudo-science, and so not taken seriously, though it continued to be useful to poets as a source of metaphor (Poe, Emerson, Whitman, to name only a few). Thoreau's conceit is clearly touched with wit. It begins: "As I was desirous to recover the long lost bottom of Walden Pond, I surveyed it carefully," and so on. (315) He found its bottom and at the same time discovered the foundation of his own faith. He differed from contemporary sounders of the pond not by being scientific while they were superstitious. It was not by failing to plumb some mystery in nature that he came to believe in the infinite but by measuring "the depth of his own nature."

In a direction opposite to this downward probing is the erection of his chimney. Of course, the chimney is a fact as well as an image, the building of it being part of the "economy" of the Walden experiment, postponed for several months after the cabin was completed since he did not need it until cold weather came. This delay throws it into the chapter called "House-Warming," and the verbal play of that title is echoed all through the passage describing its construction. He concludes with a significant metaphor. After commenting on the fact that one often sees chimneys still standing long after the houses are gone, he says: "The chimney is to some extent an independent structure, standing on the ground, and rising through the house to the heavens." (267) Part of the effectiveness here is that the chimney is by its very nature symbolic and requires little contrivance on the part of the writer to make it so. Thoreau was quick to exploit its other possibilities. "I took a poet to board for a fortnight about those times," he says. It is well known that Ellery Channing was a guest at Walden during the fall of 1845, and presumably helped with building the chimney. But Thoreau was a poet too, as well as a mason, and once again he gives us a figure that can be reckoned as his double. At any rate, it was he and not Channing who wrote the poem "Smoke," that concludes his chapter and his metaphor:

> Light-winged Smoke, Icarian bird,
> Melting thy pinions in thy upward flight,
> Lark without song, and messenger of dawn,
> Circling above the hamlets as thy nest;
> Or else, departing dream, and shadowy form
> Of midnight vision, gathering up thy skirts;
> By night star-veiling, and by day
> Darkening the light and blotting out the sun;
> Go thou my incense upward from this hearth,
> And ask the gods to pardon this clear flame. (279)

Of the many poems written by Thoreau, in the conventional sense of verse-poems, this is one of the very few that is successful —possibly because it rises directly out of the text of *Walden*, his one really great "poem." The sentence that launches it is part of its meaning: "When the villagers were lighting their fires beyond the horizon, I too gave notice to the various wild inhabitants of Walden vale, by a smoky streamer from my chimney, that I was awake." The woodland solitude makes an appropriate setting for his morning ritual of kindling a fire, his ever-fresh renewal of purpose; "awake" is his constant term for being alive, the "dead" being those who are always asleep. The sentence that follows (previously quoted in another context) is also a gloss on the poem: "It was I and Fire that lived there." "Fire" is another double for the narrator, also a double symbol, as has been shown: the vital heat for sustaining life through the winter and the "flame" of his thought or inner self. Its use in the poem proves this.

If the chimney is only indirectly a symbol for Thoreau, the smoke is made directly so: "Go thou *my incense* upward from this hearth." Not quite his prayer, but his fragrant burnt offering that might stand for it, and offered quite safely in a Christian land to the plural "gods," without specifying which ones. But why does he ask the gods "to *pardon* this clear flame"? The last line is the crux of the poem, and one must circle back to the first to clarify its meaning by asking why he calls the smoke "Icarian bird"? The allusion brings in the legend of Icarus, the arrogant demi-god who defied the laws of nature and hence the gods by trying to fly on man-made wings, came too near heaven and, burned by the sun's heat, fell to his death in the sea. Thoreau's smoke in its "upward flight" like a bird also challenges heaven and might seem to risk a similar fate—except that it is quickly transformed through a series of images into a lark, dawn's messenger, a dream, a vision. Still the "clear flame" of his spirit burns so brightly that its smoke "blots out the sun," and it needs a plea for pardon to keep him from verging on hubris. It is almost like a prayer from one god to another, from an earthly Apollo to the heavenly one.

If Thoreau could hint at his own divinity by identifying with Apollo from time to time, he could also suggest that he has already achieved immortality. He does so by fashioning a legend of the artist of Kouroo that is a parable of his own life and vocation. It sounds like a Hindu myth, but no one has been able to discover a source for it. Happily it must be taken as an original creation, but rendered so perfectly in the guise of an Oriental scripture as to be mistaken for one. All that came directly from his reading is that Kouroo (Kooroo, Kuru) is mentioned in the *Mahabharata* and in the *Bhagvat-Geeta* as a sacred land or nation, and is referred to in the *Laws of Menu* as the country of Brahmanical sages. When Thoreau published his extracts from the last named in the *Dial* for January 1843, he included that reference and, significantly, cited Menu's dictum: "The hand of an artist employed in his art is always pure." All the rest of this legend is Thoreau's own, his most impressive leap of the imagination. It begins:

There was an artist in the city of Kouroo who was disposed to strive after perfection. One day it came into his mind to make a staff. Having considered that in an imperfect work time is an ingredient, but into a perfect work time does not enter, he said to himself, It shall be perfect in all respects, though I should do nothing else in my life. . . . His singleness of purpose and resolution, and his elevated piety, endowed him, without his knowledge, with perennial youth. As he made no compromise with Time, Time kept out of his way. (359)

By the time this artist had found a stick suitable for carving, his friends had deserted him, or died, and the city itself was a hoary ruin. Before he had given it proper shape, the dynasty of the Candahars was over, and with the point of his stick he wrote the name of the last of them in the sand. Before he had polished and adorned it, Brahma had slept and waked many times:

But why do I stay to mention these things? When the finishing stroke was put to his work, it suddenly expanded before the eyes of the astonished artist into the fairest of all the creations of Brahma. He had made a new system in making a staff, a world with full and fair proportions. . . . And now he saw by the heap of shavings still fresh at his feet, that, for him and his work, the former lapse of time had been an illusion. . . . The material was pure, and his art was pure; how could the result be other than wonderful? (360)

A final clue identifying the artist of Kouroo as Thoreau, if any were needed, can be found in his letter to a friend, in the context of his own life and work and with a reference to Brahmans: "How admirably the artist is made to accomplish his self-culture by devotion to his art!" The letter was written in December 1853, about the same time the legend was being added to the book. It is clearly a parable of Thoreau's own labors to create a perfect work of art in *Walden*, polishing and revising it through eight separate drafts over a period of as many years—all but literally devoting his life to it. His dedication and singleness of purpose endowed him also "with perennial youth." As the carver of Kouroo aspired upward, fashioning his simple staff, as the original Creator of the pond rounded it with his hand into an object of natural beauty and symbolic significance, so Thoreau shaped his own experience into the magic circle of *Walden*—and then made his leap out of it by translating his facts from earth to heaven. If man is to escape from the trap of time and the limitations of nature, according to this book, he will be able to do so only through the immortality of art.

One might prefer that *Walden* should end here, but there is a tailpiece that risks anticlimax and escapes it by a hair. It brings the flight back to earth, and by returning to the issues of "Economy" brings the book full circle. Following the Kouroo passage there are six pages of sharp comments on the hurry and waste and desperation of life in the modern world. This starts Thoreau's great book running downhill rather fast, to the reader's dismay. But it is stopped just in time, by another legend. This one is not original, but a new version of one that was widely known in that age. It deals with the New World, instead of the Old, and provides a needed final dimension:

> Every one has heard the story which has gone the rounds of New England, of a strong and beautiful bug which came out of the dry leaf of an old table of apple-tree wood, which had stood in a farmer's kitchen for sixty years, first in Connecticut, and afterward in Massachusetts,—from an egg deposited in the living tree many years earlier still, as appeared by counting the annual layers beyond it; which was heard gnawing out for several weeks, hatched perchance by the heat of an urn. Who does not feel his faith in resurrection and immortality strengthened by hearing of this? Who knows what beautiful and winged life, whose egg has been buried for ages under many concentric layers of woodenness in the dead dry life of society, deposited at first in the alburnum of the green and living tree, which has been gradually converted into the semblance of its well-seasoned tomb,—heard perchance gnawing out now for years by the astonished family of man, as they sat round the festive board,—may unexpectedly come forth from amidst society's most trivial and handselled furniture, to enjoy its perfect summer life at last! (366–367)

Here is one more miniature version of *Walden*. This one has the right homely New England touch for the conclusion, and

Thoreau would probably enjoy the wit of being symbolized by "a strong and beautiful bug." After all, the book is about society and how to escape from that too. Like the bug he makes his way out by a horizontal linear image, through the concentric circles of convention. And the metaphor of his emergence into a perfect summer life at last earns him the right to the high hopes of the sentences with which the book ends: "There is more day to dawn. The sun is but a morning star." (367)

Abbreviations

Alcott	*The Journals of Bronson Alcott*, ed. Odell Shepard (1938)
Cameron, *Minerva*	K. W. Cameron, ed., *The Transcendentalists and Minerva* (1958), 3 vols.
Cameron, *Notebook*	K. W. Cameron, ed., *Thoreau's Literary Notebook in the Library of Congress* (1964)
Christy	Arthur Christy, *The Orient in American Transcendentalism* (1932)
Correspondence	*The Correspondence of Henry David Thoreau*, ed. Walter Harding and Carl Bode (1958)
Emerson, *Journals*	*The Journals of Ralph Waldo Emerson*, eds. E. W. Emerson and W. E. Forbes (1909–14), 10 vols.
Emerson, *Works*	*The Complete Works of Ralph Waldo Emerson*, ed. E. W. Emerson (1903–04), 12 vols.
Harding	Walter Harding, *The Days of Henry Thoreau* (1965)
Iamblicus	Iamblicus, *The Life of Pythagoras*, tr. Thomas Taylor (London, 1818)
LJ	Perry Miller, *Consciousness in Concord* [Thoreau's "Lost Journal"] (1958)
Paul	Sherman Paul, *The Shores of America: Thoreau's Inward Exploration* (1958)
Porphyry	Porphyry, *Abstinence from Animal Food* (in *Select Works of Porphyry*), tr. Thomas Taylor (London, 1823)
Seybold	Ethel Seybold, *Thoreau: The Quest and the Classics* (1951)
Shanley	J. L. Shanley, *The Making of Walden* (1957)

Notes

References to *The Writings of Thoreau* (Boston, 1906), 20 vols., will be found in the text, in parentheses immediately following the quotation or citation. All other references will be found in these notes. They have been kept to a minimum by citing only those works that have proved helpful. In the interests of conciseness I have used a shortened form for those items listed in the table of abbreviations (opposite); also, I have omitted the publisher and place for book titles, except when they were necessary to identify a particular edition.

The notes that follow are cued back to the text by page number and key phrase (the last words of quotations and several of the most important words for other than quoted matter). No superscript numerals are used in the text, since in a book of this sort there are few occasions that call for annotation and these will be readily apparent. To facilitate location of the notes, running heads for this section indicate where they fit in the text (*e.g.*, "Notes for pp. 7–15," etc.).

NOTES FOR *THOREAU AND "I"*

1 *Holmes: Ralph Waldo Emerson* (1885), 86.

1 *Lowell:* "Thoreau," *My Study Windows* (1871), 199.

1 *Stevenson See* Walter Harding, ed., *Thoreau: A Century of Criticism* (1955), 59–83, for a convenient reprinting of Stevenson's essay.

1 *Emerson:* his essay on Thoreau is conveniently reprinted as the "Biographical Sketch" in *The Writings of Thoreau* (1906); *see* I, xxxvii.

5 *"what I have done once"* The anecdote is reported in Emerson's "Biographical Sketch" (*see* Thoreau's *Writings,* I, xv). But he did return to the family business, off and on, until the end of his life. In 1847, replying to a questionnaire as to what he had been doing in the way of a trade or

profession during the ten years since his graduation from Harvard, Thoreau wrote: "I have found out a way to live without what is commonly called employment or industry, attractive or otherwise. Indeed my steadiest employment, if such it can be called, is to keep myself at the top of my condition, and ready for whatever may turn up in heaven or earth." Then he added a one-sentence summary of the Walden experiment, just completed. (*Correspondence*, 186)

7 *Beck Stow's swamp See* Emerson's "Biographical Sketch" in Thoreau's *Writings*, I, xxix.

7 *"an elm tree" See* Emerson, *Journals*, VI, 371; VII, 498.

8 *love affair* The strongest case for it is made by Harding (94–104); the strongest case against, by Perry Miller (LJ, 82–86).

8 *"in my career" See* Thoreau's *Correspondence*, 190–191.

9 *Concord Lyceum lectures See* Harding, 187–188.

10 *Journal is not autobiography* See J, VIII, 64: "In a true history or biography, of how little consequence those events of which so much is commonly made! . . . I find in my Journal that the most important events in my life, if recorded at all, are not dated."

There are only 76 pages in the *Journal* for the two-year period, 1845–1847, plus 50 more pages of undated fragments for the decade of 1837–1847 (J, I, 361–437 and 438–488). From 1850 on there is an average of more than 500 pages a year, about ten times as much as for the crucial Walden years. Thoreau's *Correspondence* for the same period includes only eight letters, six of which are very brief.

10 *facts for Walden years See* Harding, 179–199. His next chapter also covers the years 1845–1847, but deals with Thoreau's experiences away from the pond: the jail episode, the excursion to Maine, etc.

NOTES FOR CHAPTER 1: THE WEB

14 *"take part in it"* The translation is Thoreau's. J, I, 4–5. Cameron, *Minerva*, I, 237, says that Thoreau read Goethe's *Torquato Tasso* in German in Emerson's set of the *Werke* (Stuttgart, 1828–33). Leonora's description of the poet can be found in Vol. IX, pp. 107–108, lines 167–169:

In diesem eignen Zauberkreise wandelt
Der wunderbare Mann und zieht uns an,
Mit ihm zu wandeln, teil an ihm zu
nehmen . . .

15 *"contain them all"* J, III, 311 (18 Feb. 1852). Version IV, the first significant re-writing of *Walden*, was begun about the middle of January 1852. (Shanley, 30–31)

17 *"I sat outside"* See Thoreau's *Correspondence*, 290.

22 *"where to lay his head"* Matthew 8.20.

25 *letter scarcely clarifies it* In a letter of 1857, replying to a friend's inquiry as to the meaning of "a hound, a bay horse, and a turtle-dove," Thoreau said: "How shall we account for our pursuits if they are original? We get our language with which to describe our various lives out of a common mint. If others have their losses, which they are busy repairing, so have I *mine*, & their hound & horse may *perhaps* be the symbol of some of them. But also I have lost, or am in danger of losing, a far finer & more ethereal treasure, which commonly no loss of which they are conscious will symbolize—this I answer hastily & with some hesitation, according as I now understand my own words." (*Correspondence*, 478)

26 *"necessity of selling them"* This fable of the Indian baskets was not added to *Walden* until Version IV, summer 1852, after Thoreau knew of the failure of *A Week*. (Shanley, 31, 72)

27 *book on food reform* William Alcott, *The Young Housekeeper* (1838), 362. See the discussion by Joseph Jones, "Transcendental Grocery Bills," UTSE, XXXVI (1957), 141–154.

28 *"sweats easier than I do"* *Cf.* Genesis 3. 19. It is interesting to compare at this point one of the very earliest known writings of Thoreau, his part in a "Conference" at the time of his graduation from Harvard, August 1837, under the title of "The Commercial Spirit of Modern Times." One paragraph of it reads: "This curious world which we inhabit is more wonderful than it is convenient, more beautiful than it is useful—it is more to be admired and enjoyed then, than used. The order of things should be somewhat reversed. —the seventh should be man's day of toil, wherein to earn his living by the sweat of his brow, and the other six his sabbath of the affections and the soul, in which to range this widespread garden, and drink in the soft influences and sublime revelations of nature." (Reprinted in Cameron, *Minerva*, I, 234.)

28 *Walden digresses* See pp. 50–53, 55–60, 62–65, 79–87. Thoreau admits his digressive tendency by reminding himself in the midst of these criticisms of society, "But to proceed with my statistics." (65)

29 *"Economy" is a witty fable* The great difference made by the mode of wit in the presentation of the Walden experiment in economy may be illustrated by comparing the more serious treatment of such matters in the *Journal*. Thoreau's discussion of the problem ranges over a period of twenty

years, from 1841 (LJ, 214) to 1861 (J, XIV, 306–307). There is a long recapitulation in the *Journal* for 1855, probably inspired by the publication of *Walden* the year before. A sample will suffice: "The world will never find out why you don't love to have your bed tucked up for you—why you will be so perverse. I enjoy more drinking water at a clear spring than out of a goblet at a gentleman's table. I like best the bread which I have baked, the garment which I have made, the shelter which I have constructed, the fuel which I have gathered," (J, VII, 502–503. See also VII, 519–520; VIII, 7–8, 18–19, 30–31—all in 1855). If *Walden* were written like this, readers might indeed think it perverse.

33 *"the mountain cabin transformed"* In Version I of *Walden* (Shanley, 138), written in 1847 presumably, the passage is closer to the *Journal* than to the book text. When the final revisions were made is not known.

35 *"most important words"* F. O. Matthiessen, *American Renaissance* (1941), 95–96. Several of the points in my explication are indebted to him.

35 *"God and Him only"* See Shanley, 141.

38 *seventeenth-century meaning of wit* John Locke, *Essay Concerning the Human Understanding*, Chap. XI, 2. See J, V, 242, for an excellent example: "Murder will out. I find, in the dry excrement of a fox left on a rock, the vertebrae and talons of a partridge (?) which he has consumed. They are *memoires pour servir*."

42 *parody of the New Testament* "For what shall it profit a man, if he shall gain the whole world, and lose his own soul?" (Mark 8.36)

"For whosoever . . . will lose his life for my sake shall find it." (Matthew 16.25)

"He that loveth his life shall lose it; and he that hateth his life in this world shall keep it unto life eternal." (John 12.25)

42 *"to suffer and to work"* See Emerson, *Works*, I, 95.

43 *"a huckleberry-party"* See Emerson's "Biographical Sketch," *The Writings of Thoreau*, I, xxxvii.

45 *Walden Pond a symbol* There are a dozen brief but brilliant circle images in this chapter (treated in "Circles," pp. 213–257, below), it is true, but most of its thirty pages are unadorned and factual. Another matter of special interest is the curious fact that only two or three pages of "The Ponds" are included in Version I of *Walden*, written during the actual residence there. All the rest was first drafted in the *Journal* during the summer and fall of 1852, based on trips back to the pond for this particular purpose, and then included in Versions IV-VI, 1852–1853. (See J, IV, 320–21, 335–41, 357–58, 387, 406–08, 411, 423–25, 447; V, 260, 265.) There are other symbolic passages on Walden in the *Journal*, ranging all the way from 1840 to 1860 (LJ, 185; J, XIV, 60–61).

45 *"law for thing"* Emerson, "Ode Inscribed to W. H. Channing." Transcendentalists would probably have interpreted Thoreau's triad of being-nonbeing-becoming as an example of the Hegelian triad of thesis-antithesis-synthesis.

47 *"hatches his own schemes"* Northrop Frye, *Anatomy of Criticism* (1957), 174; 39–40, 172–176.

49 *"his enthusiasm abated"* *See* Harding, 362, 265–266.

49 *"has trodden our woods"* Alcott, 193.

49 *"lying on the air"* *Quoted* by Rose Hawthorne Lathrop, *Memories of Hawthorne* (1897), 53.

54 *analogue of eiron-alazon* J. J. Moldenhauer, "Paradox in *Walden*," *Graduate Journal*, VI (1964), 132–46. I am indebted to him for the basic idea of *eiron-alazon* and the summary on this page and the following.

55 *"wretched to read it"* Emerson, *Journals*, VI, 440; the quotation in the next sentence is from IX, 15. In submitting the essay, "A Winter Walk," Thoreau had defended his style indirectly by saying: "In writing, conversation should be folded many times thick. It is the height of art that on the first perusal plain common sense should appear—on the second severe truth—and on a third beauty." *Correspondence*, 125; Emerson's reply, cited above, is printed on p. 137.

NOTES FOR CHAPTER 2: CHRYSALIS

57 *"like an infant for sleep"* *See* Thoreau's *Correspondence*, 493.

58 *Launched on a literary career* "Sympathy" and "Persius" were published in the *Dial* for July 1840. Thoreau was of course thoroughly conscious of following the romantic tradition of literary withdrawal. More specifically, he may have been influenced by Johann Zimmerman's *Solitude* (Albany, N.Y., 1796), a compendium of renaissance and eighteenth-century views on the subject. This volume was in Thoreau's library, though just when he acquired it is not known. But he would certainly have been drawn to it because of Zimmerman's emphasis on solitude as an escape from economic servitude, especially as illustrated in his long sections on Petrarch and Rousseau.

59 *letter to Emerson's wife* On June 20, 1843, Thoreau wrote from Staten Island: "My actual life is unspeakably mean, compared with what I know and see it might be." (*Correspondence*, 120)

60 *"I thirst for it"* *See* LJ, 185–186. The editor, Perry Miller, comments on p. 198: "It is entirely evident that Thoreau's yearning for Walden Pond . . . has psychological origins long anterior to any 'economical' decision to go live with it."

61 *"nor anything else"* *See* Thoreau's *Correspondence*, 161.

66 *"none at all"* *See* Thoreau's *Correspondence*, 424, letter to H. G. O. Blake.

67 *Journal tirades against society* *See* J, III, 460–461, for an example from 1852, when *Walden* was in progress.

69 *"every degree of wit"* That a similar account of this halfwit pauper appears in the *Journal* (III, 198–200) is no proof of an actual visit. Many of the entries at this period—January 1852, when work on *Walden* had been resumed—are written "as if" in 1845–1847; they are not parts of a diary but first drafts for the book. The relation of *Journal* passages on Alek Therien to the woodchopper figure in *Walden* is similarly literary in spite of the fact that Therein was an actual person, known in and around Concord.

70 *Thoreau's "raisers" identified* G. W. Cooke, *Early Letters of George Wm. Curtis to John S. Dwight* (1898), 81.

71 *Edmund Hosmer identified* *See* Mary Hosmer Brown, *Memories of Concord* (1926), 88–111.

73 *visitors to Walden Pond* The only other known records of visits to Thoreau at the pond are those reprinted in Walter Harding's *Thoreau: Man of Concord* (1960), 50–52, 134, 143, 149–151, supplemented by a few brief reminiscences in *The Days of Henry Thoreau* (1965), 190–196. Only one is by a coeval, a friend of Thoreau's brother; the others are by people who were children at the time, all written as reminiscences late in life, many years after *Walden* had appeared—to prompt their memories. The most interesting, by a youth of seventeen, is quoted on pp. 186–187 of my book.

74 *"rhyming her steps"* *See* Alcott, 190–193.

75 *"come into Nature"* *See* Alcott, 213–214.

75 *"Emerson's Poems and Thoreau's Week"* *See* Alcott, 214–215. Although Thoreau wrote a partial first draft of *Walden* before he left the pond in September 1847, there is no evidence that Alcott read this in manuscript at the time. Under date of January 22, 1851, however, there is a response to it in his *Journals* (p. 238): "Thoreau passed this morning and dined with me. He was on

the way to read a paper at Medford this evening—his "Life in the Woods at Walden"; and as refreshing a piece as the Lyceum will get from any lecturer going at present in New England—a whole forest, with forester and all, imported into the citizen's and villager's brain. A sylvan man accomplished in the virtues of an aboriginal civility, and quite superior to the urbanities of cities, Thoreau is himself a wood, and its inhabitants. There is more in him of sod and shade and sky lights, of the genuine mold and moistures of the green grey earth, than in any person I know. Self dependent and sagacious as any denizen of the elements, he has the key to every animal's brain, every flower and shrub; and were an Indian to flower forth, and reveal the secrets hidden in the wilds of his cranium, it would not be more surprising than the speech of this Sylvanus."

80 *temporary insanity See* J, IX, 200: "Staying in the house breeds a sort of insanity always. Every house is in this sense a hospital. A night and a forenoon is as much confinement to those wards as I can stand. I am aware that I recover some sanity which I had lost almost the instant that I come abroad."

85 *"even I am a yogin" See* Thoreau's *Correspondence*, 251; letter to H. G. O. Blake, 20 November 1849. Though the editors make no identification of the quoted passages, they appear again in the *Journal* (II, 191) where they are identified as coming from the *Harivansa*. This work, an appendix to the *Mahabharata*, Thoreau borrowed from the Harvard Library on 5 November 1849, in the French translation of A. Langlois. He copied these and other passages into his "Note Book" (MS, New York Public Library) and translated a long story from it which has been published posthumously as *The Transmigration of the Seven Brahmans* (1931).

85 *"Yoga is to quibble" See* Christy, 221; 204. Bibliographical data in the following notes and suggestions for several minor points in my text are taken from this book.

86 *Emerson discovers the Bhagvat-Geeta See* R. L. Rusk, ed., *The Letters of Ralph Waldo Emerson* (1939), III, 288. Thoreau transcribed into his "Note Book" (MS, New York Public Library) some passages from Rammohun Roy's *Translation of Several Principal Books . . . of the Veds* (London, 1832), which he borrowed from the Harvard Library on 26 April 1850; it includes the *Upanishads*. A few passages from H. T. Colebrooke's *The Sankhya Karika* (Oxford, 1837) can be found in Cameron, *Notebook*, 358; Thoreau had borrowed

this volume from Harvard on 28 January 1851, and was still transcribing from it into his *Journal* the following May. (J, II, 192)

86 *"the fruits thereof"* Quoted from *A Week*, 146, 145 (my italics). See pp. 140–145 for the whole commentary on the *Bhagvat-Geeta*. Thoreau identifies the edition he is quoting from as that "translated by Charles Wilkins," which was published in London, 1785.

87 *"absorbed in my nature"* Charles Wilkins, *The Bhagvat-Geeta* (London, 1785), 63, 131–132. These quotations follow the wording in Wilkins' edition, the one Thoreau used. But transcriptions from the Sanskrit differ widely, as is well known, and it will be interesting to compare a modern version of the latter passage to show how much more closely it fits Thoreau's language, as if the translator had been a devotee of *Walden* and had recognized the kinship of the two books:

"Dwelling in solitude, eating but little, controlling speech, body and mind, and ever engaged in meditation and concentration and taking refuge in dispassion.

"And casting aside self-sense, force, arrogance, desire, anger, possession, egoless and tranquil in mind, he becomes worthy of becoming one with *Brahman*."

Quoted in W. B. Stein, "Thoreau's *Walden* and the *Bhagavad Gita*," *Topic*, VI (1963), 53–54.

87 *Thoreau as Brahman* His aloofness and increasing self-absorption in later years made at least one contemporary (a transcendentalist clergyman who had been an acquaintance of Thoreau's since college days) comment: "He went about like a priest of Buddha who expects to arrive soon at the summit of a life of contemplation, where the divine absorbs the human." John Weiss, in the *Christian Examiner*, July 1865; reprinted in Walter Harding, ed., *Thoreau: Man of Concord* (1960), 33. Christy (232–233) quotes Weiss' comment as anticipating the conclusion to which his own evidence had led.

90 *"maya falls from his eyes" See* W. B. Stein, "Thoreau's *Walden* and the *Bhagavad Gita*," *Topic*, VI (1963), 52–53.

90 *Thoreau's reading* He borrowed from Harvard on 28 January 1850 H. H. Wilson's translation of *The Vishnu Purana, A System of Hindu Mythology and Tradition* (London, 1840). Of its more than 700 pages he made some 30 pages of extracts in his "Note Book" (MS, New York Public Library). The two quoted by me are from the Note Book, p. 188 and p. 213, with one

sentence added from p. 199.

The "spectator" paragraph in *Walden* was not added until Version IV, in 1852 (see Shanley, 31, 72). The *Journal* draft of it (J, IV, 290; August 1852) is preceded by an interesting paragraph, not included in the book, which may be epitomized as follows: "I know, for instance, that Sadi entertained once identically the same thought that I do, and thereafter I can find no essential difference between Sadi and myself. He is not Persian, he is not ancient, he is not strange to me. . . . By sympathy with Sadi I have embowelled him."

91 classic Indian dramas In Thoreau's "Note Book" for 1849–50 (MS, NYPL) there are four pages of extracts from *Sacontala*, or *The Fatal Ring* (London, 1790), the edition translated by Sir Wm. Jones. A copy of H. H. Wilson's *Select Specimens of the Theatre of the Hindus* (London, 1835), 2 vols., was included in the Cholmondeley collection that reached Thoreau in the fall of 1854, but he had probably been acquainted with it earlier.

NOTES FOR CHAPTER 3: MAYA

94 "form in the formless" See Christy, 89–90.

94 Thoreau reads Emerson's Nature See Harding, 60.

95 "generalized concept" See Perry Miller, "Thoreau in the Context of International Romanticism," *New England Quarterly*, XXXIV (1961), 150.

95 "part or parcel of God" See Emerson, *Works*, I, 10.

97 "a creative soul" Wordsworth, *The Prelude*, XII, 93–101, 118–120, 126–131, 203–207. The italics are Wordsworth's.

98 "desirable to the mind" See Emerson, *Works*, I, 59.

99 "pencils would draw no other" See Emerson, *Journals*, VI, 515 (1844).

101 "manifested herself to soul" The sentence is copied down in a commonplace book he kept in the 1840's, which identifies the source. See Cameron, *Notebook*, 358.

101 the dancer is Maya-Shakti See the interpretation by W. B. Stein, "Thoreau's First Book: A Spoor of Yoga," *Emerson Society Quarterly*, No. 41 (1965), 23. A *Journal* passage in March 1852 is relevant at this point: "The gods can never afford to leave a man in the world who is privy to any of their secrets. They cannot have a spy here. They will at once send him packing. How can you walk on ground when you see through it?" (J, III, 349)

102 "unfold its great proportions" See Emerson, *Works*, I, 76 (my italics).

114 a recent critic See Nina Baym, "Thoreau's View of Science," *Journal of the History of Ideas*, XXVI (1965), 221–33.

123 "these twenty years" See Emerson, *Works*, I, 51.

123 "quite originally drest" See Emerson's *Journals*, VI, 74.

124 "in a sleepy generality" See Emerson, *Journals*, IX, 522.

NOTES FOR CHAPTER 4: BOG-TROTTER

137 "delights were dolphin-like" Shakespeare, *Antony and Cleopatra*, V, ii, 88–89.

137 "The last still loveliest" Byron, *Childe Harold*, IV, xxix. (*See* Herbert, "Giddinesse," V.)

137 dolphin in classical mythology Though there is no reference in Thoreau's writing to this specific myth, the *Journal* for 1845 does record a kindred one: "When we read that Bacchus made the Tyrrhenian mariners mad, so that they leaped into the sea, mistaking it for 'a meadow full of flowers,' and so became dolphins, we are not concerned about the historical truth of this, but rather a higher, poetical truth." (J, I, 393; transcribed verbatim into *A Week*, 58)

140 "clouds return after the rain" Ecclesiastes 11.9, 12.1–2.

141 "bereave my soul of good" Ecclesiastes 12.12; 1.3; 4.8.

NOTES FOR CHAPTER 5: TALARIA

147 Alek Therien See J, I, 365. In the book's first version his identity was retained, even as he was being transformed into a legendary figure (*see* Shanley, 170).

149 "mighty hunter" See Genesis 10.9; Micah 5.6. E. A. Speiser, *Genesis* (Anchor Bible, vol. I, 1964), 51, 67, translates "before the Lord" as "by the will of Yaweh," equivalent to *deo volente.*

149 "fishers of men" Mark 1.17.

150 "Higher Laws" a late chapter See Shanley, 67–68, 72–73.

152 the modern critic . . . food-cranks See Joseph Jones, "Transcendental Grocery Bills," *University of Texas Studies in English*, XXXVI (1957), 141–154.

152 the best classicist See Seybold, 14–26 and *passim.*

152 read Oriental scriptures Paul, 69–75.

153 Iamblicus and Porphyry See Cameron, *Notebook*, 11–51; *see also* Cameron, *Minerva.* Seybold, 41, 98, identifies the editions Thoreau read as Thomas Taylor's translations of Iamblicus' *Life of Pythagoras* (London, 1818) and *Select Works of Porphyry* (London, 1823). That both are now considered untrustworthy is beside the point. These were the versions Thoreau read, and references throughout this chapter to Iamblicus and Porphyry are simply to his understanding of them from Taylor's translations.

153 "*assumed a human form*" Iamblicus, 67–68.

153 "*mandates of reason*" Iamblicus, xi, 7.

154 "*wealth, and the like*" Iamblicus, 48–49.

154 "*familiars and friends*" Iamblicus, 17–18, 69–73, 123.

154 *laws regulating men's lives* Iamblicus, 77, 119.

155 "*as long as they lived*" Iamblicus, 183. *Cf.* Cameron, *Notebook*, 32.

155 "*kindred nature with us*" Porphyry, 4, 125.

155 "*hunters, or fishermen*" Porphyry, 116, 39.

156 "*a small and hard bed*" Porphyry, 19–20.

157 "*be truly immortal*" Porphyry, 28, 166.

157 "*they were in want*" Porphyry, 28, 41, 42, 38.

158 "*association with the body*" Porphyry, 21, 22, 43.

158 "*assimilation to divinity*" Porphyry, 81, 41.

159 "*to become somnolent*" Porphyry, 34.

161 "*go down at one swallow*" *See* Thoreau, *Correspondence*, 220.

162 "*the savor of food*" (241). Thoreau was translating from the French version by M. G. Pauthier of *Confucius et Mencius, Les Quatre Livres* (Paris, 1841), 19; *cf.* Cameron, *Notebook*, iv.

162 "*this defileth a man*" Matthew 15.11, 17–19.

162 "*when they eat bread*" Matthew 15.2, 20.

163 "*betray my peculiar defects*" *Correspondence*, 288. The "essay," properly excluded from the volume of his letters, may be found in the *Writings*, VI, 198–209. The section on chastity in *Walden* was first included in Versions IV and V, late 1852 to mid-1853. (*See* Shanley, 67–68, 72–73; *also* J, II, 186, for a passage on "purity.")

164 "*preservative of health*" Porphyry, 39.

164 *Essenes and Egyptian priests* Porphyry, 138, 147.

165 "*female with the male*" Porphyry, 163.

165 *Brahmin, the "superior man"* Paul, 71.

165 *Laws of Menu See* LJ, 156 (17 August 1840); Cameron, *Minerva*, I, 310–321; *Dial*, III, 331–340; *A Week*, 154–161.

166 "*ascended . . . to heaven*" *Institutes of Hindu Law; or the Ordinances of Menu*, trans. by Sir Wm. Jones (London, 1825), 168. This was the edition given to Thoreau by Thomas Cholmondeley in 1854. There was also a copy of it in Emerson's library, where Thoreau probably first read it (Christy, 284). It is cited hereafter as "Menu."

166 "a signal compensation" Menu, op. cit., 152.

166 "impurities of the human frame" Menu, op. cit., 164.

167 "by clear knowledge" See Dial, III, 332.

167 "a man may be found" See Cameron, *Minerva,* I, 315, transcribing the Morgan MS.

168 Thoreau's use of Oriental scriptures See Paul, 73, 74; and Shanley, 30.

168 "superior men preserve it carefully" (242) *See Confucius et Mencius. Les quatre livres.* Traduit par M. G. Pauthier (Paris, 1841), 333. Thoreau's translations from this edition were made in a Notebook, MS now in the Berg Collection, NYPL.

169 Peter the Venerable See Patrologia Latina, vol. 189, col. 943–945.

169 "come, follow me" Luke 18.22.

170 Oriental and Western monastic systems Spence Hardy, *Eastern Monachism* (London, 1850). This was one volume in the large collection of Oriental books (44 volumes in all) sent to Thoreau in the fall of 1854 by his English friend, Thomas Cholmondeley. Though it arrived after the publication of *Walden,* it was published in 1850 and may have been read earlier. The passages quoted following are taken from Christy, 292–295, who furnished the ingenious argument for attributing the markings to Thoreau.

174 "effected by mortal sounds" Iamblicus, 44; *see* Cameron, *Notebook,* 31. The passage was transcribed into *A Week,* 184–185.

174 "in intellectual perception" Iamblicus, 48; *see* his footnote on pp. 44–45.

176 "sinks into the farmer" See Emerson, *Works,* I, 83. Such an ideal farmer is one of the "Winter Visitors," described on p. 70–71 above.

176 "hovering around me" (193) This *Walden* passage, interestingly enough, is transcribed from a *Journal* entry written four years before he began his residence at the pond. His Orpheus-like experience on that occasion prompted him to add: "[I] feel that nothing but the wildest imagination can conceive of the manner of life we are living. Nature is a wizard. The Concord nights are stranger than the Arabian nights." (J, I, 260–261)

177 John Farmer There is a *Journal* source for the John Farmer episode with an interesting difference, the flute being played by the "poor hind" himself, who is Apollo in disguise. It seems to take off from an actual experience, but quickly soars: "I hear now from Bear Garden Hill—I rarely walk by moonlight without hearing—the sound of a flute, or a horn, or a human voice. It is a performer I never see by day; should not recognize him if pointed out; but you may hear his performance in every horizon. He plays but one strain and goes to bed early, but I know by the character of that strain that he is deeply dissatisfied with the manner in which he spends his day. He is a slave who is purchasing his freedom. He is Apollo watching the flocks of Admetus on every hill, and this strain he plays every evening to remind him of his heavenly descent. It is all that saves him,—his one redeeming trait." (J, II, 373) The subtle changes made in transmuting this from *Journal* to *Walden* are an instructive example of how Thoreau assimilated random fragments into a thoroughly integrated book.

Another and more exotic source has been suggested by W. B. Stein, "Thoreau's *Walden* and the *Bhagavad Gita*," *Topic*, VI (1963), 51: "The pattern of Mr. Farmer's experience follows the classic outlines of *Siddhasana* ecstacy, and the mystical voice of this meditative trance is the resonance of the mystical syllable *Om*, the word or *mantra* of the incarnate *Vishnu*, BG, XVII, 23–28. According to the beliefs of *yoga*, this utterance is an announcement of the divine presence." A fascinating extension of the episode's meaning, if one could believe it.

178 *"another furrow than you see"* (I, 54) One of the few favorable passage on farmers in all his writings describes some primitive ones such as might be seen if one voyaged far enough up the Concord, in a new version of the mute-inglorious-Miltons: "Look at their fields, and imagine what they might write, if ever they should put pen to paper. Or what have they not written on the face of the earth already. . . scratching, and harrowing, and plowing. . . again and again, erasing what they had already written for want of parchment." (I, 6)

NOTES FOR CHAPTER 6: WILDNESS

180 *"need not work"* *Cf.* "He who will not work shall not eat," Captain John Smith, *Travels and Works* (Edinburgh, 1910), Pt. I, 194.

180 *Saint Bavo* Alban Butler, *The Lives of the Saints* (London, 1936), X, 7–8, gives an account of this hermit, a nobleman of Belgium who gave away all his money to found a monastery. But being a monk himself was not enough, so he appealed to the abbot: "To satisfy his devotion, St. Amandus after some time gave him leave to live an eremetical life, and he is said first to have chosen for his abode a hollow trunk of a large tree . . . where vegetables and water were his chief subsistence."

Emerson, in his fictive role as Osman, the Ideal Man, claimed acquaintance with a similar saint, recording in his *Journals* for 1841: "Seemed to me that I had the keeping of a secret too great to be confided to one man; that a divine man dwelt near me in a hollow tree." (*Journals*, VI, 137)

181 "*This silence is eloquent*" *See Dial*, III, 494 (April 1843).

182 "*in the divine essence*" *See Dial*, III, 337–338 (January 1843).

183 "*Apologues in the world*" Charles Wilkins, Preface, *The Heetopades of Veeshnoo-Sama* (Bath, 1787), viii-ix. This English edition is the one read by Thoreau (and used by Emerson in 1842 for some extracts in the *Dial*, III, 82–85).

An early *Journal* entry by Thoreau is particularly relevant at this point: "yesterday I skated after a fox over the ice. . . . All brutes seem to have a genius for mystery, an Oriental aptitude for symbols and the language of signs; and this is the origin of Pilpay and Aesop. The fox manifested an almost human suspicion of mystery in my actions. While I skated directly after him, he cantered at the top of his speed; but when I stood still, though his fear was not abated, some strange but inflexible law of his nature caused him to stop also, and sit again on his haunches. While I stood motionless, he would go slowly a rod to one side, then sit and bark, then a rod to the other side, and sit and bark again, but did not retreat, as if spellbound. When, however, I commenced the pursuit again, he found himself released from his durance." (J, I, 470)

184 "*animals closely related to man*" Porphyry, 101–111.

185 "*Orpheus, over savage animals*" Iamblicus, 40–41.

187 "*hearing its special signal*" Frederick Willis, *Alcott Memmoirs* (1915), 90–91.

188 "*it interested him much*" (250) *See Correspondence*, 183.

190 "*the ant, thou sluggard*" Proverbs 6.6.

190 "*rescue his Patroclus*" (254) The preceding sentence, "[the ant] whose mother had charged him to return with his shield or upon it," is a submerged allusion to Plutarch's *Sayings of Spartan Women*: "Either this or upon this," as a shield was handed by mother to son. *See* Walter Harding, *The Variorum Walden* (1963), 303.

192 "*the epistolary form*" *See* Wm. Kirby and Wm. Spence, *An Introduction to Entomology* (1846), iii, vi. The scientific "validation" was first added to the *Walden* anecdote in Version V, dated by Shanley

1852–1853, with the words: "Since making this record I learn from Kirby and Spence . . ." (HM 924, MS Huntington Library).

192 "*trophy of his valor*" *See* Kirby, *op. cit.*, 360.

192 "*Myrmidonian valor*" *See* Kirby, *op. cit.*, 362.

192 "*to suit himself*" *See* Kirby, *op. cit.*, viii.

192 "*Eugenius the Fourth*" (256) *See* Kirby, *op. cit.*, 361–362.

193 "*Fugitive-Slave Bill*" (257) This bill was passed on September 18, 1850. Thoreau's attribution of it to Webster is satirical, stigmatizing his famous 7th of March speech as a betrayal of the liberal North.

194 "*Journal account of loon's visit*" The same is true in the first version of the book, which was written in 1846–1847. (*Cf.* Shanley, 193) This text stands midway between the *Journal* and *Walden*, with the myth-making phrase added, but without the private loon chase by Thoreau.

196 "*shape-changing as normal*" Edward A. Armstrong, *The Folklore of Birds: An Enquiry into the Origin and Distribution of Some Magico-Religious Traditions* (London, 1958), 64. A similar myth is recounted in Charles Leland's *Algonquin Legends of New England* (1884).

196 "*the diver is sacred*" *See* Armstrong, *op. cit.*, 66–67.

196 "*note-taking for Indian book*" In the Columbia University Library there are more than 1,000 typed pages transcribed by Arthur Christy in 1931 from Thoreau's Indian notebooks, drawn from 200 sources and running to nearly half-a-million words. This cache did not come to my notice in time to be searched for the present book, but it promises the happy prospect of extending this note in the future.

197 "*some of our thoughts*" *See* Shanley, 192.

197 "*fifth version of Walden*" *See* Shanley, 66, 73.

197 "*plant puts forth leaves*" *See* Thoreau's *Correspondence*, 45. Letter to Mrs. Lucy Brown, July 21, 1841.

197 "*twigs in his hand*" *See* Emerson, *Journals*, VII, 498.

198 "*locks dripping with moisture*" *See* Alcott, 193.

201 "*wild animals than we*" (III, 77–78) ("Ktaadn" is the spelling Thoreau uses in *The Maine Woods*.) *See* Harding, 210.

NOTES FOR CHAPTER 7: CIRCLES

213 "*center of being*" College Notebook, 155, in Cameron, *Minerva*, I, 284. Cameron says that Thoreau copied this in 1839 or 1840 from J. K. Lavater, *Aphorisms on Man* (London, 1794), 2.

221 "*capable of framing*" Cameron, *Notebook*, 33–43. Since the extracts from Iamblicus' *Life* are in quotation marks and this passage is not, it might be mistaken for Thoreau's commentary. But it can be found in Taylor's notes to the *Life*, p. 299, quoted from Proclus' "Dissertation on Magic."

224 *"God's Drop"* (215) *See* Emerson, *Journals*, V, 381 (1840).

225 *"shore of me detained"* MS Huntington Library, HM 924, containing the early versions of *Walden*.

228 *"Anticipation," according to this critic* Nina Baym, "Thoreau's View of Science," *Journal of the History of Ideas*, XXVI (1965), 221–234.

228 *"seasons in their order"* W. E. Channing, *Thoreau the Poet-Naturalist* (1902), 67.

229 *"tedious bird and flower lists" See* J, XIII, 218–229, for twelve pages devoted to listing the phenomena of March 1860; and J, XIII, 356–357, for a list of nine phenomena happening simultaneously on one day, June 12 of the same year.

229 *"to sound the pond" See* Baym, *op. cit.*, 228. (See third note above.) I am indebted to this article for the basic meaning of "anticipation" set forth in these two paragraphs.

231 *"turning of a leaf"* (I, 356) *See* Charles Anderson, *Emily Dickinson's Poetry* (1960), 149–158, for discussion of a group of poems on the same theme.

236 *Walden, Version VII See* Shanley, 32, 72–73.

242 *melting of pond, 1845–1854* There is no way to tell which of these ten years served as a source for the episode in his book. Only a small part of "Spring" was contained in Version I of *Walden*, presumably completed by the time he left the pond in 1847. Well over half of it was first included in Versions VI and VII, written in 1853–1854 from *Journal* drafts based on trips back to the pond in 1852–1853, surprisingly enough. (*See* Shanley, 32, 72–73; and J, III–IV, *passim.*)

242 *sounding Walden Pond* A modern scientist has vouched for Thoreau's accuracy in his soundings, surveys, temperature readings, and other scientific measurements of Walden Pond, saying that he may with justice be called "the first American limnologist." *See* Edward Deever, "A Reexamination of Thoreau's *Walden*," *Quarterly Review of Biology*, XVII (1942), 1–11.

243 *Goethe's Italienische Reise* Thoreau studied German with Orestes Brownson in 1835–1836, and two years later read several volumes of Goethe's *Werke*, which he borrowed from Emerson's library. (*See* J. A. Christie, *Thoreau As World Traveller* (1965), 65–

70.)

244 *Goethe's Metamorphosis of Plants* The translation of Goethe's sentence and the summary of his ideas here are taken from Agnes Arber, *The Natural Philosophy of Plant Form* (Cambridge, 1950), 40–43, 210. She does not mention Thoreau.

245 *sand foliage* Perry Miller, in his chapter called "The Stratagems of Consciousness—Anticipation" (LJ, 104 ff.), treats the sand foliage metaphor as a sign of the sterility of Thoreau's nature study. In the course of it, however, he makes one arresting judgment: "all *Walden* is an adroitly suspended anticipation of the climax of thawing sand and clay in the railroad cut; all the *Journal*—earnestly before the completion of *Walden*, more stridently thereafter—is a stratagem to anticipate, and so to survive, the winter."

246 *parable of the prodigal's return* Luke 15.24.

247 *symbol of the risen Christ* 1 John 1.5.

248 *"like Brahminical devotees... till night"* This analogy was first pointed out by W. B. Stein, "Thoreau's First Book: A Spoor of Yoga," *Emerson Society Quarterly*, No. 41 (1965), p. 22.

248 *Orpheus salutes the sun* Thoreau read G. H. Bode's *Orpheus Poetarum Graecorum Antiquissimus* (1824), an account of Orphic history and tradition, in 1841. (Seybold, 98.)

249 *"the perfect, and the pure"* *See* Taylor's notes in *The Description of Greece, by Pausanias* (London, 1824), III, 294, 295. (The hymn was by Callimachus.) Thoreau's use of two of Taylor's translations has been noted previously; he also presumably had access to the 24 volumes by Taylor that Alcott brought from England in 1843.

257 *Orphism, an inner mystical spring* F. M. Cornford, *From Religion to Philosophy* (1957), 220.

257 *"eternal spring"* (348) Ovid, *Metamorphoses*, I, 89–96, 107–108.

NOTES FOR CHAPTER 8: THE LEAP

260 *"Limbo, Purgatory, and Hell"* (J, III, 214–215.) That this paragraph was the original draft of paragraph No. 4 in "Conclusion" is proved by the fact that both end with an almost identically worded metaphor about going "before the mast and on the deck of the world." The paragraph was not added to *Walden* until Version VI, 1853–1854 (*see* Shanley, 32, 72–73).

261 *"boons on his fellow men"* Joseph Campbell, *The Hero with a Thousand Faces* (1949),

30.

263 *"ear can detect"* F. B. Sanborn, ed., *The Service* (1902), 15. (*Cf.* J, I, 156.)

265 *"traveler's stay in one place"* J. A. Christie, *Thoreau as World Traveller* (1965), 267.

266 *"idlers and vagabonds"* (J, II, 141) The brackets are Thoreau's, enclosing his interpolation in the quotation from an unnamed source. "Walking" is included in Vol. V of *Writings.*

268 *"the cats in Zanzibar"* (354, 352–353) Walter Harding, *The Variorum Walden* (1963), 317, n. 14, identifies the book that contained such a report as Charles Pickering's *The Races of Man* (London, 1851). Thoreau read it in 1853 (*see* J, V, 392).

270 *"home-cosmography"* (353) Walter Harding, *The Variorum Walden* (1963), 316, note 4, points out a slip in the first line: "eye right" instead of "eye-sight."

270 *"her prodigies in us"* Cameron, *Minerva*, I, 282, prints Thoreau's extracts from Browne's *Miscellaneous Works* (Cambridge, 1831), 31—including the one here quoted. Paul, 59, points out the analogy, though apparently unaware of the proof in Thoreau's commonplace book.

274 *"topographical phrenology"* Paul, 344. His analysis of the passage covers three pages, 342–345.

274 *Channing helps build chimney See* Harding, 182.

276 *"Smoke. . .verging on hubris"* This last point is made by F. O. Matthiessen in *American Renaissance* (1941), 166.

276 *"his art is always pure"* These details are summed up by Paul, 353 note.

277 *"devotion to his art" See* Thoreau's *Correspondence*, 311 (letter to H. G. O. Blake).

Index

About the Author

Charles R. Anderson, Caroline Donovan Professor of American Literature at Johns Hopkins University, is the author and editor of several acclaimed critical volumes, including his *Melville in the South Seas,* the ten-volume *Centennial Edition of Sidney Lanier,* and the two-volume *American Literary Masters.* His *Emily Dickinson's Poetry: Stairway of Surprise* won the 1961 Christian Gauss Award for literary criticism given by the United Chapters of Phi Beta Kappa. A guest professor at the University of Heidelberg in 1949, and a visiting lecturer at the Nagano Seminar in Japan in 1954, Mr. Anderson has held a number of fellowships, including a Fulbright and a Guggenheim. A member of the Advisory Board of the *Journal of American Literature,* Mr. Anderson has also served as a managing editor of *American Literature* and an editor of *Modern Language Notes.*